COMPLIMENTARY C

Oxford EAP

A course in English for Academic Purposes

ELEMENTARY / A2

Edward de Chazal & John Hughes

Contents

		LISTENING & SPEAKING	READING
1	**EDUCATION** Page 008 **Academic Focus:** Presenting information	**Presentations (1)** Understanding a short presentation and taking notes Giving a short presentation about yourself and your plans Present simple: Talking about now Present simple + *to* infinitive: Talking about future plans	**Textbooks (1)** Recognizing text types Understanding information in a textbook Taking notes from a text Present simple and imperative: Giving information and instructions or advice
2	**INFORMATION** Page 022 **Academic Focus:** Describing features	**Presentations (2)** Understanding the introduction to a presentation Noticing the language of presentations Giving a short presentation about a website Linking language (2): Sequencing and adding information	**Textbooks (2)** Understanding the purpose of a text Recognizing important information in a text and taking notes Noun phrases (1): Understanding a noun phrase
3	**LOCATION** Page 036 **Academic Focus:** Comparing and contrasting	**Lectures (1)** Making notes on the main content of a lecture Presenting and comparing cities Comparison (1): Comparative adjectives Comparison (2): Superlative adjectives	**Textbooks (3)** Understanding the parts of a text Reading for similarities and differences in a text Linking language (4): Comparing and contrasting ideas Word forms: *similar* / *different*
4	**PRODUCTION** Page 050 **Academic Focus:** Describing numbers and charts	**Presentations (3)** Understanding charts and data Presenting data with charts Data (1): Saying numbers exactly and approximately	**Textbooks (4)** Using a graph to understand a text Using numbers to focus on meaning Understanding the history of a company Past simple: Talking about events in the past
5	**DESIGN** Page 064 **Academic Focus:** Defining and explaining	**Lectures (2)** Identifying the main points of a lecture Taking notes with a mind map Defining and explaining terms Defining (1): Definitions, explanations, and examples	**Textbooks (5)** Identifying the main purpose of a text Understanding academic terms Taking notes on definitions in a text Defining (2): Identifying definitions, explanations, and examples

WRITING	VOCABULARY	ACADEMIC LANGUAGE CHECK
(1) Sentences about you Planning and writing sentences with personal information Sentences (1): Writing personal information **(2) A personal statement** Analysing a personal statement Writing a personal statement using linking language Linking language (1): *and, but, because*	Vocabulary-building: Verbs and nouns Collocation: Verb + noun	Talking about now and future plans Giving information and instructions or advice *and, but, because*
(1) Descriptive sentences Writing descriptive sentences using noun phrases Noun phrases (2): Adjectives in noun phrases **(2) A descriptive paragraph** Analysing a descriptive paragraph Writing a descriptive paragraph using linking language Linking language (3): *in addition, also, so, or*	Websites Noun suffixes Vocabulary-building: Antonyms	Sequencing and adding information Understanding a noun phrase Adjectives in noun phrases *in addition, also, so, or*
(1) Comparison sentences Writing sentences about similarity and difference Comparison (3): Expressing similarities and differences **(2) A comparison paragraph** Analysing a comparison paragraph Introducing, comparing and contrasting, and concluding Sentences (2): Writing about comparison	Location and business Compound nouns Identifying word forms	Comparative and superlative adjectives Similarity and difference
(1) Sentences about data Simplifying numbers and reporting data Data (2): Simplifying numerical information **(2) A description of a chart** Analysing a description of a chart Planning and writing a description of a chart	Nationality suffixes Identifying collocations Presentations with charts	Data: Numbers, fractions, and quantifiers Talking about events in the past
(1) Definition sentences Writing clear definitions using prepositional phrases Defining (3): Writing definitions **(2) A definition paragraph** Analysing a definition paragraph Structuring a definition paragraph using linking language Linking language (5): Structuring definitions and explanations / examples	Word order: Adjectives Vocabulary-building: Verbs and nouns Prepositions	Definitions, explanations, and examples

		LISTENING & SPEAKING	READING
6	**CHANGE** Page 078 **Academic Focus:** Describing changes and trends	**Lectures (3)** Reading to prepare for a lecture Listening for the language of trends Talking about your country's economy Changes and trends (1): Present progressive, present simple	**Textbooks (6)** Understanding the main trend in a graph Understanding changes and trends described in a text Time, place, and quantity: Prepositional phrases Changes and trends (2): Past and present tenses, *will*
7	**RESOURCES** Page 092 **Academic Focus:** Understanding fact and opinion	**Seminars (1)** Reading to prepare for a seminar Understanding facts and opinions in a seminar Discussing an issue Expressing opinions: Giving and supporting opinions, agreeing / disagreeing	**Textbooks (7)** Understanding factual information in a text Noticing features of text types Distinguishing between fact and opinion Present simple passive (1): Describing facts and processes
8	**IMPACT** Page 106 **Academic Focus:** Understanding cause and effect	**Seminars (2)** Reading to prepare for a seminar Taking notes in a seminar Discussing cause and effect in a seminar Cause and effect (1): Verbs Expressing possibility: Modals *could*, *might*, and *may*	**Textbooks (8)** Identifying the purpose of a paragraph Taking notes on cause and effect in a text Organizing information with a flowchart Cause and effect (2): Introducing cause with prepositions Cause and effect (3): Active and passive
9	**INVENTION** Page 120 **Academic Focus:** Recognizing perspective	**Seminars (3)** Understanding evidence in a presentation Giving evidence in a discussion Using evidence in a discussion Past events: Past simple and present perfect Referring to evidence: Reporting verbs	**Textbooks (9)** Evaluating text types for academic study Evaluating different texts on one topic Noticing perspective in texts Past simple passive: Describing discoveries and inventions Perspective: Expressions and vocabulary
10	**RESEARCH** Page 134 **Academic Focus:** Questioning	**Questions** Taking notes on a topic Recognizing the purpose of questions Questions (1): Open and closed questions	**Textbooks (10)** Identifying relevant information in a text Taking notes about reasons Applying information from a text Collocation: Verb + noun

Glossary of grammatical and academic terms page 007

Language reference page 148

Writing: Sample answers page 159

WRITING	VOCABULARY	ACADEMIC LANGUAGE CHECK
(1) Sentences about trends Writing sentences about trends using adverbs Describing trends (1): Adverbs **(2) A description of a graph** Analysing a description of a graph Describing trends in a graph using adverbs and adjectives Describing trends (2): Adjectives and adverbs	Vocabulary-building: Word forms Trends Economic terms	Present progressive, present simple, past simple, *will* Prepositional phrases Adverbs and adjectives
(1) Sentences about processes Writing passive sentences about steps in a process Writing an evaluative sentence Present simple passive (2): Describing a process **(2) A description of a process** Analysing a description of a process Describing a diagram using linking language Linking language (6): Describing steps in a process	Resources Vocabulary-building: Adjectives	Giving and supporting opinions, agreeing / disagreeing Describing facts and processes Describing steps in a process
(1) Cause and effect sentences Writing cause and effect sentences in a variety of patterns Sentences (3): Writing about cause and effect **(2) A cause and effect paragraph** Analysing a cause and effect paragraph Writing a paragraph describing positive and negative impacts	Noun phrases Prepositions	Cause and effect: Verbs and prepositions Modals: *could*, *might*, and *may*
(1) Sentences about invention Using active and passive sentence patterns Sentences (4): Changing emphasis with active / passive / *by* **(2) A description of an inventor** Analysing paragraph structure Writing a cohesive paragraph about an inventor Linking language (7): Using pronouns and determiners for cohesion	Vocabulary-building: Adjectives and nouns Vocabulary-building: Verbs and nouns Prepositional phrases	Past simple and present perfect Describing discoveries and inventions Using pronouns and determiners for cohesion
(1) Questions Writing a questionnaire using different question forms Questions (2): Form and tense **(2) A description of results** Analysing a paragraph about survey results Writing a paragraph about the results of research Sentences (5): The language of reports	Research Collocation: Verb + noun	Open and closed questions Questions: Form and tense The language of reports
Additional material from units *page 161*	**Answer key** *page 164*	**Video and audio transcripts** *page 168* **List of sources for texts** *page 175*

Introduction

Welcome to *Oxford English for Academic Purposes* – a complete course for anyone preparing to study in English at university level.

What is Oxford EAP?

Oxford EAP is designed to improve your ability to study effectively in English, whether you are planning to study on an undergraduate or postgraduate programme. Whatever your academic background, and whatever your chosen subject, *Oxford EAP* will help you develop your knowledge and skills in all of the following areas:

- reading and understanding authentic academic texts
- listening to lectures and presentations
- writing sentences, paragraphs, and different essay types
- participating in seminar and group discussions
- preparing and giving simple presentations
- improving your study skills, such as note-taking, critical thinking, and working independently
- recognizing and using academic grammar and vocabulary.

What is in a unit?

Oxford EAP A2 has ten units. Each unit starts with a preview page which shows the learning objectives for that unit, plus a short discussion task to get you thinking about the unit theme.

The **academic focus** of each unit covers an important aspect of academic study relevant to all subject areas – for example, presenting information, comparing and contrasting, and understanding cause and effect. This focus is maintained throughout the unit.

The units are divided into three main modules – Listening & Speaking, Reading, and Writing – plus one-page Vocabulary and Academic Language Check modules. Each module starts with a short list of learning objectives and includes a number of carefully sequenced tasks which help you to meet the objectives for that module.

Listening & Speaking focuses on the aural and oral skills needed to communicate successfully in an academic environment. The initial part of the module focuses mainly on listening to lectures and presentations. It uses short video extracts to help you understand key information and language, as well as how the lecture or presentation material is organized. Note-taking is a key feature, and the module often includes a critical thinking task.

The Speaking focus of the module includes participating in seminars and discussions, and giving presentations. It covers communication strategies for these situations, and presents and practises useful language. Usually you will do a short listening task to introduce the context and learn examples of useful language.

Reading uses adapted extracts from authentic academic textbooks. It usually starts with a short task to get you thinking about the topic or to predict the content of the text. Further tasks will help you to identify important features of the text, such as the main ideas or specific language, and demonstrate how you can read and understand an academic text even if you don't understand every word.

Writing focuses on the basics of academic writing. The writing modules are in two parts. The first part focuses on sentence level work, building confidence with appropriate structures and language. The second part focuses on simple paragraphs, including work on paragraph structure and linking language, and ends with a paragraph writing task. Each final task includes a 'check your writing' activity.

Vocabulary consolidates useful areas of academic vocabulary from the unit and includes regular vocabulary-building activities and vocabulary-learning strategies.

Academic Language Check provides the opportunity to further practise the academic language covered in the main modules.

What else is included?

Each unit includes:

- **Academic language** (grammar, vocabulary, and useful phrases) related to the academic focus of the unit, with examples taken from the texts or video / audio transcripts. There is a cross-reference to the Language reference.
- **Critical thinking** tasks which encourage you to think about the content of a module and about your own performance in writing and speaking tasks.
- **What is …?** boxes introducing key academic terms to A2 learners.
- **Independent study** tips suggesting how to transfer the skills from the course to your own studies.

At the front of the book:

- **Glossary** of grammatical and academic terms used in this book

At the back of the book:

- **Language reference** with more detailed information on the language covered in the units
- **Sample answers** for the tasks from Writing (2)
- **Answer key** for Vocabulary and Academic Language Check sections
- **Video and audio transcripts**

Glossary

Words and phrases used to refer to grammar and other aspects of language in this book.

Active voice the form of the verb which indicates what the subject does to the object, e.g. *The wind drives the turbines.*

Adjective a word which describes a noun, e.g. *a useful website*, or gives more information, e.g. *This website is useful.*

Adverb a word which describes a verb, e.g. *is rising slowly*, or functions as a linker in a sentence, e.g. *Firstly, However*

Agent who or what does the action in a passive sentence, e.g. *Water is heated by the Sun.*

Article (1) the most frequent determiners: definite article *the*; indefinite article *a / an*

Article (2) a type of text, e.g. in a magazine, newspaper, or online

Auxiliary verb a verb which combines with another verb to show the tense, e.g. *is / was changing*; the passive voice, e.g. *is used*; or a modal verb, e.g. *can / will produce*

Cause and effect the relationship between one action and another

Closed question a question with a limited answer, usually Yes / No, e.g. *Do / Is / Can ...?*

Cohesion how a text is connected in terms of meaning and language

Collocation two words which commonly go together, e.g. *do research, give a presentation*

Compound noun two nouns put together to create one meaning, e.g. *public transport*

Conclusion the final part of a written or spoken text which sums up the whole text

Content word a word which has real meaning rather than grammatical meaning; nouns, verbs, adjectives, and adverbs are content words

Contraction the short form of a verb form, often used in spoken English, e.g. *I'm, they're, don't*

Data factual and numerical information such as figures, charts, and graphs

Definite article the determiner *the*, which specifies definite meaning

Determiner a word before a head noun which gives information about it, e.g. *the, some, this*

Evaluation an opinion or comment on an idea from a text, presentation, or discussion, e.g. *This is an effective way to deliver data.*

Head noun the main noun in a noun phrase, e.g. *a large global organization*

Imperative a form of the verb (the same as the infinitive form) used to give instructions or advice, e.g. *Listen, Make notes*

Indefinite article the determiner *a* (*an* before vowels), which specifies indefinite meaning

Infinitive the base form of the verb, with or without *to*, e.g. *write, to write*

Introduction the first part of a written or spoken text which introduces the topic and aims of a text

Irregular verb a verb that doesn't follow regular patterns, e.g. *go–went–gone*

Linking language words / phrases which help make text cohesive: which join sentences, e.g. *and, but, However*; which add information, e.g. *in addition*; which add explanation, e.g. *because, so*; or which signpost order, e.g. *First of all, Finally*

Modal verb an auxiliary verb such as *can, could, might, may* – these are often used to express possibility

Noun a word which can refer to anything concrete, e.g. *university*, or abstract, e.g. *growth*

Object the part of a sentence, often a noun phrase, which is affected by the action of the verb and which normally comes after the main verb; an object can become the subject in the passive form of the sentence, e.g. *Tourism creates new jobs.*; *New jobs are created by tourism.*

Open question a question with any answer, e.g. *Why are you studying Portuguese?*

Participle the form of the verb which ends in *-ing* or *-ed*; used to form the progressive (*-ing*), the perfect (*-ed*), and the passive (*-ed*)

Passive voice the form of the verb which is used to indicate something being done to the subject, e.g. *The turbines are driven by the wind.*

Perspective how a topic is linked to its academic context, e.g. *from a medical perspective*

Phrase a structure built round a noun, verb, adjective, and/or adverb, e.g. *a similar problem*

Possessive determiner a word before a head noun which specifies possession, e.g. *my, your, their*

Prefix the first part of some words, which expresses a particular meaning or grammatical function, e.g. *un-, dis-*

Preposition a word or group of words before a noun or pronoun, e.g. *in, from, by, due to, as a result of*

Prepositional phrase a structure built round a preposition, e.g. *on the internet*

Pronoun a word which takes the place of another noun or noun phrase, e.g. *he, it*

Quantifier a determiner or pronoun that expresses quantity, e.g. *some, a few, all*

Regular verb a verb that follows normal past tense / past participle endings, e.g. *work–worked–worked*

Reporting verb a verb used to refer to information or evidence from another source, e.g. *state, believe, suggest*

Sequencing language words / phrases which put information in order, e.g. *First, Next, Then*

Source the original text from which information is taken

Subject the part of a sentence which performs the action of the main verb, e.g. *Our teacher uses new technology.*

Suffix the last part of some words, which expresses a particular meaning or grammatical function, e.g. *-tion, -ment*

Tense the form of the verb which relates to time; English has two tenses: present, e.g. *he works*, and past, e.g. *he worked*; future time is referred to with modal verbs, e.g. *will*, and time expressions

Verb the part of a sentence which typically comes between the subject and the object and can be in the present or past tense, e.g. *Millions of people move to cities every year.*

UNIT 1 Education

ACADEMIC FOCUS: PRESENTING INFORMATION

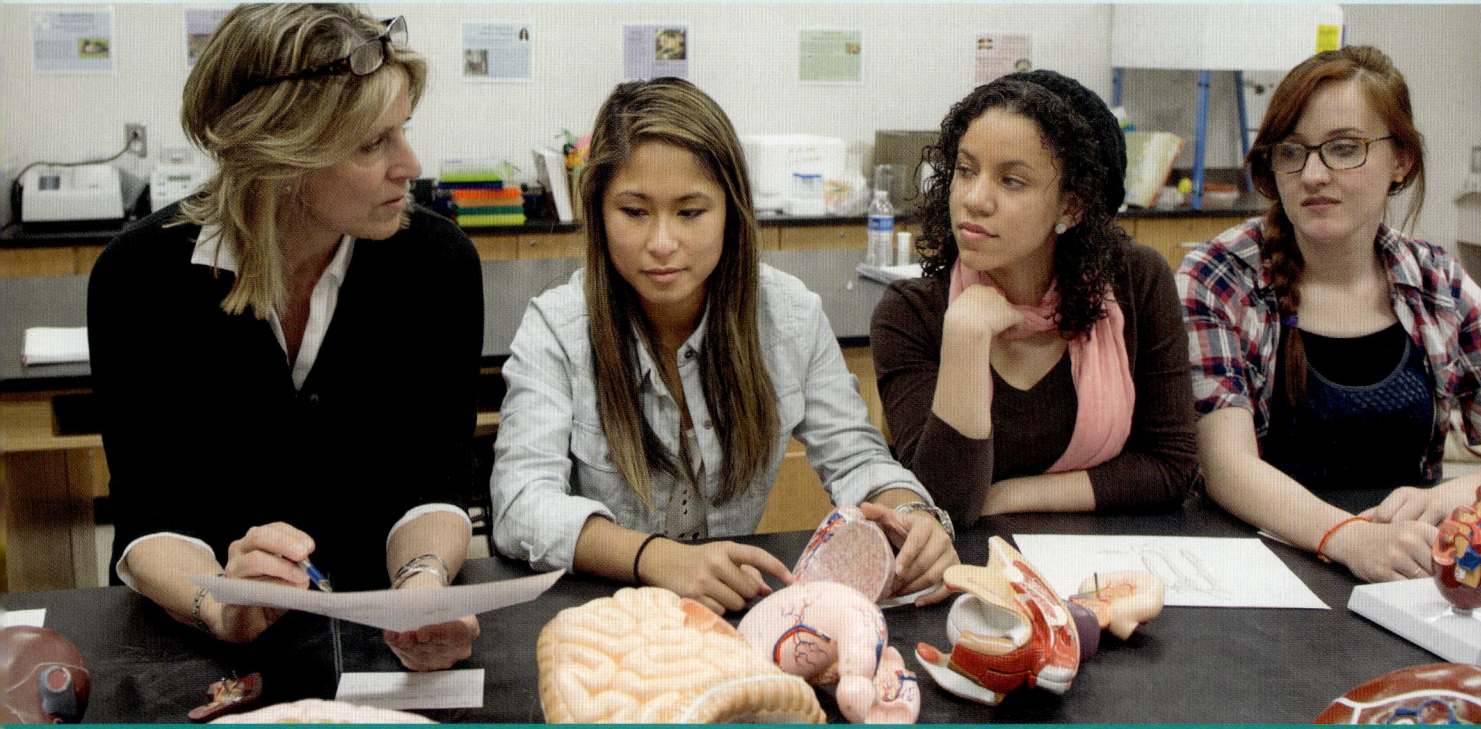

LEARNING OBJECTIVES
This unit covers:

Listening and Speaking
- Understanding a short presentation and taking notes
- Giving a short presentation about yourself and your plans

Reading
- Recognizing text types
- Understanding information in a textbook
- Taking notes from a text

Writing
- Planning and writing sentences with personal information
- Analysing a personal statement
- Writing a personal statement using linking language

Vocabulary
- Vocabulary-building: Verbs and nouns
- Collocation: Verb + noun

Academic Language Check
- Talking about now and future plans
- Giving information and instructions or advice
- *and, but, because*

Discussion

1 Work in pairs. Look at the picture. Who are the people? Which subject is it?

design   engineering   English   geography   history   information technology   mathematics   media studies   physical education   science

2 🔊 1.1 Listen and repeat the subjects in 1.

3 Match the lecturers' words a–j with the subjects in 1.

Example: 'We use plastic in lots of products.' – design

a ~~'We use plastic in lots of products.'~~
b 'Young people watch more videos online than on TV.'
c 'Next, we heat the chemicals.'
d 'The first man in space was in 1961.'
e 'The population of Peru is 32 million.'
f 'Multiply this number by five.'
g 'The verb comes after the subject of the sentence.'
h 'Kick the ball to your partner.'
i 'The Burj Khalifa is an example of a skyscraper.'
j 'Today, our topic is HTML for the web.'

4 Work in pairs. What subjects do you study? What subjects do you like? Why?

Example: *I study English, geography, and history. My favourite subject is geography because I like learning about other countries.*

1A Listening & Speaking Presentations (1)

This module covers:
- Understanding a short presentation and taking notes
- Giving a short presentation about yourself and your plans

TASK 1 Talking about how you learn

1 Look at activities 1–6. When you study, which activities do you do? Tick (✓) the ones you like.
   1 reading academic textbooks ☐
   2 listening to lectures ☐
   3 watching videos online ☐
   4 making notes ☐
   5 doing exercises ☐
   6 discussing information in groups ☐

2 Think about learning English. What activities work for you? Say what you like / don't like doing.
   Example: *I like watching videos online. I don't like working in groups.*

TASK 2 Understanding key information in a presentation

1 ▶1.2 Watch a student presentation. Circle the correct words / phrases.
   Name: Steve Pacher / Shaun Pallet / (Shri Patel)
   Country: Indiana / India / Indonesia
   Favourite school subjects: mathematics / science / history
   Future university subject: mathematics / biology / management
   Likes: doing exercises / reading academic textbooks / working in groups

2 ▶1.2 Watch again and match 1–6 with a–f.
   Example: *I'm from India.*
   1 I'm from *c*
   2 We study ____
   3 You need ____
   4 Maths and science are ____
   5 I like ____
   6 I don't like ____

   a hard at school.
   b reading academic textbooks.
   c ~~India.~~
   d management because the course is very practical.
   e high grades to enter the best universities.
   f my favourite subjects.

3 Look at the sentences in 2. Are they about the present or the future?

> **What is an academic presentation?**
> As part of academic study, students sometimes give presentations, i.e. they give short talks about their subject to their tutor and other students.

UNIT 1A LISTENING & SPEAKING 009

ACADEMIC LANGUAGE

▶ Language reference page 148

Present simple Talking about now

To talk about now, use verbs in the present simple.

	+ Positive	− Negative	? Question
be	I'**m** a student at university. It'**s** difficult. Maths and science **are** my favourite subjects.	I'**m not** at university. It **isn't** difficult. They **aren't** my favourite subjects.	**Are** you a student? **Is** she a lecturer?
other verbs	I **like** history. They **like** watching videos. She **studies** maths.	I **don't like** working in groups. They **don't like** history. She **doesn't study** English.	**Do** you **study** science? **Do** they **like** English? **Does** he **like** reading?

🔊 **1.3** Listen and repeat the sentences and questions.

TASK 3 Practising the present simple

1 Underline the correct verb forms.
1. I *'m* / *is* from Mexico.
2. In China, students *study* / *studies* for many hours a day.
3. He *need* / *needs* a good grade in his English exam.
4. Design and geography *is* / *are* my favourite subjects.
5. Maths and science *aren't* / *isn't* difficult.
6. She *like* / *likes* working with other students, but she *don't like* / *doesn't like* reading textbooks.

2 Make questions with *Are* or *Do*.
1. you / a university student?
2. you / study maths?
3. you / like / read / textbooks?
4. you / like / work / in groups or on your own?

3 Work in pairs. Ask and answer the questions in 2.
Example: A *Are you a university student?*
B *Yes, I am. / No, I'm not.*

TASK 4 Noting down key information

1 ▶ **1.4** Watch another student presentation. Complete the notes.
Name: *Leila Wong*
From: ....
Future subject: ....
Likes: .... / .... / ....
Future plans: become a ....

2 ▶ **1.4** Watch again and complete the sentences with the correct verb.
1. I .... to do a Master's degree.
2. I .... to study business.
3. I .... to become a project manager.
4. I .... to work with people on international projects.

010 UNIT 1A LISTENING & SPEAKING

ACADEMIC LANGUAGE
▶ Language reference page 148

Present simple + *to* infinitive Talking about future plans

To talk about future hopes and plans, use the verbs *plan, hope, want* in the present tense + *to* infinitive:
 I **plan to study** business.
 I **hope to become** a project manager.
 She **plans to work** in logistics.
 I **don't want to study** maths at university. I **want to study** management.

You can also use *would like* + *to* infinitive:
 I**'d like to study** problems and find solutions.

To ask about hopes and plans, use *Do / Does* … or a *Wh-* question:
 Do you plan to study engineering?
 Does she want to work in America?
 What do you want to study?
 Where does he hope to work?

🔊 **1.5** Listen and repeat the sentences and questions.

TASK 5 Practising the present simple for future plans

1 🔊 **1.6** Complete the conversation. Use the words in brackets. Listen and check.
 Teacher ¹*Do you plan to study* (you / plan / study) history at university?
 Student No, I don't. I ² _____ (like) history, but I ³ _____ ('d like / work) in business, so I ⁴ _____ (want / do) a business degree.
 Teacher OK. Where ⁵ _____ (you / hope / study)?
 Student Well, my brother ⁶ _____ (plan / go) to an American university next year. I ⁷ _____ ('d like / go) there too.

2 Make sentences about your future plans. Use *plan to, want to, hope to, would like to*.

3 Work in pairs. Ask each other questions about your plans in 2.
 Example: **A** *What do you plan to do?*
  B *I plan to …*

TASK 6 Preparing and giving a short presentation

1 Read Stefan's presentation. Complete the same information about yourself.

> 'I'm Stefan and I'm from Germany. I plan to study engineering at university because I like solving problems and doing experiments. I don't like lectures, but I like studying with other students. In the future I hope to work abroad. I want to be a project manager. I'd like to work for an international company.'

 1 Your name: _____
 2 From: _____
 3 Future subject: _____
 4 Likes: _____
 5 Future plans: _____

2 Work in pairs and practise your presentations. Give feedback.

3 Take turns to give your presentations. Watch the presenter and make short notes.

> **INDEPENDENT STUDY**
> It is useful to practise giving a presentation.
> ▶ Record or video a short presentation about yourself. Listen or watch and note down any mistakes. Then do the presentation again.

1B Reading Textbooks (1)

This module covers:
- Recognizing text types
- Understanding information in a textbook
- Taking notes from a text

TASK 1 Recognizing text types

1 Look at the words in the list. Label text types 1–5.

examination essay   lecture slides   magazine article   ~~report~~   textbook

> **What is a text type?**
> A text type is a written or spoken text. Written text types: an essay, an article, a report, etc. Spoken text types: a presentation, a discussion, a lecture, etc.

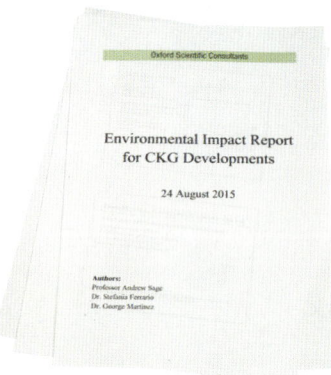

1 _report_

2 ....

3 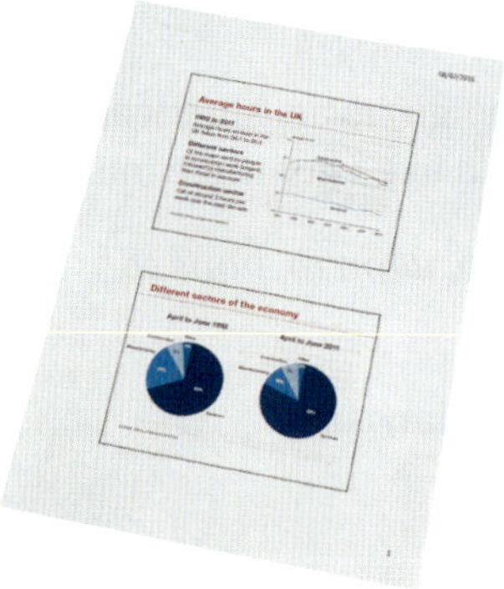 ....   4 ....   5 ....

2 Work in pairs. Which texts in 1 do you read?

Example: I read magazine articles in my language.

I read .... in my language.
I read .... in English.
I need to read .... in English in the future.

TASK 2 Understanding information in a textbook

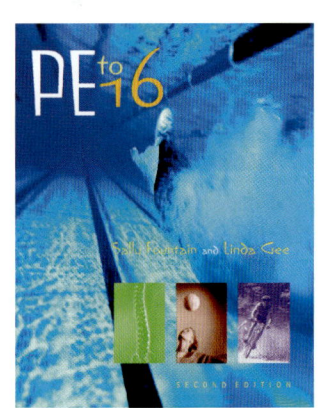

1 Look at the book cover. Are the sentences true (T) or false (F)?
  1 The textbook is about physical education. ......
  2 The textbook is only about swimming. ......
  3 The textbook is for sixteen-year-old students. ......

2 Read Text 1, from the textbook *PE to 16*. What is the text about?
  1 how to learn new skills
  2 how to run faster
  3 how to study

TEXT 1

Learning new skills

You learn new skills in PE in different ways.

Copying

You often learn a new skill by copying. For example, in a PE lesson, the teacher shows you what to do and then you copy it. Four things are important here:
- Watch carefully.
- Remember what you see.
- Practise and repeat the activity.
- Develop your physical ability (e.g. to run faster).

Learning from your mistakes

You also learn from your mistakes. For example, if you practise something and it doesn't work, then your PE teachers help you; they watch you and then they give you feedback. If you make a mistake, your teacher tells you. In this way, you learn from your mistakes.

SOURCE: Adapted from Fountain, S. & Goodwin, L. 2009. p.126. *PE to 16* 3rd ed. Oxford: Oxford University Press.

3 Match the pairs of words with definitions a or b.

1 skill / subject
   a an ability
   b an area of knowledge (at school / university)
2 copy / repeat
   a to do the same thing more than once
   b to do something in the same way
3 learn / practise
   a to do an activity and improve your skills
   b to gain a skill or knowledge of a subject
4 remember / develop
   a to have something in your memory
   b to become better or stronger
5 mistake / feedback
   a an incorrect action
   b information about correct or incorrect actions

4 Read Text 1 again. Are the sentences true (T) or false (F)?

1 There is one way to learn a new skill. ....
2 In PE, watch the teacher carefully. ....
3 Copy the activity and repeat it. ....
4 Mistakes are bad for learning. ....
5 A PE teacher says what you do correctly and incorrectly. ....

TASK 3 Taking notes from a text

1 Complete the notes with words / phrases from Text 1.

> **Copying**
> watch carefully → ¹............................ → practise and repeat → ²............................
> **Learning from your mistakes**
> practise something → ³............................ → your PE teacher tells you → ⁴............................

> **ACADEMIC LANGUAGE** ▶ Language reference page 148
>
> **Present simple and imperative** Giving information and instructions or advice
>
> To give information that is generally true, use the present simple:
>   You **learn** from your mistakes. The teacher **shows** you what to do.
>
> To give instructions or advice, use the imperative. The imperative form is the same as the infinitive form without *to*:
>   **Watch** carefully. **Remember** what you see.

TASK 4 Practising giving information and instructions

1 Read Text 1 again. Underline verbs in the present simple and circle verbs in the imperative.

2 Underline the correct form of the verbs.
   1 Copying *be / is* a good way to learn a new skill.
   2 A teacher *give / gives* you feedback on your English.
   3 Please *watch / to watch* the other students carefully.
   4 *Remember / To remember* what you see and then *copy / copies* it.
   5 First your teacher *show / shows* you what to do and then you *do / does* it.
   6 When you *learn / learns* something new, *try / tries* to remember it.

3 Complete the sentences with the verbs in brackets in the correct form.
   1 Watching my teacher .... the best way for me to learn. (be)
   2 Always .... to the instructions carefully. (listen)
   3 A good teacher always .... helpful feedback. (give)
   4 The students .... all good at watching and copying. (be)
   5 .... from your mistakes. (learn)

TASK 5 Understanding the main information and taking notes

1 Read Text 2, the next part of the text from *PE to 16*. Does it:
   1 give instructions to teachers?
   2 give information and advice about learning new skills?
   3 explain how to learn new football skills?

> **TEXT 2**
>
> There are two more ways of learning a new skill.
>
> **Role models**
> You also learn skills from role models. A role model is an important person in our lives like a good friend, parent, teacher, or even someone famous. For example, when a young footballer likes a famous player from their favourite team, they watch this role model play and then try to copy him or her.
>
> **Changing learned skills**
> Sometimes you learn a new skill and it is very difficult to change it. This is a problem if you learn the skill incorrectly the first time. Here is some useful advice:
> - Go back to the beginning and learn the skill again.
> - Don't make the same mistakes.
> - Be patient and do lots of practice.
>
> SOURCE: Adapted from Fountain, S. & Goodwin, L. 2009. p.126. *PE to 16* 3rd ed. Oxford: Oxford University Press.

2 Read Text 2 again. Take notes on 'Role models' and 'Changing learned skills'. Write your notes as flowcharts.

> **Role models**
> ¹ *You like a role model* → ² _____ → ³ _____
> **Changing learned skills**
> ⁴ _____ → ⁵ _____ → ⁶ _____

3 Work in pairs and compare your notes in 2. Did you write the same notes?

TASK 6 Critical thinking – summarizing information

1 Work in pairs. Match the sentence halves to summarize Texts 1 and 2.

Example: *Texts 1 and 2 are about how to learn new skills.*

1 Texts 1 and 2 are about ...   *c*
2 Copying is when you ...   ____
3 Learning from your mistakes is when you ...   ____
4 Learning from role models is when you ...   ____
5 Changing learned skills is when you ...   ____

a try something, listen to feedback, and try it again.
b start learning a skill again from the beginning.
c ~~how to learn new skills.~~
d watch, remember, and learn.
e choose an important person in your life and learn from them.

2 Think about learning English. Which advice from Texts 1 and 2 is true for you?

Example: *I copy my teacher when I learn new words.*

3 Work in groups. Talk about learning English. Write five sentences for a new student. Use the ideas below or your own ideas. Give advice or instructions using the present simple and imperative forms.

making mistakes   working with other students   using dictionaries
learning new words   time for studying   asking your teacher for help

Example: *When you make a mistake in English, write the sentence again correctly.*

> **INDEPENDENT STUDY**
>
> Find different ways of learning new words.
>
> ▶ Think about how you learn new words in English. Ask other students and try their ideas. Which way do you like best?

1C Writing (1) Sentences about you

This module covers:
- Planning and writing sentences with personal information

TASK 1 Understanding a personal statement

1 Read the student's personal statement. What is it for?

   a an application for a job at a sports centre
   b a university application to study business
   c an application for a job at a university

> **What is a personal statement?**
> A personal statement is a written description of a person's qualifications, experience, and other positive things. You write it on an application form for a university course or a new job.

Personal statement
Nur Sadik

I am 18 years old and I'm from Turkey. I study mathematics, science, and geography at the British International School in Istanbul. In my free time I like sport and volunteering. I am a member of the local basketball team and I'm good at tennis. Every Saturday I work at a special centre for children with disabilities. I want to study business at university. I hope to develop my academic and personal skills. I'd like to work as a project manager in construction.

2 Read the statement again and tick (✓) the information Nur gives.

Age and country	☐	Address	☐
Date of birth	☐	Interests and hobbies	☐
School subjects	☐	Future plans	☐

3 Answer the questions about Nur.
1. Where does Nur go to school?
2. What subjects does she study?
3. What does she do in her free time?
4. What are her future plans?

ACADEMIC LANGUAGE ▸ Language reference page 149

Sentences (1) Writing personal information

We often give personal information in the present simple.
Use *I am* + information about you:

I	am	18 years old.
		good at maths and science.
		a member of the local handball team.

Use verbs *like, enjoy, want, need*, etc. to give information about your interests and future plans. Use a **subject-verb-object (svo)** sentence pattern:

subject	verb	object
	like	sport.
I	study	mathematics, science, and geography.
	want	to study business at university.

It is common to start with a sentence with *be* and write the next sentence with another verb:
*I **am** 19 years old. I **want** to study engineering at university.*

TASK 2 Practising present simple sentences

1 Complete the personal statement with verbs.

Personal statement

Mohammed Al Jabri

I ¹ _am_ 17 years old and I'm from Oman. I ² _____ English, physical education, and economics at the British School in Muscat. In my free time I ³ _____ watching films and writing stories. I ⁴ _____ a member of the local film club and I ⁵ _____ as a journalist for our school newspaper. I ⁶ _____ to study English at university. I'd ⁷ _____ to become a professional journalist in the future.

2 Correct the sentences.

Example: I an engineering student. *I am an engineering student.*

1 I 20 years old. _____
2 I'm Yemen. _____
3 Am a student at Birmingham University. _____
4 I studies mathematics. _____
5 I like read books. _____
6 I'm a member local football team. _____
7 I plan go to university. _____
8 In the future, I like to study economics. _____

TASK 3 Planning and writing personal information

1 Note down your personal information for points 1–5.

1 Age: _____
2 Nationality: _____
3 Secondary school: _____
4 Interests: _____
5 University / Job plans: _____

2 Write one sentence for each point in 1.

Example: *I'm 19 years old. I'm from Dubai. …*

TASK 4 Checking your writing

1 Read your sentences in Task 3.2 again. Use this checklist to check your writing. Did you:

- use the correct verbs? ☐
- use the present simple? ☐
- give interesting information? ☐

2 Work in pairs. Read your partner's sentences. Use the checklist in 1 and give feedback.

1C Writing (2) A personal statement

This module covers:
- Analysing a personal statement
- Writing a personal statement using linking language

TASK 1 Analysing a personal statement

1 Read two personal statements, A and B. Answer questions a–c.
a Which statement has more sentences?
b Which words are different in B?
c Which statement do you prefer? Why?

Statement A

I am 19. I am from Malaysia. I have an international baccalaureate from the Kuala Lumpur International School. School exams are very difficult in Malaysia. I have grade A in all my subjects.

In my free time I like sport. I often go running. I always play football on Saturdays. I am a member of my local football team. We play against other teams.

My favourite subjects are history and geography. In the future, I hope to study management at university. I'm interested in business.

Statement B

I am 19 and I am from Malaysia. I have an international baccalaureate from the Kuala Lumpur International School. School exams are very difficult in Malaysia, but I have grade A in all my subjects.

In my free time I like sport and I often go running. I always play football on Saturdays because I am a member of my local football team and we play against other teams.

My favourite subjects are history and geography, but in the future, I hope to study management at university because I'm interested in business.

ACADEMIC LANGUAGE ▶ Language reference page 149

Linking language (1) *and, but, because*

We often join simple sentences together or add information with linking language. This makes writing easier to read.
Join two sentences with *and* and *but*.
Use *and* to add information:
  I like sport. I am a member of a basketball team.
  *I like sport **and** I am a member of a basketball team.*
Use *but* to show contrast:
  I study English. I don't study mathematics.
  *I study English, **but** I don't study mathematics.*
Use *because* to give a reason:
  I study English. I want to work in the USA.
  *I study English **because** I want to work in the USA.*
Use a capital letter (e.g. A, B) at the beginning of the sentence. Use a full stop (.) at the end. Use a comma (,) before *but*:
  ***I** study English**,** but I don't study mathematics. **M**athematics is difficult.*

018 UNIT 1C WRITING (2)

TASK 2 Practising joining sentences

1 Read personal statement B again and circle the linking language.

2 Choose the correct word in brackets and join the two sentences.
   Example: I am good at maths and science. I have A grades in these subjects.
   (and / but)
   I am good at maths and science and I have A grades in these subjects.
   1 I enjoy most sports. I don't like football. (and / but)
   2 I like studying languages. I have a C grade in English. (because / but)
   3 I am interested in travel. I enjoy meeting people from different countries. (but / because)
   4 I am in the athletics team at school. I am a member of a local athletics club. (because / and)
   5 I study music at school. I learn the piano at home. (but / and)
   6 I plan to study engineering at university. I hope to be a project manager. (and / but)
   7 I hope to become a journalist. I like writing and meeting new people. (because / and)

3 Complete the sentences with personal information.
   1 I'm .... I'm from ....
   2 I like .... I don't like ....
   3 I study .... I like it.
   4 In my free time I play .... I play ....
   5 My favourite subject is .... I don't like ....
   6 I plan to study .... at university. I want to become a .... in the future.

4 Write each pair of sentences in 3 as one sentence. Use *and, but,* or *because*.

5 Check your sentences in 4.
   1 Does each sentence start with a capital letter?
   2 Does each sentence end with a full stop?
   3 Is there a comma before *but*?

TASK 3 Writing a personal statement

1 Note down answers to the questions.
   How old are you? ....
   Where are you from? ....
   Where do you go to school? ....
   What subjects do you study? Why? ....
   What do you like doing in your free time? Why? ....
   What are your future plans? What job do you hope to do? ....

2 Write a paragraph using your notes in 1. Use personal statement B in Task 1 as a model. Remember to use linking language.

3 Read your paragraph again. Check the capital letters and punctuation in each sentence.

> **INDEPENDENT STUDY**
>
> After you write in English, it's important to check your work.
> ▶ When you write, always check grammar, spelling, and punctuation and correct any mistakes.
>
> *Sample answer:*
> page 159

UNIT 1C WRITING (2) 019

1D Vocabulary

TASK 1 Vocabulary-building: Verbs and nouns

1 Look at the words in bold in the pairs of sentences. Write verb (V) or noun (N).

   Example: A *After the lecture, we **discuss** the topic.* V
   B *The **discussion** after the lecture was interesting.* N

   1 A I want to **teach** geography when I leave university. ___
   B We have two **teachers** for mathematics. ___
   2 A Most people **study** English nowadays. ___
   B One area of media **studies** is how we communicate online. ___
   3 A I hope to **manage** my own department one day. ___
   B I'd like to study **management** at university. ___
   4 A What are your **plans** for the future? ___
   B What subjects do you **plan** to study? ___
   5 A I work at Oxford University and I **lecture** in history. ___
   B My father is a **lecturer** at Oxford University. ___
   6 A My **presentation** is about my plans for the future. ___
   B I'd like to **present** some information about me. ___

2 Rewrite the sentences so they are true for you.

   Example: *I study engineering at university.*
   1 I study English at university.
   ....
   2 I have two teachers for my English lessons.
   ....
   3 In the future I hope to study management.
   ....
   4 I also plan to open my own business.
   ....

TASK 2 Collocation: Verb + noun

1 Underline the verb in each sentence. Write the noun that collocates with each verb.

   exercises   lectures   notes   solutions   ~~subjects~~   textbooks   videos

   Example: Which *subjects* do you <u>study</u>?
   1 For my course, I read a lot of different ....
   2 Please make .... on the lecture.
   3 How often do you do the .... in the book?
   4 Do you watch .... on your course?
   5 In engineering, we find .... to the problem.
   6 At university, students listen to ....

2 Choose the correct verbs in italics.
   1 Listen to the teacher and *repeat / do* the sentence.
   2 I want to *do / become* a Master's degree.
   3 You can *develop / copy* your physical ability with lots of practice.
   4 Your teachers *give / make* you feedback.
   5 I *learn / practise* the piano twice a week.
   6 How many words can you *study / remember* from the last lesson?

> **INDEPENDENT STUDY**
> It is important to learn the word class of a new word, e.g. *verb* (v), *noun* (n), *adjective* (adj).
> ▶ Write down new words from this unit and write the word class afterwards, for example: *study* (v), *student* (n).

1E Academic Language Check

TASK 1 Talking about now and future plans

1 Write the verbs in brackets in the present simple.

1. I _____ (be) from Oman.
2. Aziz _____ (want / not) to become a project manager.
3. History and geography _____ (be / not) difficult subjects.
4. They _____ (plan) to study science at university.
5. He _____ (be) interested in information technology.
6. We _____ (hope) to work in the USA next year.
7. She _____ (study) economics at a business school.
8. You _____ (like / not) doing examinations.

2 Which sentences in 1 are about now (N)? Which are about the future (F)?

1 ___ 2 ___ 3 ___ 4 ___ 5 ___ 6 ___ 7 ___ 8 ___

3 Write a question for each sentence in 1.

1. *Are you from Oman?*
2. *Does Aziz want to become a project manager?*
3. _____
4. _____
5. _____
6. _____
7. _____
8. _____

TASK 2 Giving information and instructions or advice

1 Read a paragraph from a university guide. Choose the correct verb form in italics.

When ¹*start / you start* a new course at university, ²*need / you need* to go to every lecture. Before the lecture, ³*try / you try* to read about the subject in the textbooks. During the lecture, ⁴*make / you make* notes and ⁵*listen / you listen* carefully. After the lecture, ⁶*talk / you talk* to other students about the subject. It ⁷*'s / be* a good way to learn and think about the main points.

TASK 3 *and, but, because*

1 Match the sentence halves.

1. I'm Spanish and …
2. I'm good at history, but …
3. I plan to do media studies because …
4. I enjoy sport and …
5. Geography is my favourite subject because …
6. I'm at school at the moment, but …

a. the teacher is good.
b. I'm from Madrid.
c. I play football and tennis.
d. I'm not good at mathematics.
e. I like films and TV.
f. I plan to start university in September.

2 Complete the sentence in three different ways.

1. I study English and _____ .
2. I study English, but _____ .
3. I study English because _____ .

UNIT 2 Information

ACADEMIC FOCUS: DESCRIBING FEATURES

LEARNING OBJECTIVES

This unit covers:

Listening and Speaking
- Understanding the introduction to a presentation
- Noticing the language of presentations
- Giving a short presentation about a website

Reading
- Understanding the purpose of a text
- Recognizing important information in a text and taking notes

Writing
- Writing descriptive sentences using noun phrases
- Analysing a descriptive paragraph
- Writing a descriptive paragraph using linking language

Vocabulary
- Websites
- Noun suffixes
- Vocabulary-building: Antonyms

Academic Language Check
- Sequencing and adding information
- Understanding a noun phrase
- Adjectives in noun phrases
- *in addition, also, so, or*

Discussion

1 Look at the phrases. At school or university, where do you find information for your studies?

from my teacher or lecturer   in a textbook
in a library   on the TV and radio   on websites
from friends   on my mobile phone   other: ....

2 Work in pairs. Look at the diagram and make six sentences about information. Use each verb once.

Example: *We find information on websites.*

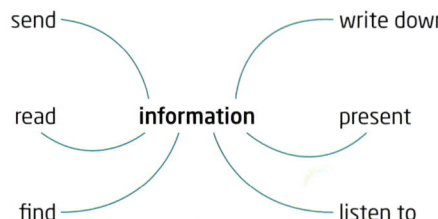

3 Work in pairs. Which is your favourite website for …?

entertainment   general information   news
sport   travel information   work or study

4 Tick (✓) the important features of your favourite website.

easy to use ☐   useful links ☐
factual information ☐   videos ☐
interesting podcasts ☐   other ☐

5 Work in groups. Discuss websites you often use.

Example: *Udacity is my favourite website for study. You can listen to podcasts of lectures.*

2A Listening & Speaking Presentations (2)

This module covers:
- Understanding the introduction to a presentation
- Noticing the language of presentations
- Giving a short presentation about a website

TASK 1 Understanding the introduction to a presentation

1 Look at the categories in the table. They refer to features of academic websites. Match students' comments 1–6 about different academic websites to the correct category.

Category	Comments
Information (What is it about?)	1
Authority (Who writes it?)	
Design (How does it look?)	

1 'All the texts have useful facts.'
2 'It's a university website so I think it's reliable.'
3 'It's really easy to find links.'
4 'I like the colours and it uses great photos.'
5 'All the writers are qualified lecturers and researchers.'
6 'It has articles on hundreds of different subjects.'

2 ▶2.1 Watch the introduction to a student's presentation.
1 What is the presentation about?
2 In what order does he talk about the categories in **1**?

> **What is authority?**
> An academic resource (e.g. a textbook or a website) has authority when its writers are experts in the subject and the information is reliable, i.e. it's true and you can believe it.

TASK 2 Understanding the features of a web page

1 Match the words / phrases in the list with the parts of the web page 1–8.

domain name   heading   home page   image   link   logo   PDF   search box

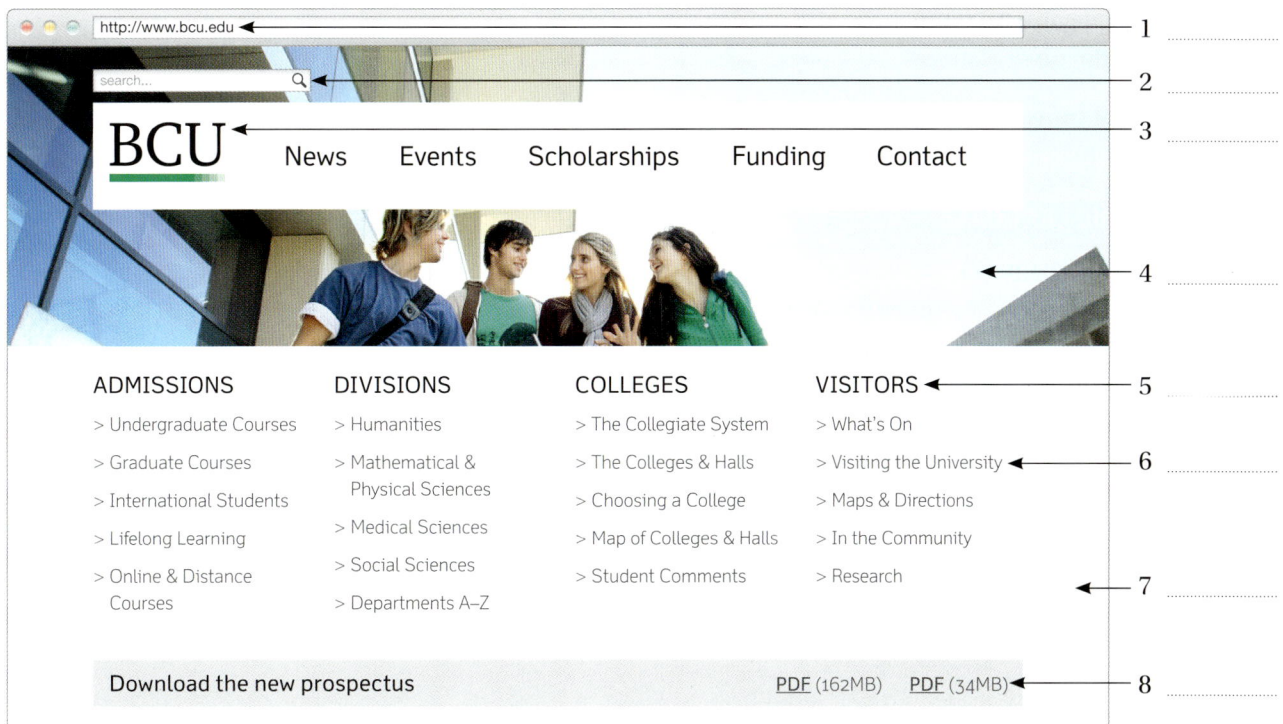

2 ▶2.2 Watch the main part of the student's presentation. Complete the notes.

Authority
On an academic website, look for:
- a ¹_____ ending with the letters .edu
- a ²_____ for the university
- ³_____ for different subject areas

Design
Look at the design:
- The ⁴_____ is simple. It uses one ⁵_____ and one or two colours.
- You can use the ⁶_____ to find information quickly.
- The ⁷_____ are easy to read.

Information
Check the information on the site:
- click on the ⁸_____ to open an article
- look at the title
- quickly read about the author

3 Work in pairs. Do you agree with the student's advice? Which things do you think are most important?

TASK 3 Noticing the language of presentations

1 ▶2.1, 2.2 Watch the presentation again. Number the expressions 1–8 in the order you hear them.

Firstly, I'm going to talk about … ____   My talk is in three parts: … ____
Today I'd like to talk about … ____   To sum up … ____
Hello. My name's … __1__   Are there any questions? ____
Finally, I'll talk about … ____   Secondly, we'll look at … ____

2 Which expressions in 1 do you use for:
   a introducing the presentation?
   b sequencing information?
   c ending the presentation?

3 Look at the transcript on page 168. Find three expressions for adding information.

ACADEMIC LANGUAGE ▶Language reference page 149

Linking language (2) Sequencing and adding information
Make a presentation clear for your audience with linking words and phrases.
Sequence information with *Firstly, …, Secondly, …, Finally, …*:
   Firstly, *I'm going to talk about the authority of a website.*
   Secondly, *we'll look at the design.*
   Finally, *I'll talk about the information on a subject page.*
Add information with *It also has …, In addition, …,* and *Also, …*:
   The domain name ends in .edu. **It also has** *a university logo.*
   In addition, *it has subject headings.* **Also,** *the links are easy to read.*

🔊 2.3 Listen and repeat the linking language and sentences.

024 UNIT 2A LISTENING & SPEAKING

TASK 4 Practising sequencing and adding information

1 🔊 2.4 Complete another introduction with words from Academic Language. Then listen and check.

I'm going to talk about the library's online resource. ¹ _Firstly_, we'll look at how you register on our website. ² _____, I'll talk about using the home page. And ³ _____, I'll talk about the information on the site. In ⁴ _____, I'll show you how to find specific information for your courses. We'll ⁵ _____ have time for questions at the end.

2 Look at the features of an academic website. For each section, decide on phrases you can use to sequence and add information.

Authority	Design	Information
• a domain name ending with the letters *.edu* • a university logo • the authors are qualified lecturers	• one main image on the home page • only two colours • a search box to find information quickly • the links are easy to read	• includes articles as PDFs • there is information on many different subjects • the articles are very useful

3 Work in pairs. Take turns to talk about features of the website. How confident do you feel about using presenting language?

TASK 5 Preparing and giving a short presentation

1 Prepare a short presentation about a website you often use for studying. You can show the website during the presentation. Make notes about:
- the authority of the website
- the design
- the information.

2 Work in pairs and practise your presentations. When you listen to your partner, do they use language for:
- introducing the presentation?
- sequencing and adding information?
- ending the presentation?

3 Take turns to give your presentations. Watch the presenter. Do they:
- talk about the authority, design, and information?
- use expressions to introduce, sequence, and add information, and end the presentation?

> **INDEPENDENT STUDY**
>
> It is useful to practise giving a presentation to another person, to check what you say and how you say it.
>
> ▶ Prepare a short presentation. Ask another student to watch and give feedback. Do you include the important information? Do you use the correct expressions to organize the presentation?

UNIT 2A LISTENING & SPEAKING 025

2B Reading Textbooks (2)

This module covers:
- Understanding the purpose of a text
- Recognizing important information in a text and taking notes

TASK 1 Thinking about the purpose of reading

1 Think about what you read. What texts do you often read:
- in your free time?
- for your studies?

2 Tick (✓) the purpose(s) of each text type in the table.

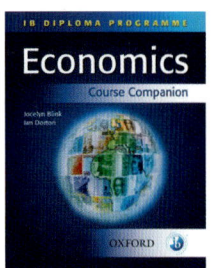   

	a textbook	a magazine	a news website	an advertisement
to inform	✓			
to entertain				
to give an opinion				

3 Work in pairs. Compare your answers in 2 and give reasons.

Example: *A textbook informs students because it gives information about their subject.*

TASK 2 Understanding the purpose of a text

1 Read Text 1 and choose the correct option a–c to complete sentences 1 and 2.
  1 The reading text is from …
    a a magazine about new technology.
    b a textbook about media studies.
    c a news website.
  2 The purpose of the text is to …
    a inform you about different types of websites.
    b entertain you.
    c give an opinion about good and bad websites.

The reasons for a website

TEXT 1

Some websites provide information and others are for entertainment. Many websites do both; they present information in an entertaining way. News websites, in particular, present news stories in this way. They make the news interesting by using text and interactive features such as video.

Other websites such as Amazon offer a service or sell products. You can also have your own blog, or a personal home page on sites like Facebook and Twitter. These social networking websites are very popular nowadays because the people who use the website provide the information.

SOURCE: Adapted from Morris, R. et al. 2009. p.76. *GCSE Media Studies*. Cheltenham: Nelson Thornes.

GLOSSARY

entertainment *(n)* activities for interest and relaxation

interactive *(adj)* allowing communication in both directions (between the computer and the person)

ACADEMIC LANGUAGE   ▶ Language reference page 149

Noun phrases (1) Understanding a noun phrase

Noun phrases give the main information in a sentence. When you make notes from a textbook, you can use the noun phrases in the text.

A noun phrase always has a **head noun** (= the main noun), e.g. *website / features / information*. A noun phrase can be very short, or much longer:

Head noun: **website**
news **website** (noun + head noun)
a **website**, the **features**, some **information** (determiner + head noun)
important **information** (adjective + head noun)
a personal **website**, the interactive **features** (determiner + adjective + head noun)

A noun phrase can be the subject or object of a sentence:

subject	verb	object
Websites	provide	information.
News websites	provide	important information.

TASK 3 Practising using noun phrases to make notes

1 Read Text 1 again and underline nouns and noun phrases.

2 Complete the notes about Text 1 with noun phrases.

Four types of websites:
- 1 *information*
- 2 ....
  (Some websites do both; e.g. a .... presents news stories as information and entertainment)
- ³offer .... or sell ....
- ⁴blogs and .... home pages on .... networking

3 Use the notes in 2. Tell a partner about different types of websites.

TASK 4 Recognizing important information in a text

1 Read Text 2. Are the sentences true (T) or false (F)?
   1 Most websites have completely different features. ....
   2 Headings on a website can make the text more difficult to understand. ....
   3 Many websites include videos. ....
   4 Banners often have advertisements for products. ....
   5 The design of the home page should interest the user. ....
   6 Designers usually put website features in different positions on every home page. ....
   7 Users of a new website look at headings and links first. ....
   8 The search box is the last feature they look at. ....

Features of websites
TEXT 2

Different websites have different information, but the main features of websites and their home pages are often the same. Most websites have these features:
- **Headings** These divide the information into easy-to-read sections.
- **Text** The main body of the text is often presented in a box.
5 • **Links** These can be words or images. When you click them, you go to another page.
- **Video** Nowadays, many websites also include moving images and video.
- **Banners** These are usually across the top of the website's home page. They often have adverts for products and services.
- **Search box** You can type a word or words to find important information.

10 Design features are very important on a home page. Web designers use different colours, images, video, and interactive features, so users find it more interesting. The position of the different features is often the same on a website, so it's easier to read. As a result, when a user looks at a homepage for the first time, their eyes usually follow the pattern below.

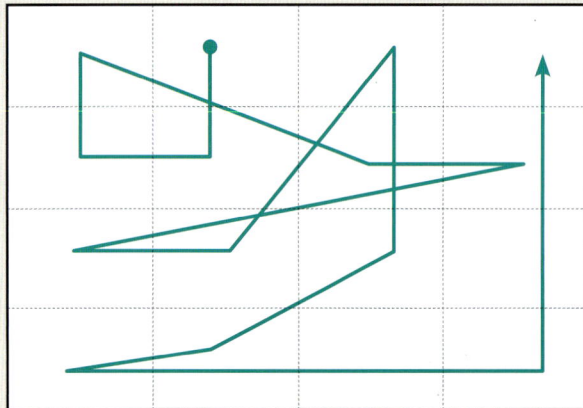

15   According to research, users first look near the top left-hand corner on a website. Usually, this is where you find a logo or name. Next, the eyes look at the headings and link buttons to other pages. The final place is the top right hand corner, where you find the search box.

SOURCE: Adapted from Morris, R. et al. 2009. pp.77-9. *GCSE Media Studies*. Cheltenham: Nelson Thornes.

GLOSSARY
pattern *(n)* the usual way sth happens

2 Read Text 2 again. Make short notes about the features, design, and layout of websites.
   Types of features: *headings, text,* ....

   Design: ....

   Layout: ....

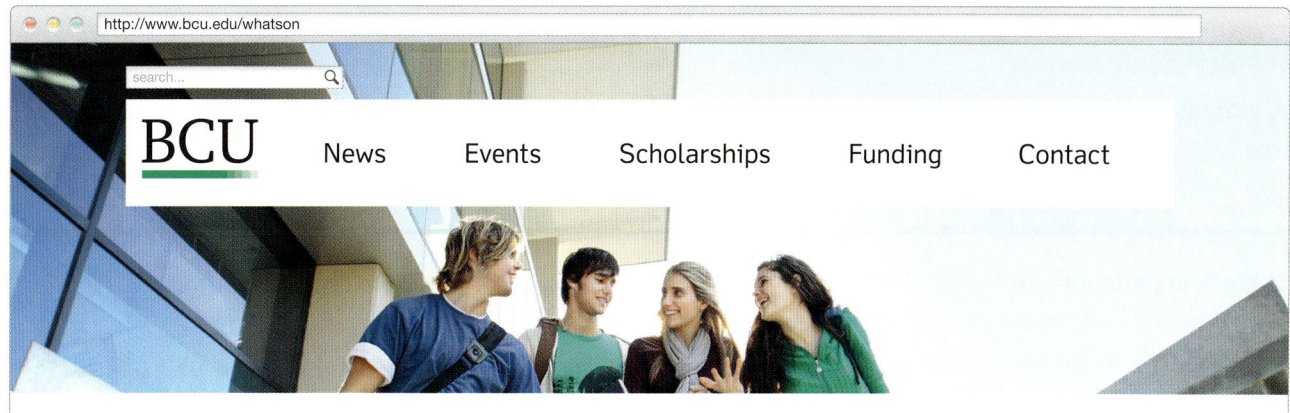

TASK 5 Critical thinking – discussing a website

1 Work in pairs. Look at the university web page above, or find another example online. Make notes about these questions.
   - What kind of information is on the website?
   - Do you like the design? Why? / Why not?
   - What features are on the home page? Are they in the normal position for a website?

2 Compare your answers with another pair. Then work in a group and discuss the points in 1. Agree answers to these questions.
   - Do you think this website is useful and easy to use? Why? / Why not?
   - What other features would you add?

What is critical thinking?
Critical thinking is asking questions about what you read and listen to, e.g. *Is the new information useful to me? Is it reliable? How can I use the information in my studies?*

INDEPENDENT STUDY
Use noun phrases to find the main information in texts that you read.

▶ **Read an article in English from a textbook, newspaper, or website. Find all the noun phrases in the text.**

UNIT 2B READING 029

2C Writing (1) Descriptive sentences

This module covers:
- Writing descriptive sentences using noun phrases

TASK 1 Understanding a description

1 **Work in pairs. Ask and answer the questions.**
  1 Which TV and radio stations are famous in your country?
  2 What TV programmes do you often watch, e.g. sport, films, news, etc.?
  3 Do you watch TV programmes from other countries, e.g. TV programmes from the USA or the UK?

2 **Read a description of the BBC and answer the questions.**
  1 Why is the BBC famous?
  2 How many users visit its news website?
  3 What information is on its website?

The BBC (British Broadcasting Corporation) is a large organization. It's famous because people watch BBC television programmes and listen to BBC radio stations around the world. It also has a popular news website with 40 million users per day. In addition, other BBC websites provide free information about weather, sport, culture, and entertainment.

ACADEMIC LANGUAGE ▸ Language reference page 149

Noun phrases (2) Adjectives in noun phrases

We often use adjectives in a description, e.g. *The BBC is **famous***.
Sometimes, the adjective is part of a noun phrase, e.g. *The BBC is **a large** organization*.
You can use one or more adjectives in a noun phrase. With two adjectives, use them in this order:

   *It's a **large British** organization.* NOT *It's a ~~British large~~ organization.*

There are some common groups for ordering adjectives. Type A adjectives come before Type B adjectives.

	Examples
Type **A** adjectives describe the qualities of a noun, e.g. colour, size, or age.	red, small, large, modern, expensive, famous, free, popular
Type **B** adjectives often end in *-al* or *-ic* and refer to area, subject, or nationality.	educational, global, international, local, medical, political, social, historic, online, British

TASK 2 Practising adjectives in noun phrases

1 Underline the two adjectives in each sentence.
CNN is a popular American TV news channel. It also has a large international audience.

2 Put the words in the noun phrase in the correct order.
Example: CNN is a ... American / news channel / popular.
CNN is a popular American news channel.

1 Al Jazeera is a ... news channel / large / international.

2 The Huffington Post is a ... online / modern / news blog.

3 Handmade Films is a ... film company / small / British.

4 Facebook is a ... global / free / social networking site.

5 Oxford University is a ... university / famous / historic.

3 Underline the adjectives in the description of the BBC in Task 1. Which adjectives are part of a noun phrase? Which adjective is not part of a noun phrase?
Example: *The BBC is a <u>large</u> organization.*

4 Complete the text with an adjective or adjective + noun in the list.
expensive   famous   free   international broadcaster   local office   main headquarters

CNN is an ¹_____ with audiences in over 200 countries. It is ²_____ for its 24-hour-a-day news. It is ³_____ for viewers, but TV advertising on the channel is ⁴_____. It has its ⁵_____ in Atlanta, but it also has a ⁶_____ in every major capital city in the world.

TASK 3 Describing an organization

1 Think of a company or organization in your country. Write three sentences about it using an adjective or an adjective + noun.
1 It's _____
2 It's a _____
3 It has _____

2 Work in pairs. Compare your sentences in 1.

INDEPENDENT STUDY

Use noun phrases to make your writing interesting.

▶ Look at a piece of your writing, e.g. your writing in unit 1. Can you add any adjectives to the noun phrases?

2C Writing (2) A descriptive paragraph

This module covers:
- Analysing a descriptive paragraph
- Writing a descriptive paragraph using linking language

TASK 1 Analysing a descriptive paragraph

1 **Read a paragraph about a media company. Are sentences 1-3 true (T) or false (F)?**
   1 News Corporation is a small American company. ......
   2 It has TV channels and newspapers. ......
   3 It also makes TV shows. ......

¹News Corporation is a large media organization. ²Its headquarters is in New York, but it also has offices all over the world, so it's a global company. ³Every day, people in different countries watch its international TV news channels, or they read one of its many newspapers. ⁴In addition, the company is famous because it produces popular TV shows such as *House* and *The Simpsons*.

2 **Read the paragraph again. Which sentence (1-4) gives information about:**
   a the company's locations? sentence ......
   b the company's name and business? sentence ......
   c the company's other activities? sentence ......
   d the company's main business activities? sentence ......

ACADEMIC LANGUAGE ▶ Language reference page 149

Linking language (3) *in addition, also, so, or*

In descriptive paragraphs we use linking language to add details or explain more about something.

Join sentences with *and* and *but*, and give a reason with *because* (see Unit 1, page 18).
Use *In addition* and *also* to add information:
   News Corporation has TV news channels. **In addition**, it has newspapers.
                              It **also** has newspapers.
Use *so* to give the result:
   Millions of people watch the TV show, **so** it's very famous.
Use *or* to give an alternative.
   People watch the news on TV, **or** they read it in newspapers.

TASK 2 Practising adding information and joining sentences

1 Read the paragraph about News Corporation again. Circle the linking language.

2 Join sentences 1-5 to a-e with the word / phrase in brackets.

Example: *Al Jazeera's headquarters is in Qatar. In addition, it has 70 offices in six continents.*

1 Al Jazeera's headquarters is in Qatar. (In addition) *b*
2 Al Jazeera broadcasts news in the Middle East, Europe, Asia, and the USA. (so) ....
3 You can watch the Al Jazeera news in Arabic. (or) ....
4 Al Jazeera has a website. (also) ....
5 Al Jazeera is popular in the United States. (because) ....

a It's a global TV news network.
b ~~It has 70 offices in six continents.~~
c It has a special channel called 'Al Jazeera America'.
d It has a mobile app.
e You can watch it in English.

3 Underline the correct linking words.

Spire FM is a small radio station ¹*and / so* it's based in the English city of Salisbury. It's popular with local people ²*also / because* you can listen to music, the news, and traffic information. You can receive Spire FM on your radio ³*or / so* you can listen online on the Spire FM website. It's a commercial radio station, ⁴*but / so* it advertises local shops and businesses. ⁵*Because / In addition*, there are advertisements on the website, ⁶*but / or* this only provides about 3% of the station's income.

4 Use the notes to write a similar paragraph about the Walt Disney company. Join the sentences with linking language.

> the Walt Disney company
> large media conglomerate
> famous for children's films (*Snow White*, *The Lion King*)
> other media: Disney TV channel, Radio Disney, theme parks (Disneyland)

TASK 3 Researching and writing about a company

1 Choose a company. Find information about:
   type of company   size of company   location   products or services

2 Write a paragraph of three or four sentences about the company. Use the paragraph in Task 1 as a model.

3 Read your paragraph again and use this checklist to check your writing. Did you:
   • describe the company with adjectives and noun phrases?   ☐
   • join sentences and add more information with linking language?   ☐
   • use capital letters and punctuation correctly?   ☐

4 Work in pairs. Read your partner's paragraph. Use the checklist in 3 and give feedback.

What is research?
Academic research is finding information on a topic and then checking it, e.g. students find information on a website, then check it on another website, or in the library.

Sample answer: page 159

UNIT 2C WRITING (2) 033

2D Vocabulary

TASK 1 Websites

1 **Complete the text about an academic website with the words in the list.**

home   links   names   PDFs   search   website

The ¹_____ www.educause.edu is for managers and users of IT at colleges and universities. At the top of the ²_____ page, there are headings for the main pages. Then, below this, there is a range of ³_____ to different topics including research and publications, conferences and events, and career development. Under 'research and publications' there are book references and ⁴_____ of articles. You can type a subject in the ⁵_____ box in the top right-hand corner and it provides results. The site also lists the domain ⁶_____ of other useful sites.

TASK 2 Noun suffixes

1 **Write the verbs in the table as nouns. Use the suffixes -tion, -ation, or -ment.**

Verbs	Nouns	Verbs	Nouns
inform	¹ *information*	present	⁴
organize	²	advertise	⁵
entertain	³	educate	⁶

2 **Write six sentences with the noun forms in the table.**

TASK 3 Vocabulary-building: Antonyms

1 **An antonym is a word that means the opposite of another word. Match adjectives 1–8 with their antonyms a–h.**

1 interesting _____
2 reliable _____
3 useful _____
4 easy _____
5 expensive _____
6 important _____
7 large _____
8 modern _____

a unimportant
b old
c boring
d small
e difficult
f useless
g unreliable
h cheap

2 **Choose the correct adjective in italics.**

1 Design features are *important / unimportant* on a home page.
2 This textbook is really *useful / useless*. It has lots of factual information.
3 It's *easy / difficult* to find the information with the search box. Just type the word and it gives you useful links.
4 This university was built in 2014, so it's very *old / modern*.
5 This journal is very *cheap / expensive*, but the articles are very good, so it's worth the money.
6 The links on this website are *reliable / unreliable*. They often don't work.

> **INDEPENDENT STUDY**
>
> An antonym is a word that means the opposite of another word. You can remember adjectives in antonym pairs, e.g. *easy / difficult*.
>
> ▶ Write down new adjectives from this unit and then write down the antonym (if there is one). Use a dictionary to help you.

034   UNIT 2D VOCABULARY

2E Academic Language Check

TASK 1 Sequencing and adding information

1 Read the introduction to a presentation. Complete the linking language.

Good morning everyone. Today I'm going to present the changes to our new university website. ¹F_____, I'll talk about the new design and layout. ²S_____, we'll look at the new features.
³F_____, I'll show you how to log on to the resources section.
⁴In a_____, you'll have the chance to use this part of the site.
⁵A_____, there'll be time for questions.

TASK 2 Understanding a noun phrase

1 Underline the nouns / noun phrases in each sentence.

Example: <u>Design</u> is important on <u>a home page</u>.
1 A search box is an important feature.
2 A news website has information.
3 A website has different links.
4 A modern university has good resources.

2 Match the underlined nouns / noun phrases in 1 with a–e.

a head noun: _____design_____, _____
b determiner + noun + head noun: _____a home page_____, _____, _____
c adjective + head noun: _____, _____
d determiner + head noun: _____
e determiner + adjective + head noun: _____, _____

TASK 3 Adjectives in noun phrases

1 Rewrite the two sentences as one sentence with a noun phrase.

Example: The BBC is a media organization. It is large.
         The BBC is a large media organization.
1 Apple is an IT company. It is global. _____
2 Al Jazeera is a TV news channel. It is international. _____
3 Harvard is a famous university. It is American. _____
4 Google is a search engine. It is free. _____
5 *The Economist* is a weekly magazine. It is popular. _____

TASK 4 in addition, also, so, or

1 Read about a company. Choose the correct linking word in brackets.

1 Time Warner is an American media corporation, _____ people watch its TV programmes and films all over the world. (but / so)
2 You can watch its programmes in English _____ in other languages. (or / also)
3 It has over 26,000 employees, _____ it's very big. (or / so)
4 The headquarters is in New York; _____, it has offices in many other countries. (in addition / because)
5 The company has divisions called Warner Brothers Films and Turner Broadcasting Systems. It _____ has a division called HBO. (and / also)

UNIT 3 Location

ACADEMIC FOCUS: COMPARING AND CONTRASTING

LEARNING OBJECTIVES
This unit covers:

Listening and Speaking
- Making notes on the main content of a lecture
- Presenting and comparing cities

Reading
- Understanding the parts of a text
- Reading for similarities and differences in a text

Writing
- Writing sentences about similarity and difference
- Analysing a comparison paragraph
- Introducing, comparing and contrasting, and concluding

Vocabulary
- Location and business
- Compound nouns
- Identifying word forms

Academic Language Check
- Comparative and superlative adjectives
- Similarity and difference

Discussion

1 Work in pairs. Look at the picture of a building. Choose adjectives to describe it.

bad   beautiful   big   boring   busy   cheap   clean
dirty   expensive   good   high   interesting   low
modern   old   quiet   small   ugly

2 Find pairs of opposite adjectives in the list in 1.

Example: *bad ≠ good*

3 Think about your town or city, or your country's capital city. Describe the items in the list. Use adjectives from 1 or your own adjectives.

Example: *Public transport is clean and modern, but it's also expensive.*

public transport   the city centre   the university
housing   shopping   hotels and restaurants
the airport   sports facilities (e.g. swimming pools, gyms)
the roads   entertainment and nightlife

036

3A Listening & Speaking Lectures (1)

This module covers:
- Making notes on the main content of a lecture
- Presenting and comparing cities

TASK 1 Focusing on a topic to prepare for a lecture

1 Work in pairs and discuss questions 1 and 2.
  1 Where is the next Olympic Games?
  2 Is the Olympic Games good for a city? Why? / Why not?
     Example: *The Olympic Games is good for a city because lots of people visit the city.*

2 Think about the next Olympic Games. Number factors a–g in order of importance 1–7 (1= more important, 7 = less important).
  a hotels and restaurants ……
  b location (or city) ……
  c local people ……
  d entertainment and nightlife ……
  e transport links ……
  f cost ……
  g sports facilities ……

3 Work in groups. Compare your answers and give reasons.
  Example: *I think location is an important factor. It's important for the Olympic Games to be in a large city, so it's interesting for visitors. For example, London and Tokyo are very popular locations.*

4 ▶3.1 Look at the slide and watch the introduction to a lecture. Which three factors in 2 does the lecturer talk about?

> **What is a lecture?**
> A lecture is a long talk by a tutor on an academic topic. A presentation is different – it is a short talk about a topic or to present research.

Planning the Olympic Games

TASK 2 Making notes on the main content of a lecture

1 ▶3.2 Watch the main part of the lecture. Complete the notes with adjectives.

Location
- Location is ^{1}……………… because you need space for the sports facilities, e.g. the stadium.
- The location has to be a ^{2}……………… city, e.g. London, Beijing, Rio de Janeiro, etc.

Transport links
- The location needs ^{3}……………… air, rail, and road links, e.g. Atlanta has a very ^{4}……………… international airport.

Cost
- The Olympic Games are very ^{5}………………, so a city needs a lot of money from its government and sponsors.
- The cost of the 2014 Winter Olympics in the Russian city of Sochi was very ^{6}………………, at around $50 billion.

ACADEMIC LANGUAGE
▶ Language reference page 150

Comparison (1) Comparative adjectives

We use comparative structures to compare people, places, and ideas.
To compare two things, use adjective + -er + than:
   London is **older than** Atlanta.
   The cost of transport is **higher than** the cost of many facilities.
Some adjectives have different spellings, e.g. busy - bus**ier**, big - big**ger**, etc. (For rules for forming comparative adjectives, see p.150.)
For adjectives with two or more syllables (e.g. important, interesting), use more / less + adjective + than:
   The location is **more important than** the size of the city.
   Paris is **less expensive than** London.
Some adjectives are irregular, e.g. good - better, bad - worse:
   This location is **better** because it has good transport links.
   Road and rail transport are **worse** in this city.

🔊 **3.3** Listen and repeat the sentences with comparative adjectives.

TASK 3 Practising comparative adjectives

1 **Underline the comparative structures.**
   1 Beijing is smaller than Shanghai.
   2 São Paulo is bigger than Rio.
   3 Transport links are more important than the size of the city.

2 **Complete the sentences with the adjectives in brackets in the comparative form.**
   1 Paris is _bigger_ (big) than Frankfurt.
   2 Dubai has _____ (new) buildings than London.
   3 Traffic into the city is _____ (busy) this summer because of the Olympics.
   4 The city centre is _____ (quiet) at the weekend than during the week.
   5 The cost of police and security is _____ (important) than people think.
   6 I think the new Olympic village is _____ (beautiful) than the old city.
   7 Air transport links from Atlanta are _____ (good) than from other US cities.
   8 Housing for local people is _____ (bad) than before the Olympic Games.

3 **Work in pairs. Compare different cities in your country or around the world.**
   Example: *Istanbul is bigger than Ankara, but Izmir is smaller than Ankara.*

ACADEMIC LANGUAGE
▶ Language reference page 150

Comparison (2) Superlative adjectives

To compare three or more things, use the + adjective + -est:
   Berlin is **the biggest** city in Germany.
   Shinjuku station in Tokyo is **the busiest** train station in the world.
(For rules for forming superlative adjectives, see p.150.)
For adjectives with two or more syllables (e.g. modern, interesting), use the most / least + adjective:
   I think location is **the most important** factor.
   People say that Bucharest is **the least expensive** city in Europe.
Some adjectives are irregular, e.g. good - best, bad - worst:
   Is Rome, Sydney, or Delhi **the best** city for the next Olympic Games?

🔊 **3.4** Listen and repeat the sentences with superlative adjectives.

TASK 4 Practising superlative adjectives

1 Read three sentences from the lecture. Which city did they describe?
   1 It's the biggest city in the UK. ....
   2 It's probably the busiest airport in the world. ....
   3 It was the most expensive Olympic Games in history. ....

2 Three cities want to be Olympic cities. Look at the table and read sentences 1–6. Are the sentences true (T) or false (F)?

Example: Madrid is the oldest city. _F_

	Madrid (Spain)	Doha (Qatar)	Istanbul (Turkey)
Founded	9th century	1825	Byzantium in 660 BCE Constantinople in 4th century Istanbul in 1930
Population	6.5 million	1 million	14 million
August temperature	31°C	40°C	34°C
Transport links	Airport has 49 million passengers per year. Metro system with 300 stations.	New airport with capacity for 29 million passengers per year. Metro system under construction.	Airport has 51 million passengers per year. Metro system with 65 stations.

Madrid

Doha

1 Doha is the newest city. ....
2 Istanbul is bigger than Doha but smaller than Madrid. ....
3 In August, Doha is the hottest city. ....
4 Madrid is hotter than Istanbul in August. ....
5 Doha has the biggest airport. ....
6 The Madrid metro has the highest number of stations. ....

3 Rewrite the false sentences in 2 using comparative and superlative forms.

Example: Madrid is the oldest city. _F_
          Madrid is older than Doha, but Istanbul is the oldest city.

4 Work in groups. Use the information in the table in 2 and discuss the three cities. Choose the best city for the Olympic Games. Give reasons.

Example: _I think Istanbul is the most interesting city, but Madrid has a better Metro._

Istanbul

TASK 5 Presenting your city

1 Choose a big city in your country to have the next Olympic Games. Prepare a two-minute presentation about the city. Note down the following information:
- Age
- Population
- Average summer temperature
- Transport links (air, rail, and road)
- Other information?
- Reasons why it's a good city for the Olympics

2 Work in groups. Present your city and give reasons. Make notes about other cities.

3 Look at your notes from the presentations. Write sentences to compare the cities.

Example: _Jeddah has a bigger population than Dammam, but it's smaller than Riyadh._

> **INDEPENDENT STUDY**
>
> Prepare good reasons to support your opinions and listen to the reasons of other students.
>
> ▸ Make a list of opinions from the presentations in Task 5. Note at least one reason for each opinion.

3B Reading Textbooks (3)

This module covers:
- Understanding the parts of a text
- Reading for similarities and differences in a text

TASK 1 Comparing locations

1 Work in groups. Read about two business locations. Compare these factors:
- location (nearer to / further from a city centre / railway station)
- cost (cheaper / more expensive)
- transport links (better / worse)

Example: *The high street shop rent is more expensive than the business park rent.*

High street shop
Location: central London
Rent: £50,000 per month
Transport links: near 3 railways and 5 underground stations

Business park
Location: 25 km from Birmingham
Rent: £10,000 per month
Transport links: 5 km from two motorways; 15km from railway

2 Which location is better for the following businesses? Give reasons.

a bookshop   a café   a car dealer   a company selling products over the internet
a gym   a high-class clothes shop   a laboratory   a university

Example: *A business park is better for a car dealer because it's cheaper.*

TASK 2 Understanding the parts of a text

1 Match each of the business words with definitions a or b.
1. cost / price
   a the amount of money you need to pay for a product or service (e.g. *the ~ of a bag*)
   b the amount of money you need to buy, make, or do something (e.g. *labour ~*)
2. profit / income
   a the money a person gets from doing work, etc.
   b the money a business gets from selling a product or service, after it pays for its costs
3. to rent / to own
   a to pay money every week / month, etc. so you can use something
   b to have something because you paid for it
4. suppliers / customers
   a the people who sell things to business (e.g. *~ of office equipment*)
   b the people who buy things from business
5. employees / labour
   a the people who work (e.g. *~ force*)
   b the people who work for a business (e.g. *company ~*)

2 Look at the title of Text 1 and read the text. Match sub-headings a–e with paragraphs 1–5.

a **Labour costs**   c **Individual needs**   e **Building costs**
b **Transport costs**   d **Income**

> **What is a title?**
> The title of a text is at the beginning; it gives the topic of the text. A sub-heading is a title for a section or paragraph of the text. This helps the reader find information.

Business location   TEXT 1

Location is very important for a business. There are a number of factors in choosing a location:

- ¹ .... This is the cost of buying the building, such as a shop or a factory, or the cost of renting it. For example, a company selling products over the internet can use a cheap building because customers do not see the location. However, a shop in the high street or in a shopping centre is more expensive.

- ² .... Employee salaries are higher in some regions than others. For example, in the UK, a business near London will have high labour costs, but salaries in other regions are lower.

- ³ .... Some businesses need high-income customers, for example, a shop selling expensive food or clothes. High-class shops are usually located in the centre of major cities. Similarly, some businesses, like a gym and fitness centre, need to be near to the city centre.

- ⁴ .... Some businesses pay higher transport costs than others, for example, businesses making large or heavy products. In contrast, a business which is near to its suppliers and customers can keep the costs lower.

- ⁵ .... Some businesses also choose a location for other reasons, for example, the location is more beautiful, or the travel time to work is shorter. In addition, maybe the area has better schools and it's easier to find qualified employees.

SOURCE: Adapted from Stimpson, P. et al. 2009. pp.106–7. *GCSE Business Studies*. Cheltenham: Nelson Thornes.

ACADEMIC LANGUAGE   ▸ Language reference page 150

Linking language (4) Comparing and contrasting ideas

Linking words and comparative adjectives are common in texts which compare and contrast two ideas.

Similarities

Use *Similarly* to add similar ideas:
> The high street is a *better* location for selling luxury brands than a business park. *Similarly*, airports are a good location for selling luxury items such as perfume.
> **Idea 1:** the high street is good for luxury items (a positive idea)
> **Idea 2:** airports are good for luxury brands (a similar positive idea)

You can add a similar idea with *in addition* or *also*:
> *In addition*, airports are ... / Airports are *also* ...

Differences

Use *However, On the other hand, In contrast,* or *But* to contrast different ideas:
> You want a cheap business location with low rent. *However*, a *cheaper* location can be *more expensive* because of high transport costs.
> **Idea 1:** low rent (a positive idea)
> **Idea 2:** high transport costs (a negative idea)

But can start a new sentence:
> ... with low rent. ***But*** a cheaper location ...

We use a comma before *but* when it continues the same sentence:
> ... with low rent, ***but*** a cheaper location ...

TASK 3 Noticing comparison and contrast

1 Read Text 1 again. Complete the table about the ideas in each paragraph. Find the linking word(s) and comparatives in each paragraph to support your answers.

Paragraph	Adds similar ideas	Contrasts different ideas	Linking word(s) and comparative adjectives
1		✓	However, more expensive
2			
3			
4			
5			

TASK 4 Reading for similarities and differences in a text

1 Read Text 2. What is the main idea of the text?
   a to compare land costs and labour costs in the UK
   b to compare locating in the UK and not locating in the UK
   c to compare transport costs to and from the UK

TEXT 2

Locating in the UK and in another country

Many UK companies think about relocating their businesses to other countries in order to lower their costs and increase their profits. However, there are some points to consider first before moving overseas:

5 • **Land costs** UK cities such as London are expensive for office space, so locating to other countries can often cost less. However, it is not easier for working with UK customers or suppliers.

• **Labour costs** Some businesses use a lot of labour; for example, telephone answering services, clothing manufacturers, and other similar businesses have high labour costs.
10 For these businesses the cost of staff in the UK is often higher than the cost overseas. On the other hand, sometimes the quality of manufacturing in another country is worse.

• **Tariffs** There are different tariffs on products coming into a country or area like the European Union (EU). So even if manufacturing costs are cheaper, with tariffs it can be
15 more expensive to produce items in another country.

• **Language** In another country language differences sometimes make communication with workers difficult. Similarly, there are sometimes problems with cultural differences.

• **Transport costs** Locating to another country means these costs are higher because the goods need to be transported back to the UK.

SOURCE: Adapted from Stimpson, P. et al. 2009. pp.108-9. *GCSE Business Studies*. Cheltenham: Nelson Thornes.

GLOSSARY
relocate *(v)* move to a new location
tariff *(n)* a tax on products coming into or going out of a country

---

2 Read Text 2 again and look at factors a–h. Do they describe the UK (UK) or overseas (O)?
   a expensive office space *UK*
   b more difficult for working with suppliers and customers ....
   c higher salaries ....
   d sometimes the quality is worse ....
   e manufacturing costs lower ....
   f no tariffs on products ....
   g language and cultural differences ....
   h longer distances to transport ....

042 UNIT 3B READING

3 Underline the comparative forms and linking words in Text 2 for comparing and contrasting ideas.

Example: *UK cities such as London are expensive for office space, so locating to other countries can often <u>cost less</u>. <u>However</u>, it is <u>not easier</u> for working with UK customers or suppliers.*

ACADEMIC LANGUAGE ▶ Language reference page 150

Word forms *similar / different*

Notice the forms of *similar* and *different* for comparing and contrasting.

similarly (adverb)
Language problems can be difficult. **Similarly**, there are sometimes problems with cultural differences.

similar / different (adjective)
Land costs in the two countries are **similar**. / You can find high-class shops in London, Paris, and other **similar** cities.
The quality is often very **different**. / **Different** countries have **different** tariffs.

similarity / difference (noun)
There is no **similarity** between a London shopping street and a Birmingham business park.
There is a big **difference** between land costs in London and Warsaw.

TASK 5 Practising word forms for comparing and contrasting

1 Underline the correct form of the words in italics.

There are many ¹*similar / similarities* between the capital cities of France and the UK. London and Paris are very old cities on famous rivers and they are also commercial and industrial centres. ²*Similar / Similarly*, London and Paris are the largest cities in their country; they are also international cities for business and tourism. On the other hand, there are a number of ³*different / differences*. One ⁴*difference / different*, of course, is language; in addition, the political culture and the food are also ⁵*difference / different*. Overall, there are probably more ⁶*similarly / similarities* between the two cities than differences.

2 Look at the notes on London. Make notes about the capital city of your country.

	London	Your country's capital city
Age	very old	
Location	– in the south of the UK – on a river	
Population	about 10 million	
Business and tourism	very good	
Other important information	– the government is here – international food and restaurants – good entertainment and nightlife	

3 Work in pairs. Present the information in your table and talk about the similarities and differences between the two capital cities.

INDEPENDENT STUDY

Look for comparison when you read.
▶ Read a website article that compares and contrasts information. Note down the language of comparison, e.g. comparative and superlative forms, linking language, and forms of *similar / different*.

3C Writing (1) Comparison sentences

This module covers:
- Writing sentences about similarity and difference

TASK 1 Understanding similarities and differences

1 Look at the table of information. What does it compare?

	Durham University	Bristol University
Founded	1832	1876
Number of students	15,000	21,000
Average annual rent for accommodation	£5,000	£5,000
Percentage of overseas students	21%	13%
International airport	yes	yes

(Information is approximate.)

2 Read a student's notes about the two universities in 1. Correct the wrong information.

> **Durham or Bristol?**
> 1 Durham is newer than Bristol.
> 2 There are more students at Bristol.
> 3 Student accommodation at Durham is as expensive as at Bristol.
> 4 The percentage of overseas students at Durham is lower.
> 5 Both cities are near an international airport.

3 Which sentences in 2 describe differences? Which sentences describe similarities?

ACADEMIC LANGUAGE ▶ Language reference page 150

Comparison (3) Expressing similarities and differences

Use these structures to describe **similarities**.
as + adjective + *as*:
   Student accommodation at Durham is **as expensive as** at Bristol.
both + plural noun:
   Both cities have an airport.

Use these structures to describe **differences**.
Comparative adjectives:
   Durham University is **older** (than Bristol).
more + plural noun:
   Bristol University has **more students** (than Durham).
not as + adjective + *as*:
   Bristol University is **not as old as** Durham University.

044 UNIT 3C WRITING (1)

TASK 2 Practising comparison sentences

1 Read the information about Oxford and Cambridge in the UK. Complete the sentences with the words in the list.

as   beautiful   ~~bigger~~   both   more   people   than   universities

1 Oxford is _bigger_ than Cambridge.
2 Oxford University has _____ students than Cambridge University.
3 More _____ live in Oxford.
4 Cambridge is an older city _____ Oxford.
5 Student accommodation in Cambridge is as expensive _____ in Oxford.
6 _____ cities are about 100 kilometres from London.
7 The university buildings in Oxford are as _____ as in Cambridge.
8 Around the world, both _____ are very famous.

2 Look at the information about two universities in the USA. Write sentences using the words given.

	Harvard University	Yale University
Founded	1636	1701
Number of students	21,000	11,900
Annual student fees	$42,000	$42,000
Percentage of overseas students	20%	18%

(Information is approximate.)

1 Harvard / old / Yale
   Harvard is older than Yale.
2 Yale / new / Harvard

3 the number of students / high / at Harvard

4 the number of students / low / at Yale

5 there are / students at Harvard than at Yale

6 student fees at Yale are / expensive / student fees at Harvard

7 there are / overseas students at Harvard

Harvard University

Yale University

TASK 3 Comparing universities

1 Find out about two universities in your country. Make notes about:
   - location and age
   - the number of students (including overseas students)
   - costs (education, accommodation, travel, etc.)
   - travel links.

2 Write sentences about the two universities. Describe their similarities and differences. Work in pairs and compare your sentences.

> **INDEPENDENT STUDY**
>
> Memorize real information to help you remember comparison expressions.
>
> ▶ Look at the information about different universities in this module. Write down and memorize five different sentences comparing them. Say them to yourself every day for five days.

UNIT 3C WRITING (1) 045

3C Writing (2) A comparison paragraph

This module covers:
- Analysing a comparison paragraph
- Introducing, comparing and contrasting, and concluding

TASK 1 Analysing a comparison paragraph

1 Read the paragraph. Are sentences 1–3 true (T) or false (F)?
  1 The purpose of the paragraph is to compare working in Hong Kong and Singapore. ....
  2 The writer thinks the education at HKU is better than NUS. ....
  3 The writer thinks HKU and NUS have more similarities than differences. ....

> There are a number of similarities between the University of Hong Kong (HKU) and the National University of Singapore (NUS). Both universities are over 100 years old and located in Asia. Similarly, both universities are always in the top ten of Asian universities and the teaching at HKU is as good as at NUS. In addition, English is the main language of instruction, so there are a lot of international students. Singapore's population is not as large Hong Kong's. On the other hand, Singapore is a capital city and the centre of the country's government and economy. Hong Kong is not a capital city; however, it is a centre for trade and business. So overall, the universities are very similar because they are exciting places to live and study and offer a good university education.

University of Hong Kong

National University of Singapore

2 Read the paragraph again. What is similar and different? Tick (✓) the table.

	Age	Location	Level of education	Language	Population	Type of city
Similar	✓					
Different						

ACADEMIC LANGUAGE ▶ Language reference page 151

Sentences (2) Writing about comparison

When we write about comparison, we often use the following sentence patterns:

Introducing the comparison
   There are a number of similarities / differences between (HKU) and (NUS).

Describing similarities
   Similarly, both universities … (are located in Asia).
   and …, / In addition, … / It also …
   It is as good / big / modern as …

Describing differences
   On the other hand, … / However, … (Singapore is a capital city and Hong Kong is not).
   It is better / bigger / more modern than …
   It is the best / biggest / most modern …

Concluding
   Overall, they are similar / different because …
   In conclusion, (Harvard) is better than (Yale) because …

Ankara   Riyadh

TASK 2 Practising comparison

1 Complete the comparison paragraph with the words in the list.

bigger   both   ~~differences~~   important   largest   on the other hand
overall   similarly

There are a number of similarities and ¹ _differences_ between Ankara in Turkey and Riyadh in Saudi Arabia. They are ² _____ capital cities and their location is in the centre of their country. ³ _____, both cities have about 15 universities, and education in the two cities is as ⁴ _____ as in most other large modern cities. ⁵ _____, Riyadh has a ⁶ _____ population and it has the ⁷ _____ women's university in the world. However, ⁸ _____, both cities are interesting places to live and study.

2 Complete sentences 1–5 about Harvard and Yale Universities. Use the information in Task 2 on page 045.
   1 There are a number of similarities and differences between …
   2 Both universities are …
   3 Similarly, both universities …
   4 On the other hand, Harvard …
   5 However, overall, both universities …

TASK 3 Writing a comparison paragraph

1 Look back at the sentences you wrote about two universities in your country in Task 3 on page 045. Now write these sentences as a paragraph. Use the paragraph in Task 1 on page 046 as a model. Remember to:
   • introduce the paragraph
   • describe similarities
   • describe differences
   • conclude the paragraph.

2 Work in pairs. Read your partner's paragraph. Use this checklist and give feedback. Does the paragraph:
   • introduce the cities or universities?   ☐
   • describe similarities and then differences?   ☐
   • conclude clearly?   ☐
   • use the language of comparison accurately?   ☐

Sample answer:
page 159

UNIT 3C WRITING (2)   047

3D Vocabulary

TASK 1 Location and business

1 Complete the summary about business relocation with the words in the list.

cost   customers   employees   expensive   location   profit   rent

Many companies are leaving the cities and choosing a new ¹_____ in the countryside. There are a number of reasons for this. First of all, there's the ²_____ of a building in a city; even if you don't own the building, the ³_____ can be very high. Secondly, more and more ⁴_____ buy their products and services online, so companies don't need ⁵_____ retail stores. Thirdly, it's often easier to attract more qualified ⁶_____ to a more beautiful region. So, overall, the costs can be lower, but ⁷_____ can stay the same.

TASK 2 Compound nouns

1 Complete sentences 1–5 with one noun from A and one from B.

A individual   ~~labour~~   land   office   sports   transport

B ~~costs~~   costs   facilities   links   needs   space

Example: Call centres employ a lot of people so they have high _labour costs_.

1 Cities with conferences centres must have good _____ _____, for example, an international airport and fast trains.
2 Companies can reduce the costs of _____ _____ if employees can work from home.
3 One advantage of being an Olympic city is that you have excellent _____ _____, including stadiums and swimming pools.
4 Employees may want good schools or a short travel time, so sometimes a business chooses a location according to _____ _____.
5 The _____ _____ in UK cities such as London are very high for new buildings.

> **INDEPENDENT STUDY**
>
> Some nouns often appear together. We call these **compound nouns**, e.g. *public + transport = public transport*.
>
> ▶ Look back at the unit and find more compound nouns.

TASK 3 Identifying word forms

1 Match the words in bold in sentences 1–7 with word forms a–g.
1 There's a big **difference** between Bonn and Berlin. ____
2 Bonn isn't as **old** as Berlin. ____
3 Both **cities** have an airport. ____
4 Berlin has the **biggest** population. ____
5 **Similarly**, building costs are higher. ____
6 Accommodation **costs** a lot of money. ____
7 Accommodation in the old town is **cheaper** than in the new town. ____

a verb
b adjective
c comparative adjective
d superlative adjective
e adverb
f singular noun
g plural noun

3E Academic Language Check

TASK 1 Comparative and superlative adjectives

1 Complete the table.

Adjective	Comparative adjective	Superlative adjective
old	¹ _older_	oldest
²	higher	³ ....
big	⁴	biggest
⁵	busier	busiest
modern	more modern	⁶ ....
⁷	⁸	most important
expensive	less expensive	⁹ ....
¹⁰	better	¹¹ ....
bad	¹²	worst

2 Correct one mistake in each sentence.

Example: Paris is larger ~~as~~ Frankfurt. *Paris is larger than Frankfurt.*

1 The population of Los Angeles is more larger than the population of Atlanta.
2 São Paulo is biger than Rio de Janeiro.
3 Dubai is modern than Rome.
4 Shopping online is less expensiver than shopping in the high street.
5 Accommodation in London is the more expensive in the UK.
6 Athens is one of oldest cities in Europe.
7 I'm the more youngest in my family.
8 My city has the most good transport links in the world.

TASK 2 Similarity and difference

1 Choose the correct linking language in italics.

1 People often buy luxury items in the high street. *Similarly / However*, they often buy them in airports.
2 Rome is a beautiful city for tourists. *But / Also* transportation around the city can be slow if you live there.
3 Taking public transport into the city is easier than driving. In *contrast / addition*, it's usually cheaper than parking a car.
4 There are many *similar / similarities* between New York and Chicago.
5 One *difference / different* between St Petersburg and Moscow is the age of the buildings.

2 Match the sentence halves.

1 The exam results this year are as high ... .
2 The exam results are good for both ... .
3 The exam results are higher ... .
4 More ... .
5 Overall, the exam results this year aren't as ... .

a high as two years ago.
b than last year.
c years.
d students took the exam this year.
e as last year.

UNIT 4 Production

ACADEMIC FOCUS: DESCRIBING NUMBERS AND CHARTS

LEARNING OBJECTIVES

This unit covers:

Listening and Speaking
- Understanding charts and data
- Presenting data with charts

Reading
- Using a graph to understand a text
- Using numbers to focus on meaning
- Understanding the history of a company

Writing
- Simplifying numbers and reporting data
- Analysing a description of a chart
- Planning and writing a description of a chart

Vocabulary
- Nationality suffixes
- Identifying collocations
- Presentations with charts

Academic Language Check
- Data: Numbers, fractions, and quantifiers
- Talking about events in the past

Discussion

1 Work in pairs. Match the countries with regions in the world.

Countries:	Regions:
Brazil	Africa
Canada	Asia
Germany	Europe
Ghana	the Middle East
Indonesia	Latin America
Oman	North America

2 ◀))4.1 Compare with the class. Then listen and check.

3 Work in groups.
- Think of two more countries in each region.
- Decide which countries / regions are famous for certain products.
   Example: *Brazil and Colombia are famous for coffee.*
- What famous products are made in your country? What products does it export?

4 Choose three products with you today. Tell the group where they are made.
   Example: *My textbook is from an English company, but it's printed in China. My T-shirt is made in Vietnam. I don't know where my bag is from.*

4A Listening & Speaking Presentations (3)

This module covers:
- Understanding charts and data
- Presenting data with charts

TASK 1 Understanding the purpose of a chart

1 Match the verbs in A with opposites in B. Complete sentences 1–4 with each pair.

A	B
~~import~~	consume
produce	~~export~~
earn	sell
buy	spend

Example: *import – export*

1 The USA *imports* a lot of cars from other countries, but it also *exports* cars around the world.
2 People _____ money by working and then they _____ it at the weekend.
3 Manufacturing businesses _____ materials, make products, and then _____ them.
4 Farmers _____ food, sell it, and people _____ it.

2 Look at the charts about cocoa production. Match titles 1–3 with charts A–C.
1 Major cocoa consumers in the world, by amount _____
2 Cocoa exports of the world's main producers, by percentage _____
3 Where your money goes when you buy a bar of chocolate for £1 in the UK _____

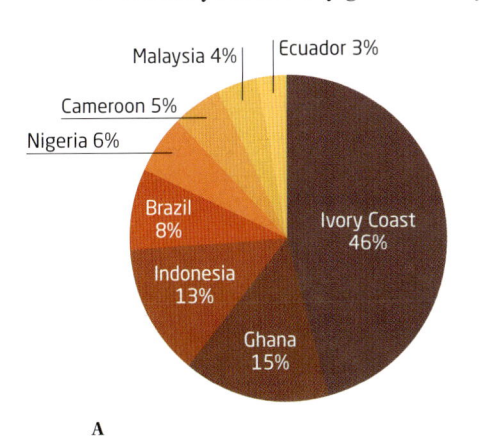

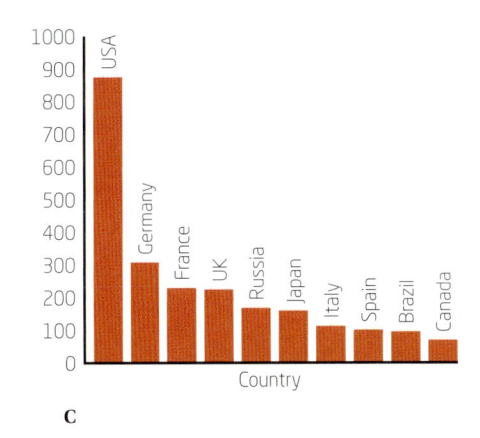

A
- Ivory Coast 46%
- Ghana 15%
- Indonesia 13%
- Brazil 8%
- Nigeria 6%
- Cameroon 5%
- Malaysia 4%
- Ecuador 3%

B
- Cocoa farmers 7p
- Non-cocoa ingredients 13p
- Chocolate company costs and profits 43p
- Shop costs and profits 22p
- UK Government tax 15p

C (bar chart by Country): USA, Germany, France, UK, Russia, Japan, Italy, Spain, Brazil, Canada

3 Look at the charts again. Which country:
a exports the most cocoa?
b buys and consumes the most cocoa?
c exports and consumes cocoa?
d taxes 15 pence on a bar of chocolate?

TASK 2 Understanding data

What is data?
Data is factual and numerical information from research. You often report data in the form of charts or graphs.

1 ▶4.2 Watch part of a student presentation about global cocoa production and consumption. Number the information in the correct order (1–3).
   a how much a cocoa farmer earns and why ....
   b world exporters of cocoa ....
   c world importers of cocoa ....

2 ▶4.2 Watch again and note down the information for numbers and phrases 1–7.

Chart 1
- thirteen per cent – cocoa Indonesia exports
- fifteen per cent – [1] ....
- eight per cent – [2] ....
- nearly a half of the world's cocoa – [3] ....

Chart 2
- around nine hundred thousand tonnes per year – cocoa the USA imports
- about one hundred and fifty thousand tonnes – [4] ....

Chart 3
- one pound – cost of a bar of chocolate in UK shops
- about half – money for the [5] ....
- more than a fifth – money for the [6] ....
- seven pence per pound – money for the [7] ....

3 Use the notes in 2 to write complete sentences about the presentation.

Example: *Indonesia exports 13% of the world's cocoa.*

ACADEMIC LANGUAGE ▶Language reference page 151

Data (1) Saying numbers exactly and approximately

In presentations, you can use exact numbers, or approximate numbers / percentages / fractions.

Saying numbers exactly
  0 = zero   11 = eleven   15 = fifteen   71 = seventy-one   101 = one hundred and one
  1,010 = one thousand and ten   101,000 = one hundred and one thousand
  1,000,000 = one million
  3% = three per cent   13% = thirteen per cent   33% = thirty-three per cent

Saying numbers approximately and in fractions
We sometimes say numbers approximately in presentations because it's easier for listeners to understand the data.
  99.2 = **approximately** one hundred / **about** one hundred / **around** one hundred
We use fractions a lot when we say numbers approximately.
  ½ = a half, ¼ = a quarter, ¾ = three quarters, ⅓ = a third, ⅔ two thirds, ⅕ = a fifth
  35% = **more than** a third   24% = **nearly** a quarter   22% = **less than** a quarter

🔊 4.3 Listen and repeat the numbers and fractions.

052 UNIT 4A LISTENING & SPEAKING

TASK 3 Practising saying numbers

1 How many different ways can you say these percentages?

   Example: 24% – *twenty-four per cent, nearly a quarter, around twenty-five per cent*

   19%   48%   51%   66%   75%   99%

2 🔊 4.4 Listen to an example answer for each number in 1.

3 🔊 4.5 Listen and write the numbers you hear.

   1 ....   3 ....   5 ....
   2 ....   4 ....   6 ....

4 Look at the charts in Task 1.2 again. Write sentences about the data. Use different ways to say the numbers. Then read your sentences to a partner.

   Example: *France consumes around 200,000 tonnes of cocoa per year.*

TASK 4 Referring to charts in presentations

1 ▶ 4.2 Watch the presentation again. Tick (✓) when you hear the phrase.

1	2	3 ....
Let's look at this chart. ☐	It shows … ☐	Notice this. ☐
Moving on … ☐	Here, you can see … ☐	This is interesting because … ☐
This is my final chart. ☐	It's a chart of … ☐	Look at this number. ☐

2 Complete headings 1–3 in the table in 1 with a–c.

   a Explain what the chart shows
   b Introduce a new chart
   c Present specific numbers and information

TASK 5 Presenting data with charts

1 Look at three charts. What do they show?

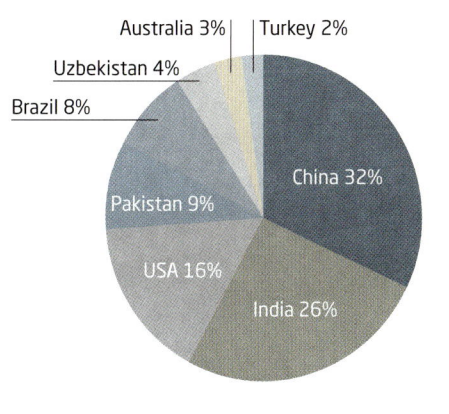

The world's eight major cotton producers by percentage
- Australia 3%
- Turkey 2%
- Uzbekistan 4%
- Brazil 8%
- China 32%
- Pakistan 9%
- USA 16%
- India 26%

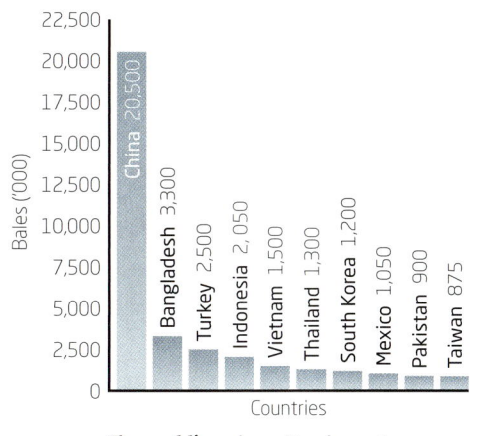

The world's major cotton importers, by amount (Source: www.statista.com 2011)
- China 20,500
- Bangladesh 3,300
- Turkey 2,500
- Indonesia 2,050
- Vietnam 1,500
- Thailand 1,300
- South Korea 1,200
- Mexico 1,050
- Pakistan 900
- Taiwan 875

Where your money goes when you buy a pair of jeans for £10 in the UK
- Shop £5.40
- Manufacturing materials £1.90
- Manufacturing costs & profits £1.70
- Factory worker £1.00

2 Work in groups. Prepare a short presentation of each chart.

3 Take turns to present the data in the charts. As you watch the presenters, check that:
   - they introduce the charts ☐
   - they explain what the charts show ☐
   - they point out specific numbers ☐
   - they say the numbers clearly. ☐

> **INDEPENDENT STUDY**
>
> Presenters stress content words such as names of countries and important numbers, e.g. *The Ivory Coast exports nearly a half of the world's cocoa.*
>
> ▶ Listen for the stressed words when you take notes. Practise stressing content words when you present data.

4B Reading Textbooks (4)

This module covers:
- Using a graph to understand a text
- Using numbers to focus on meaning
- Understanding the history of a company

TASK 1 Recognizing types of data presentation

1 Match the words with visual ways (1–4) of presenting data in textbooks.

   bar chart   graph   pie chart   table

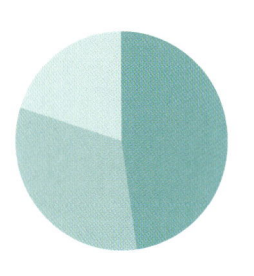

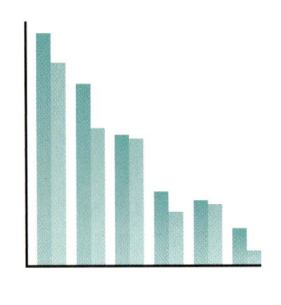

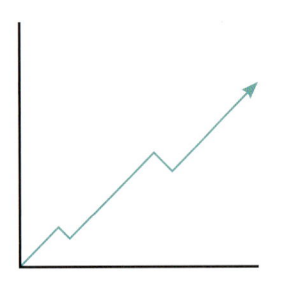

   1 ....   2 ....   3 ....   4 ....

2 Work in pairs. Chart, graph, or table? Choose the best way to present each type of information.
   - A list of 30 student names, subjects, and classes
   - Student exam results from each year from 2001 to 2015
   - Percentage of different nationalities of overseas students

TASK 2 Using a graph to understand a text

1 A graph helps you to understand a text in more detail. Read the information in the table and tick (✓) Graph, Text, or Both.

	Graph	Text	Both
Gives numbers and factual information			
Shows change over a period of time			
Explains the reasons for changes			
Presents information visually			

2 Look <u>only</u> at the graph in Text 1 and answer questions 1–5.
   1 What months does the graph show?
   2 What length of time does it show?
   3 Does it show the name of a product?
   4 What currency are the prices in?
   5 Is the Fairtrade price higher or lower than the world market price?

054   UNIT 4B READING

TEXT 1

Fairtrade is a non-profit organisation. It buys products from farmers and food producers in regions such as Africa, Asia, Latin America, and the Caribbean. It then puts the Fairtrade label on these products and sells the food in other countries. The Fairtrade label means that the food producers receive a fair price for their products.

The Fairtrade minimum price is the lowest price for a producer of Fairtrade products. This price is never lower than the world market price and it is usually higher. The Fairtrade minimum price for cocoa is $1,600/tonne. In addition, producers receive a Fairtrade premium of $150/tonne. The farmer's local community invests this money in social, environmental, or economic development projects.

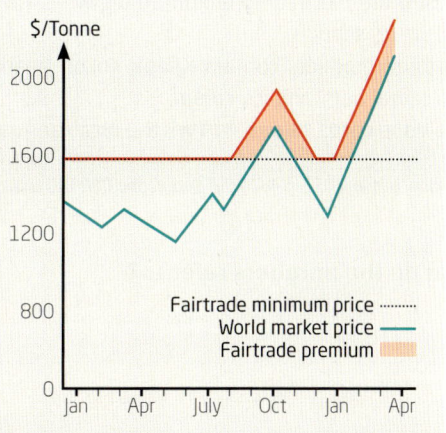

SOURCE: Adapted from Widdowson, J. et al. 2011. p.46. *GCSE Geography OCR B*. Oxford: Oxford University Press.

GLOSSARY

fair *(adj)* equal or right for everyone
label *(n)* information on a product
premium *(n)* an extra payment

3 Read Text 1 and look at the graph again. Choose the correct option in italics.
1 Fairtrade *produces / buys and sells* the food.
2 Farmers and growers with Fairtrade always receive the *minimum / world market* price or higher.
3 $1,600 per tonne is the Fairtrade *minimum price / premium* for *cocoa / cotton*.
4 The world market price was *higher / lower* than the Fairtrade minimum price in October.
5 When the world market price is higher than the minimum price, farmers *receive / don't receive* an extra $150 per tonne.
6 Farmers received the minimum price on cocoa for *ten / thirteen* months.
7 Fairtrade paid a premium for *six / eight* months.
8 The *farmer / local community* spends the premium.

4 Work in pairs. Did you find answers 1–8 in 3 in the text, in the graph, or in both?

1 .... 5 ....
2 .... 6 ....
3 .... 7 ....
4 .... 8 ....

TASK 3 Using numbers to focus on meaning

1 Read Text 2 about an organization called Kuapa Kokoo. Tick (✓) the main purpose of the text. Is it to describe the organization's:
   a products and history? ☐
   b work with Fairtrade? ☐
   c profits and prices? ☐

TEXT 2

- Kuapa Kokoo is an organisation of cocoa growers in Ghana. It began in 1993 with a small group of local farmers. Nowadays it represents approximately 50,000 cocoa growers. 28% are women.
- The average farm in Ghana is four hectares and nearly all the income comes from cocoa.
- In 1999 Kuapa Kokoo members produced 19,000 tonnes of cocoa beans. Nearly ten years later, in 2008, its members produced 35,000 tonnes – 5% of Ghana's total cocoa production.
- From 2008 to 2009 it sold 27% of its cocoa to the Fairtrade market and received a premium.
- Local communities used the Fairtrade premium to dig wells for drinking water and to build new classrooms in its schools.
- More than 300 Fairtrade products contain Kuapa Kokoo beans, including chocolate bars, cakes, biscuits, cereal bars, and ice cream.
- Kuapa Kokoo means 'good cocoa farmer' in Twi, the local language.

SOURCE: Adapted from Widdowson, J. et al. 2011. p.47. *GCSE Geography OCR B*. Oxford: Oxford University Press.

GLOSSARY
hectare *(n)* a unit for measuring an area of land (= 10,000m²)

2 Read Text 2 again. What do the numbers refer to?
   1993 ....
   50,000 ....
   4 ....
   35,000 ....
   5% ....
   27% ....
   300 ....

ACADEMIC LANGUAGE   ▶ Language reference page 151

Past simple Talking about events in the past

The past simple describes finished events in the past:
   In 1999 Kuapa Kokoo members **produced** 19,000 tonnes of cocoa beans.
   It **began** in 1993 with a group of local farmers.

Regular verbs (e.g. *produce, work, live, receive, use, export, import*)
Add *-ed* to regular verbs or *-d* to verbs ending in *e*:
   He work**ed** in Ghana in 1999.
   Farmers receive**d** a premium from Fairtrade.

Irregular verbs (e.g. *be, begin, sell, buy*)
Do not add *-ed* to irregular verbs:
   From 2008 to 2009 it **sold** 27% of its cocoa to the Fairtrade market. (= sell)
   UK consumers **bought** products with Kuapa Kokoo beans. (= buy)
Common irregular past forms: *be – was / were, go – went, make – made, do – did, grow – grew, can – could*

056 UNIT 4B READING

TASK 4 Practising the past simple

1 Complete the sentences with the verbs in brackets in the past simple.
   1 He _worked_ (work) in Oman for three years.
   2 I _____ (live) in London when I was a student.
   3 The company _____ (begin) in 1995.
   4 From 2010 to 2012, the country _____ (sell) over a half of its cotton to the USA.
   5 Last year, the UK _____ (buy) 200 tonnes of cocoa.
   6 They _____ (make) over one billion dollars last year.
   7 We _____ (receive) the payment yesterday.
   8 Sales of chocolate _____ (grow) by 25% in 2014.

2 Read about a cotton producer's cooperative. Underline the correct form of the verb in italics.

India ¹*is / was* currently the world's second biggest producer and supplier of cotton. From 1999 to 2000 it ²*exports / exported* approximately 50,000 bales of cotton. Last year, it ³*sell / sold* nearly 13 million bales of cotton overseas. Many cotton producers in India are small farmers. For example, Khim Ranchhod and his wife Jamnaben ⁴*have / had* a four-hectare family farm in the Kutch region. In the past Khim's father also ⁵*grows / grew* cotton here, but the minimum price of cotton ⁶*is / was* never guaranteed. Nowadays, farmers like Khim ⁷*are / were* in cooperatives such as the Agrocel Pure & Fair Cotton Growers' Association. This association ⁸*begin / began* in 2005 with only 50 cotton farmers. Today it ⁹*has / had* 1,930 members, including 77 women farmers. It ¹⁰*works / worked* closely with Fairtrade, and its farmers ¹¹*receive / received* a guaranteed minimum price for their cotton.

GLOSSARY
bale of cotton (n) 226kg of cotton pressed together and tied up

TASK 5 Understanding the history of a company

1 Work in pairs. Look at a timeline for the chocolate company Divine. Summarize the company's history using the past simple.

   Example: *In October 1998, Divine started in the UK.*

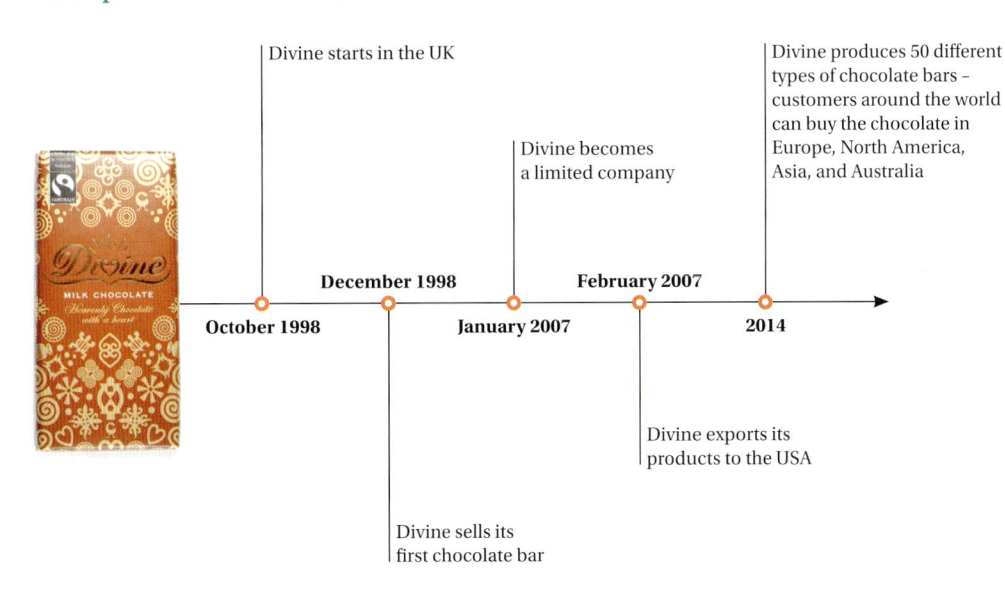

   Divine starts in the UK
   December 1998 — Divine becomes a limited company
   February 2007
   Divine produces 50 different types of chocolate bars – customers around the world can buy the chocolate in Europe, North America, Asia, and Australia
   October 1998
   January 2007 — Divine sells its first chocolate bar
   2014 — Divine exports its products to the USA

INDEPENDENT STUDY

The important information on a topic is often in the form of data.

▶ When you read information about a topic, make notes on key numbers, e.g. dates, percentages, quantities, prices.

UNIT 4B READING 057

4C Writing (1) Sentences about data

This module covers:
- Simplifying numbers and reporting data

TASK 1 Writing numbers accurately

1 Match the numbers in A with the correct terms in B.

　A　32°　75%　30 km/h　$23m　60,000,000　4 cm　4,001,965 km²　020 8675 4658

　B　area　currency　length　percentage　phone number　population　speed　temperature

2 Write numbers about your country. Write an exact number or guess the answer with an approximate number.
- What is the population?
- What is the average temperature in the summer?
- How much is £10 (UK) in your currency?
- What is the maximum speed limit on a motorway?
- What percentage of people live in cities?
- What is the international dialling code?
- What is the area of the country?

3 Work in pairs. Compare your answers in 2.

ACADEMIC LANGUAGE ▶ Language reference page 151

Data (2) Simplifying numerical information
Use fractions and quantifiers to simplify numbers.

Fractions
Use *a third, a quarter, a half, a fifth, a sixth,* etc. + *of* + plural noun:
　A fifth of cars in this country are made overseas.
　Two thirds of people use tablet computers.
You can leave out the main noun with a fraction:
　A fifth are made overseas.

Quantifiers

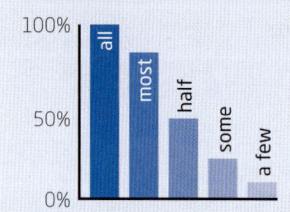

[bar chart: all 100%, most ~75%, half 50%, some ~25%, a few ~10%]

Use *all, most, some, a few, no* + plural noun:
　A few cars are made in this country. **Some cars** are also made in Asia.
You can leave out the main noun with a quantifier:
　A few are made in this country. **Some** are also made in Asia.
Be careful with *no / none*:
　No cars are made here. → **None** are made here. (NOT *No are made* ...)

Writing numbers approximately
Use *nearly, over, about, around* + fractions:
　Over (a) half of our customers are in Europe. (*over* = more than)
　Nearly a third of our customers are in Asia. (*nearly* = less than)
You can use *nearly + all*:
　Nearly all of the customers are female. (*nearly all* = 85% to 99%) but NOT *About / Around / Over all* ...

TASK 2 Practising simplifying numbers

1 Read the percentages in the report and complete the simplified information in sentences 1–5.

> The 'Global Online Shopper Report' based its findings on data from 15 countries including the UK, US, China, Spain, Finland, Japan, Russia, Brazil, Mexico, Australia, Canada, Argentina, and India.
>
> 95% of online shopping is from midday to midnight.
> 46% of online shoppers watch television when they are shopping.
> 29% of global shoppers order products at work. 6% are in the car.
> 55% use a laptop to shop. 19% use their mobile phone.
> 69% of global online shoppers use credit cards.
>
> SOURCE: bizreport.com/2012/04/10-habits-of-online-shoppers

a few   a fifth   most   nearly   over   some   two thirds

1 .... online shopping is from midday to midnight.
2 .... half of online shoppers watch television when they are shopping.
3 .... global shoppers order products at work. .... are in the car.
4 .... half use a laptop to shop. About .... use their mobile phone.
5 Over .... of global online shoppers use credit cards.

TASK 3 Reporting data

1 Read the data from a survey about British people's holidays. Write five sentences about the results. Simplify the percentages.

take one or more holidays per year	80%
take three or more holidays per year	16%
have one holiday in the UK	68%
have one holiday abroad	53%
have one holiday in the UK and one abroad	41%
book their holiday a few months in advance	36%

(Data based on information from ABTA.)

Example: *Most people take one or more holidays per year.*

1 ....
2 ....
3 ....
4 ....
5 ....

> **INDEPENDENT STUDY**
>
> Become familiar with common terms for data, e.g. *area, length, currency, temperature.*
>
> ▶ Look for charts and graphs with accurate data in your textbooks. Write sentences about the data and simplify the numerical information.

4C Writing (2) A description of a chart

This module covers:
- Analysing a description of a chart
- Planning and writing a description of a chart

TASK 1 Analysing a description of a chart

1 Look at Figure 1 and read the paragraph. Answer the questions.
1 Does the chart show every car producer in the world?
2 Look at the phrase 'half of these countries' in sentence b. Which countries does it refer to?
3 What is the difference between the numbers in the chart and the numbers in the description?

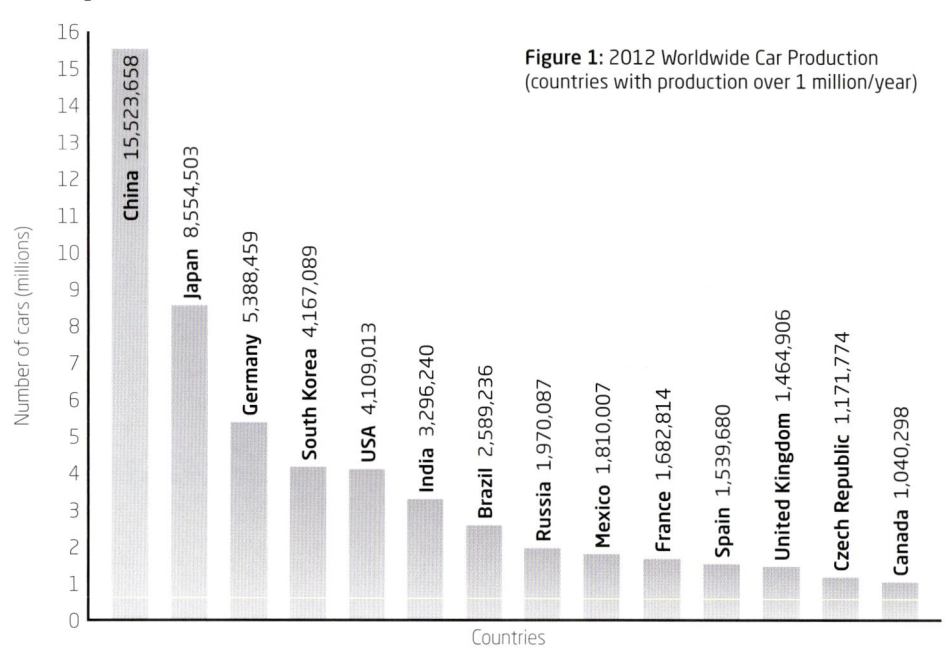

Figure 1: 2012 Worldwide Car Production (countries with production over 1 million/year)

- China 15,523,658
- Japan 8,554,503
- Germany 5,388,459
- South Korea 4,167,089
- USA 4,109,013
- India 3,296,240
- Brazil 2,589,236
- Russia 1,970,087
- Mexico 1,810,007
- France 1,682,814
- Spain 1,539,680
- United Kingdom 1,464,906
- Czech Republic 1,171,774
- Canada 1,040,298

Source: OICA (Organisation Internationale des Constructeurs d'Automobiles / International Organization of Motor Vehicle Manufacturers) 2014

> ᵃFigure 1 shows worldwide car production in 2012 for countries producing over one million cars. ᵇThere are 14 countries in total and **half of these countries** produce between one and two million cars per year. ᶜChina is the world's main producer, with over 15 million cars per year. ᵈNext, Japan produces approximately eight-and-a-half million and Germany nearly five-and-a-half million. The United States and South Korea produce around four million per year. Brazil produces over two million and India produces more than three million.

What is a source?
A source is where information comes from, e.g. the source of the data in a chart is usually given below it. A source gives the data its authority.

2 Read the paragraph again. Match each part (a–d) to its purpose 1–4.
1 gives general information about countries and numbers in the chart ....
2 introduces the title of the chart ....
3 gives information about the most important country and number in the chart ....
4 gives more information about other countries and numbers in the chart ....

060 UNIT 4C WRITING (2)

TASK 2 Planning a description of a chart

1 **Work in pairs. Look at Figure 2 and answer the questions.**
   1 What information in the chart goes into the first sentence of a paragraph?
   2 How many countries are there in the chart?
   3 How can you simplify the numbers? e.g. 495,682 = around half a million
   4 Which countries have similar numbers? Which can you put into groups?
   5 Which countries are more important? Which is the most important?

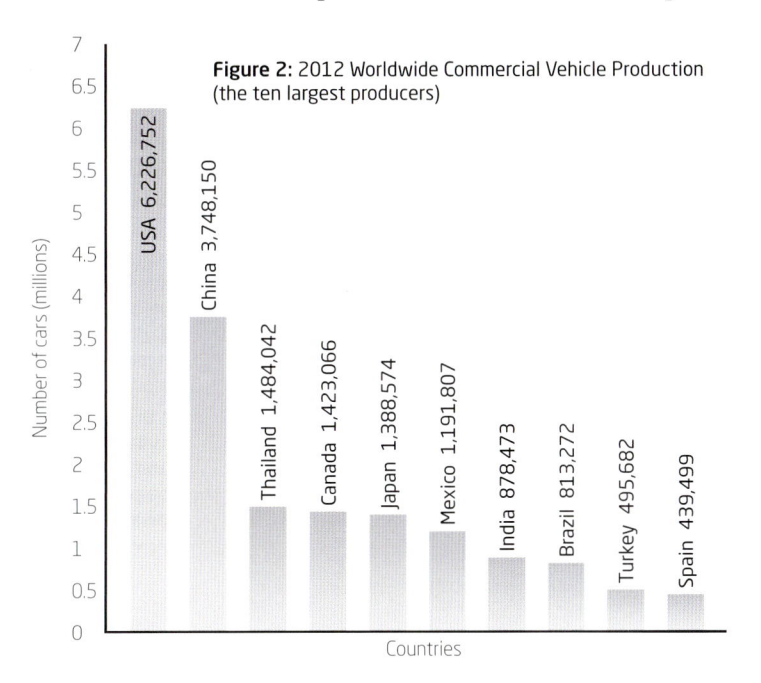

Figure 2: 2012 Worldwide Commercial Vehicle Production (the ten largest producers)

- USA 6,226,752
- China 3,748,150
- Thailand 1,484,042
- Canada 1,423,066
- Japan 1,388,574
- Mexico 1,191,807
- India 878,473
- Brazil 813,272
- Turkey 495,682
- Spain 439,499

Source: OICA (Organisation Internationale des Constructeurs d'Automobiles / International Organization of Motor Vehicle Manufacturers) 2014

GLOSSARY
commercial vehicle *(n)* a vehicle used by businesses to transport products or people (e.g. lorries, trucks)

2 **Complete the sentences about Figure 2.**
   1 The chart shows _____.
   2 There are _____ producers in total.
   3 _____ is the main producer.
   4 China produces _____ vehicles per year.
   5 _____ produces _____ one million per year.
   6 Thailand and Canada produce nearly _____ million per year.

TASK 3 Writing a description of a chart

1 Write a paragraph about the chart in Task 2. Use the paragraph in Task 1 as a model.

2 Read your paragraph again. Use this checklist to check your writing. Did you:
   • introduce the title of the chart in the first sentence? ☐
   • give general information about the countries and numbers? ☐
   • give general information about the most important country? ☐
   • give more information about countries which are less important? ☐
   • simplify the numbers? ☐

3 Work in pairs. Read your partner's paragraph. Use the checklist in 2 and give feedback.

Sample answer: page 159

4D Vocabulary

TASK 1 Nationality suffixes

> **Nationality suffixes**
> Make most countries into a nationality by using a suffix. Common nationality suffixes are
> *-ish, -n, -an, -ian,* and *-ese*:
> Britain   Brit**ish**   Canada   Canad**ian**
> America   America**n**   Japan   Japan**ese**
> Mexico   Mexic**an**
> There are some irregular forms, e.g. *France – French, Thailand – Thai*.

1 Read the information box. Complete the table.

Countries	Nationalities
Brazil	Brazilian
Britain	1
2	German
America	3
4	Canadian
China	5

Countries	Nationalities
6	Spanish
Indonesia	7
8	Turkish
Australia	9
10	Saudi (Arabian)

> **INDEPENDENT STUDY**
> With some countries and nationalities, the word stress is on the same syllable, e.g. *Bri*tain – *Bri*tish. But sometimes it moves, e.g. *Ja*pan, Japa*nese*.
> ▶ Underline the stressed syllable in the countries and nationalities on this page. Use a dictionary to help you.

2 What's your country? What's your nationality?

TASK 2 Identifying collocations

1 Match the nouns in the list with verb groups 1–5.

a company   a country   food   money   ~~products~~

1 buy, make, export   *products*
2 spend, earn, invest ___
3 grow, cook, eat   ___
4 live in, work in, visit ___
5 join, start, manage ___

2 Complete sentences 1–5 with one verb from each group in 1.
1 Brazil ___ coffee to many other parts of the world.
2 He ___ half his salary on rent.
3 Ghana ___ a lot of cocoa for chocolate.
4 One day I'd like to ___ France for a holiday.
5 I ___ a small company, but I don't own it.

TASK 3 Presentations with charts

1 Complete the presentation expressions with the words in the list.

is   look at   moving   notice   see   shows

1 Let's ___ this chart.
2 ___ on to my next slide …
3 Here you can ___ a pie chart.
4 This graph ___ the market price for five years.
5 This ___ my final chart.
6 ___ this number here.

062   UNIT 4D VOCABULARY

4E Academic Language Check

TASK 1 Data: Numbers, fractions, and quantifiers

1 Read about Morocco. Write the words in bold as numbers, percentages, or fractions.

Example: Morocco has **two** official languages: Arabic and Berber. *2*

1 The population of Morocco is around **thirty-three million**. _____
2 About **half** the population lives in cities. _____
3 The largest city is Casablanca, with nearly **three point five million** people. _____
4 Tourism is an important industry, with more than **ten million** tourists per year. _____
5 Agriculture employs around **forty-five per cent** of the population. _____
6 **Ninety-five per cent** of its mining is for phosphates. _____
7 Phosphates represent about **a quarter** of its total income from exports. _____

2 Read sentences from different surveys. Replace the information in bold with the words in the list.

a few   a fifth   a half   most   nearly a third   three quarters   two fifths   two thirds

1 About **66%** of 18-year-olds spend three hours a day on their mobile phones. _____
2 **5% of the** people didn't answer this question. _____
3 **90% of** universities offer at least one online course. _____
4 **20%** of young people now watch films online, not on TV. _____
5 Approximately **75%** of the people in the survey normally download music. _____
6 **31%** of people aged 20 and above live with their parents. _____
7 Just over **50%** plan to study online in the next 12 months. _____
8 Nearly **40%** order their weekly food shopping online. _____

TASK 2 Talking about events in the past

1 Complete the text with the verbs in brackets in the past simple.

The Manduvira Cooperative in Paraguay exports Fairtrade sugar to nearly 20 countries. The Cooperative [1]_____ (begin) in 1975 and it [2]_____ (receive) a Fairtrade certificate in 1999. The General Manager is Andres Gonzales: 'When we [3]_____ (start), we [4]_____ (not / have) anything.' Many local farmers and producers [5]_____ (join) the Cooperative and [6]_____ (sell) their food through it. Now there are around 1,750 members. In 2014 the Cooperative [7]_____ (buy) some land and [8]_____ (build) its own factory. This [9]_____ (be) because in the past they [10]_____ (rent) a factory over 100 km away and they [11]_____ (pay) for transportation. Now the farmers own their own factory and spend more money on local projects.

UNIT 5 Design

ACADEMIC FOCUS: DEFINING AND EXPLAINING

LEARNING OBJECTIVES
This unit covers:

Listening and Speaking
- Identifying the main points of a lecture
- Taking notes with a mind map
- Defining and explaining terms

Reading
- Identifying the main purpose of a text
- Understanding academic terms
- Taking notes on definitions in a text

Writing
- Writing clear definitions using prepositional phrases
- Analysing a definition paragraph
- Structuring a definition paragraph using linking language

Vocabulary
- Word order: Adjectives
- Vocabulary-building: Verbs and nouns
- Prepositions

Academic Language Check
- Definitions, explanations, and examples

Discussion

1 Read about the verb. Then look at the list below. Think of examples and make definitions.

> **to define** (v) to say or write the meaning of a word or phrase, e.g. *A train is a passenger vehicle.*

computer technology   a consumer product
a household appliance   a media company
a passenger vehicle   a scientific subject
a sports facility

2 Read about the verb. Then match the descriptive adjectives in the list to groups 1–7. Add more adjectives.

> **to describe** (v) to say or write what something is like, e.g. *It's a fast train.*

~~fast~~   modern   narrow   plastic   quiet   small   white

1	Size	
2	Shape	
3	Age	
4	Colour	
5	Speed	*fast*
6	Sound	
7	Material	

3 Read about the verb. Then look at the picture above of a Shinkansen. Take turns to explain what it is.

> **to explain** (v) to say or write about something to make it easy to understand

064

5A Listening & Speaking Lectures (2)

This module covers:
- Identifying the main points of a lecture
- Taking notes with a mind map
- Defining and explaining terms

TASK 1 Identifying the main points of a lecture

1 Look at the picture of a kingfisher.
   - Describe this bird. Use adjectives.
   - How are the bird and the Shinkansen train similar?

   Example: *The bird and the train are both ...*

2 ▶5.1 Watch three short extracts from a lecture about the science of biomimetics. Number the extracts in the correct order (1–3).

   The lecturer ...
   - explains why the Shinkansen train is similar to a kingfisher. ....
   - defines the word *biomimetics*. ....
   - gives an example of biomimetic design. ....

A kingfisher

TASK 2 Taking notes with a mind map

1 Read the script of Extract 1 from the lecture. Then look at a student's mind map of notes on Extract 1 and compare the lecturer's words with the student's notes. Delete any words the student does not write down.

'Biomimetics is the scientific study of design in nature and its application in the design of man-made objects. In other words, an engineer or an architect can get ideas for new buildings by studying design in the natural world. Let me explain by giving you a famous example ...'

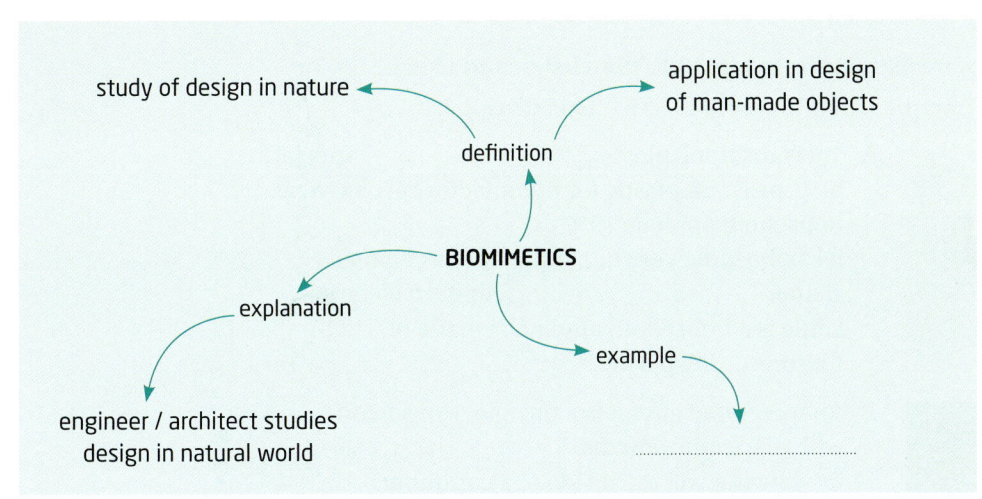

> **What is a mind map?**
> A mind map is a visual diagram of information. It's useful for taking notes and planning.

```
study of design in nature          application in design
                                   of man-made objects
                   definition

              BIOMIMETICS

    explanation
                           example

engineer / architect studies
design in natural world
```

2 Which types of word does the student <u>not</u> write in the mind map?

3 ▶5.2 Watch Extracts 2 and 3 again and note down important words about the example of biomimetics.

4 Work in pairs. Compare your notes in 3.

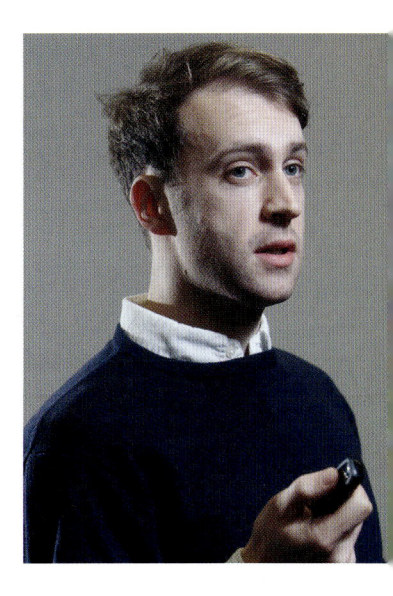

UNIT 5A LISTENING & SPEAKING 065

ACADEMIC LANGUAGE
▶ Language reference page 152

Defining (1) Definitions, explanations, and examples

Definitions
We use **new word / idea** + *is / are* + **defining phrase** to define new words or ideas:
  Biomimetics is *the scientific study of design in nature*.
  Kingfishers are *very fast birds with a long, narrow beak*.

Explanations
After a definition, we can explain the new word or idea:
  In other words, an engineer studies design in the natural world.
  Let me explain why. / **Let me explain by** giv**ing** you a famous example.

Examples
After definitions and explanations, we also give examples:
  It's a good example of 20th century engineering.
  For example … / **Let me give you an example.** / **This is a good example of** …

🔊 5.3 Listen and repeat the sentences and expressions.

TASK 3 Practising defining and explaining with examples

1 Work in pairs. Match 1–3 with a–c to make three sentences from a lecture.

1 Fibre optics is ......
2 In other words, ...
3 Let me give you an example of ......

a light can travel through cables made of fibre optics.
b fibre optics used in the telecommunications industry.
c the science of using glass or plastic fibre to transmit light.

2 🔊 5.4 Listen and check. Identify which sentences in 1 are a definition, an explanation, and an example.

3 🔊 5.5 Complete two more extracts from lectures. Then listen and check.

a good example   For example   In other words   is a   Let me explain

A Thermosetting plastic [1] .... special heat-resistant plastic for manufacturing electrical household appliances. [2] ...., it can become very hot, but it doesn't change shape. [3] ...., a modern electric kettle is a household appliance made of thermosetting plastic.

B An integrated circuit is a tiny piece of silicon with electronic circuits. [4] .... by showing you the inside of a computer. A computer has thousands of electronic components. This is [5] .... of an integrated circuit.

066 UNIT 5A LISTENING & SPEAKING

TASK 4 Defining and explaining terms

1 Work in pairs. Read two texts about design ideas.
   Student A: read the text on this page about *Anthropomorphism* in design.
   Student B: go to page 162 and read about *Smart materials* in design.

> ### Anthropomorphism
> Anthropomorphism is a design technique for giving human characteristics to non-human objects. In other words, a designer can give an object a human face, legs, arms, or speech. The robot ASIMO is a good example of this. Designers at Honda made ASIMO to help humans. ASIMO has arms and legs and it can walk and talk to humans.
>
> SOURCE: Adapted from Russell, B. et al. 2011. p.16. *Design and Technology*. Cheltenham: Nelson Thornes.

Draw a mind map and make notes about:
- the definition
- the explanation
- any examples.

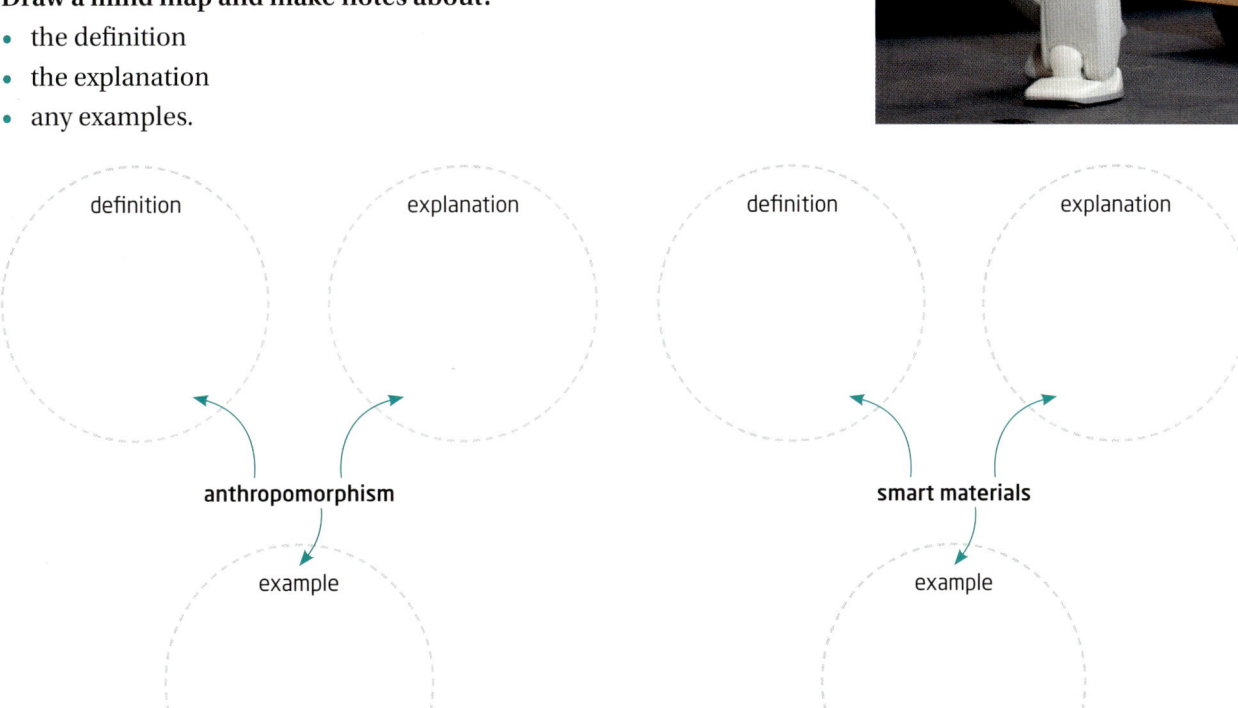

2 Take turns to define and explain *Anthropomorphism* or *Smart materials*.
   - Use your notes when you present (do not read the text).
   - Listen to your partner and take notes using a mind map.

3 When you have finished, compare your notes with the original text. Did you write down all the important information?

4 Work in pairs. Do you think a mind map is a good way to take notes? Why? / Why not?

> **INDEPENDENT STUDY**
>
> The important words in a lecture are usually verbs, nouns, and descriptive language. Less important words are often pronouns, auxiliary verbs, determiners, and repeated or obvious words.
>
> ▶ When you listen to a lecture, note down the main points and important words. Try using a mind map.

UNIT 5A LISTENING & SPEAKING 067

5B Reading Textbooks (5)

This module covers:
- Identifying the main purpose of a text
- Understanding academic terms
- Taking notes on definitions in a text

TASK 1 Identifying the main purpose of a text

1 Work in pairs and discuss. When you buy a product or service, what is most important for you?

brand (e.g. Nike)   design   price   other: ....

2 Make sentences about these products and services. You can use more than one adjective or add your own. Work in pairs. Do you agree?

Example: I prefer a practical car.

I prefer a / an	easy-to-use stylish nice-looking modern reliable practical interesting friendly comfortable clean	car. language course. house. book. tablet. restaurant. university.

3 Read Text 1. Tick (✓) the purpose of the text. Is it:
   a to compare human designs with designs in nature? ☐
   b to define and explain the idea of human factors in design? ☐
   c to describe how humans design products? ☐

Human factors in design   TEXT 1

Product designers have to consider many factors, but overall, human factors are the most important. Human factors refer to the abilities and limitations of the end user; these factors fall into three groups: **physiological**, **psychological**, and **sociological**.

   Physiological factors relate to the study of the human body and its movement; in other words, people's physical abilities, such as size, strength, and stamina, affect how they interact with a product. For example, a keyboard should not be too small for the human finger. Another word for the study of physiological factors is *ergonomics*. It comes from the Greek word *ergon*, which means 'work', and *normia*, which relates to organisation. In particular, ergonomic design considers how humans interact with many different products and environments. Ergonomics in the design of cars is a good example of this; the car driver must be able to operate the car comfortably, efficiently, and safely.

SOURCE: Adapted from Russell, B. et al. 2011. pp.40-1. *Design and Technology*. Cheltenham: Nelson Thornes.

GLOSSARY

stamina *(n)* the strength to do something difficult for a long time

---

4 Read Text 1 again. Are statements 1–4 true (T) or false (F)?
   1 Product designers need to consider human factors more than other factors. ....
   2 Human factors refer to what designers can produce. ....
   3 There are three types of human factors. ....
   4 The study of physiological factors in design is called ergonomics. ....

ACADEMIC LANGUAGE
▶ Language reference page 152

Defining (2) Identifying definitions, explanations, and examples
To recognize definitions and explanations / examples in a text, look for common verbs and expressions.

Definition verbs
With verbs *is / are, mean, refer to,* and *relate to,* the definition comes <u>after</u> the verb:
  Physiology **is** the study of the human body.
  It **refers to** the study of human movement.
  It **relates to** the design of objects in our daily lives.

With explanations and examples, look for expressions that introduce or refer to the extra information:

Explanations
  ..., **in particular**, how people use the product in their daily lives.
  ..., **in other words**, the study of how people use products in their daily lives.

Examples
  Human physiology is important in the design of furniture, **such as** an office chair.
  Human physiology is important in the design of furniture, **for example,** an office chair.
  The design of an office chair **is a good example of this**.

TASK 2 Practising definitions, explanations, and examples

1 Label the words and phrases (a) definition, (b) explanation, or (c) example.

   for example   *c*   means   ....
   in other words ....   such as ....
   in particular   ....   refer to ....
   is a good example of ....   relates to ....

2 Read six sentences from Text 1. Identify two definitions, two explanations, and two examples.

   Definition: *1* ....   Explanation: ....   Example: ....

   1 Another word for the study of physiological factors is ergonomics.
   2 In other words, people's physical abilities, such as size, strength, and stamina, affect how they interact with a product.
   3 Ergonomics in the design of cars is a good example of this; the car driver must be able to operate the car comfortably, efficiently, and safely.
   4 Physiological factors relate to the study of the human body and its movement; ...
   5 For example, a keyboard should not be too small for the human finger.
   6 In particular, ergonomic design considers how humans interact with many different products and environments.

3 Complete the paragraph with the phrases in the list.

   a good example   in other words   in particular   relates to

   Ergonomics in design [1] .... the human body and helping people to work more effectively through design. [2] ...., designers look at how they can improve the working environment of employees. [3] ...., they look at existing furniture and equipment and redesign it. The modern office chair is [4] .... of this; in the past, office chairs came in one design only, but all modern ergonomically-designed chairs can be adjusted to suit an individual person's height.

TASK 3 Understanding academic terms

1 Look at the extract from Text 1. What does *It* refer to?

> Another word for the study of physiological factors is *ergonomics*. **It** comes from the Greek word *ergon*, which means 'work', and *normia*, which relates to organisation.

2 Many terms in academic English come from Greek words. Look at these academic subjects and terms. Match the bold part to its meaning (1–7).

biology **biblio**graphy **chrono**logy **geo**graphy **psycho**logy
physiology **socio**logy

1 life _bio_
2 book ....
3 earth ....
4 group ....
5 mind ....
6 time ....
7 nature and the body ....

What does *-ology* mean?
-ology (suffix) is from the Greek word meaning 'the study of', e.g. *biology* – the study of life, *psychology* – the study of the mind.

3 🔊 5.6 Listen and repeat the words in 2.

TASK 4 Taking notes on definitions in a text

1 Read Text 2, the second part of Text 1. Complete the factors.

Sociological   Psychological

TEXT 2

> 1 .... **factors** relate to the human mind and our behaviour, and these are important in design. In particular, human senses provide information, such as the height of a step or the heat from an oven. Many products help the user to understand and respond to sensory information. Colour is a good example of this because it can change our mood: some colours are welcoming in a reception area and a neutral colour helps people in an office to think. Colour can also help the consumer understand the product; for example, safety features on an electrical product are often in red. Kitchen appliances are often white, which relates to cleanliness.
>
> 2 .... **factors** refer to human difficulty in relation to the environment, and often relate to special groups (including people with disabilities). These factors affect design on larger public projects, such as the design of public spaces. For example, small spaces can affect public stress levels, which is a major factor in public transport. Access in public buildings is also a key issue; climbing steps or opening doors can be difficult for children and the elderly.
>
> SOURCE: Adapted from Russell, B. et al. 2011. pp.40-1. *Design and Technology*. Cheltenham: Nelson Thornes.

GLOSSARY
sensory *(adj)* relating to the senses

2 Read Text 2 again. Match a–f with 1–6 in the table. Look for academic language to help you (e.g. *refer to*).
   a colour can change moods in rooms and give safety information on products
   b the study of the human mind and our behaviour
   c small spaces on public transport can affect stress levels
   d how design can improve public spaces
   e the study of human difficulty in relation to the environment
   f how sensory information in design makes products easier to use

Factor	Definition	Explanation	An example
Physiological	the study of the human body and its movement	how people live and work with products in their environment	a car driver operates a car comfortably, efficiently, and safely
Psychological	1	2	3
Sociological	4	5	6

3 Work in pairs. Use the notes in 2 and take turns to explain one of the factors in the texts.

   Example: *Physiological factors refer to the study of the human body and its movement, in particular, how …*

TASK 5 Critical thinking – responding to ideas in a text

1 Work in pairs. Look at products 1–8 and match them with the correct descriptions a–h. Which factor is more important in the design process for each item: physiological, psychological, or sociological? Give reasons.

   Example: *I think physiological factors are important for the design of a cockpit on a commercial aeroplane, because a pilot uses a lot of different controls …*

   a a new park for a city centre ......
   b a bicycle for people to travel to work ......
   c the entrance to a cinema ......
   d a smoke alarm in a building ......
   e the cockpit on a commercial aeroplane ......
   f a new type of toothpaste for children ......
   g a bus station for all types of passengers ......
   h the desktop screen on a tablet computer ......

> **INDEPENDENT STUDY**
>
> Reading texts is a good way to expand your academic vocabulary.
>
> ▶ When you read a text, look out for new words and terms. Underline words and phrases which define and explain the new term. Does the writer also include examples?

5C Writing (1) Definition sentences

This module covers:
- Writing clear definitions using prepositional phrases

TASK 1 Understanding the structure of definitions

1 Work in pairs. Look at pictures 1–4. Answer the questions for each one.
- What is it?
- Who is it for?
- How do we use it?

1 a Kevlar® helmet   2 a Mini   3 bricks and cement   4 a telecommunications satellite

2 Complete definitions 1–8 with the nouns in the list.

company   ~~materials~~   part   process   software   study   type   university

1 Cement and bricks are *materials* in the construction industry.
2 Kevlar is a .... of hard material.
3 Psychology is the .... of the human mind and behaviour.
4 Photosynthesis is the .... of turning light into energy.
5 CAD is computer .... for designing products.
6 Quality control is .... of the design process.
7 The Massachusetts Institute of Technology is a famous .... in Cambridge, USA.
8 COMSAT is a global communications .... with satellites in space.

ACADEMIC LANGUAGE   ▶ Language reference page 152

Defining (3) Writing definitions

In academic writing we often use a **new word / idea** + *be* + noun phrase to give definitions. We can give more information in the noun phrase by using a prepositional phrase:

		noun phrase	
new word / idea	be		prepositional phrase
Biology	is	the study	**of** human life.
Cement and bricks	are	materials	**in** the construction industry.
Tower Bridge	is	a famous bridge	**across** the River Thames.

With a verb + the preposition *for*, use the *-ing* form:
   Cardboard is a material **for packing**.
   HTML is a type of code **for designing** websites.

TASK 2 Practising definitions with prepositional phrases

1 Look at definitions 1–8 in Task 1.2 again. Write the noun phrase (after the verb) from each definition. Underline the prepositional phrase.
   1 *materials <u>in the construction industry</u>*.
   2
   3
   4
   5
   6
   7
   8

2 Look at the table. Write definitions.

   Example: *Sociology is the study of group behaviour.*

Sociology		intelligent technology	of academic qualification.
A degree		a type	on the internet.
Robots	is	animals	with eight legs.
Customer research	are	part	of the design process.
Google		the study	of group behaviour.
Spiders		a search engine	for helping humans.

3 Write definitions for these words. Use a noun phrase including a prepositional phrase.
   1 Smartphones are
   2 Economics is
   3 Plastic is
   4 A tablet computer is
   5 Disney is

TASK 3 Writing clear definitions

1 Think of an example of each item in the list. Write a detailed definition of each.
   - a popular product
   - a subject or area of study
   - a design material
   - modern technology
   - a university, company, or organization

   Example: *A microwave oven is a modern household appliance for heating food quickly.*

2 Work in pairs. Take turns to read your definitions in 1. Don't say the main word. Guess your partner's word from the definition.

   Example: A *It's a modern household appliance for heating food quickly.*
   B *Is it a microwave oven?*
   A *Yes, it is.*

> **INDEPENDENT STUDY**
>
> Writing definitions with examples is a good way to expand your vocabulary.
>
> ▶ When you read a new word in English, learn it by writing a definition of the word and using it in an example sentence.

5C Writing (2) A definition paragraph

This module covers:
- Analysing a definition paragraph
- Structuring a definition paragraph using linking language

TASK 1 Analysing a definition paragraph

1 Read the paragraph. Answer questions 1–4.
1 What do designers use CAD for?
2 What are two advantages of CAD for designers?
3 How does CAD help architects?
4 With CAD, what can an architect do during a meeting with a client?

> [a]Computer-aided design (CAD) is the use of computers for creating and communicating product ideas. [b]In other words, designers can use CAD software to make accurate designs and to share their plans. [c]For example, architects use CAD to design 2D and 3D plans of buildings and the software calculates accurate measurements. Then they can show the plans to their client and make immediate changes.

2 Read the paragraph again. Match each part (a–c) with its purpose (1–3).
1 explains the definition ......
2 gives an example ......
3 gives a definition of the term ......

ACADEMIC LANGUAGE ▸ Language reference page 152

Linking language (5) Structuring definitions and explanations / examples

After a definition, we can use a variety of linking language to introduce explanations and examples. This helps to structure the paragraph and make the writing flow.

> Computer-aided design is the use of computers for creating and communicating product ideas. **In other words**, designers can use CAD software to make accurate designs. **For example**, they can calculate the size of a new product using CAD.

> Smart materials are a type of material with special features. **In particular**, they can change colour, shape, and even temperature. They are important in various products **such as** sunglasses and household appliances.

074 UNIT 5C WRITING (2)

TASK 2 Practising structuring a definition paragraph

1 Number the sentences in the correct order (1–3).

In book publishing, the editors and designers might work in Oxford, but the process of printing is in Hong Kong. ......

Remote manufacturing is the process of designing and manufacturing a product in different locations. ......

Using CAD software, designers can send their designs across the world for manufacture. ......

2 Join the sentences in 1 to make a paragraph. Add linking language to two of the sentences.

3 Use the notes and write a paragraph about *Video-conferencing*.

Video-conferencing:
- type of two-way telecommunications with video and audio technology
- people in different countries speak face-to-face through webcams
- fashion designers in Paris can talk to clothes manufacturers in China

TASK 3 Writing a definition paragraph

1 Choose a type of computer technology, e.g. a mobile phone, a laptop, an iPod, a webcam, etc. Write a paragraph about the technology. Use the paragraph in Task 1 as a model. Remember to give a definition, an explanation, and an example.

2 Read your paragraph again. Use this checklist to check your writing. Did you:
- define the term in the first sentence? ☐
- explain the definition with more detail? ☐
- give an example? ☐
- structure the paragraph with linkers? ☐

3 Work in pairs. Read your partner's paragraph. Use the checklist in 2 and give feedback.

Sample answer:
page 159

5D Vocabulary

TASK 1 Word order: Adjectives

1 **Put the words in the correct order.**

   Example: It's a / fast / train / long. *It's a long, fast train.*
   1 Kevlar / hard / is a / material

   2 ASIMO is a / white / short / robot

   3 Thermosetting plastic / heat-resistant / is a / material / modern

   4 An integrated circuit / small / piece of technology / is a / square

   5 Kingfishers / beaks / narrow / have / long

   6 Time Warner / global / is a / media company / large

TASK 2 Vocabulary-building: Verbs and nouns

1 **Look at the words in bold in the pairs of sentences 1–5. Write verb (V) or noun (N).**
   1 **A** Can you give me a **definition**?
      B Can you **define** this term?
   2 **A** Let me **explain** what I mean.
      B That's a good **explanation**.
   3 **A** Biology is the **study** of living things.
      B In biomimetics, you **study** design in the natural world.
   4 **A** Write a short **description** of the design.
      B To **describe** something is to say or write what it is like.
   5 **A** Computer-aided **design** is for creating new buildings and products.
      B Architects often **design** buildings with CAD software.

TASK 3 Prepositions

1 **Complete sentences 1–10 with the prepositions in the list.**

   about   at   by   from   of (x3)   to (x2)   with

   1 Let me **explain** _____ giving you an example.
   2 It's **a good example** _____ modern engineering.
   3 Designers **look** _____ how they can improve the working environment.
   4 Physiological factors **relate** _____ the human body.
   5 Psychology is **the study** _____ the mind.
   6 Kingfishers are **birds** _____ long, narrow beaks.
   7 It **refers** _____ human organizations.
   8 Write about **a type** _____ technology.
   9 Ergonomics **comes** _____ the Greek word *ergon*.
   10 It's **a book** _____ design.

2 **Look at the words in bold before each preposition in 1. Which sentences have:**
   a verb + preposition? _____
   a noun + preposition? _____

> **INDEPENDENT STUDY**
>
> Some prepositions often come after certain verbs or nouns, e.g. *look at* (verb + preposition), *an example of* (noun + preposition).
>
> ▶ Find and note down more examples of verb + preposition or noun + preposition.

5E Academic Language Check

TASK 1 Definitions, explanations, and examples

1 Complete the paragraph with the words in the list.

example   is   particular   refers   such as

Virtual reality ¹_____ to a computer-simulated environment. For ²_____, VR technology can recreate physical objects and places on a computer screen. In ³_____, a user can wear a virtual reality headset and look at new buildings or experience new countries. Virtual reality ⁴_____ now part of computer gaming and entertainment technology, but it also has serious uses, ⁵_____ training people to work in new or dangerous environments.

2 Match the sentence halves.

1 Biomimetics is the … ____
2 Chronology refers … ____
3 Ergonomics relates to … ____
4 Nature is important in the design of products, such … ____
5 Let me give … ____
6 This is a good … ____
7 Let me explain by … ____
8 In other … ____

a you an example.
b to the order of events in time.
c giving you an example.
d study of design in nature.
e design and the human body.
f words, it is the study of nature in design.
g example of biomimetics.
h as the Shinkansen train.

3 Rewrite sentences 1–4 using the words in brackets.

Example: Biology is the study of living things. (refer to)
Biology *refers to the study of living things.*

1 The word *ergonomics* means 'work' and 'organization'. (relate to)
The Greek word *ergon* _____.

2 Kevlar has many useful features. One feature is, it's a strong material. (in particular)
Kevlar _____.

3 CAD software is for creating new products. To explain, you can use it for design. (in other words)
CAD software _____.

4 Ergonomic design refers to design for human use, such as the modern keyboard. (for example)
Ergonomic design _____.

UNIT 6 Change

ACADEMIC FOCUS: DESCRIBING CHANGES AND TRENDS

LEARNING OBJECTIVES
This unit covers:

Listening and Speaking
- Reading to prepare for a lecture
- Listening for the language of trends
- Talking about your country's economy

Reading
- Understanding the main trend in a graph
- Understanding changes and trends described in a text

Writing
- Writing sentences about trends using adverbs
- Analysing a description of a graph
- Describing trends in a graph using adverbs and adjectives

Vocabulary
- Vocabulary-building: Word forms
- Trends
- Economic terms

Academic Language Check
- Present progressive, present simple, past simple, *will*
- Prepositional phrases
- Adverbs and adjectives

Discussion

1 Look at the picture. Who are the people? Where are they? What are they doing?

2 🔊 6.1 Listen and repeat the words in the list.
employ
employee / employer
employed / unemployed / self-employed
employment / unemployment
full-time employment / part-time employment

3 Work in pairs. Say the form (noun, verb, etc.) of each word in 2 and give a definition with an explanation or example. Use a dictionary to help you.

Example: *'Employ' is a verb. It means 'to give someone a job for money.' For example, 'This company employs one hundred people.'*

4 Do you know anyone who:
- works part-time?
- is self-employed?
- employs other people?

Tell your partner about them.

5 Is unemployment a problem in your country? Why / Why not?

6A Listening & Speaking Lectures (3)

This module covers:
- Reading to prepare for a lecture
- Listening for the language of trends
- Talking about your country's economy

TASK 1 Reading to prepare for a lecture

1 Look at the different groups of people. Which groups are part of the 'working population'?

The young

Schoolchildren and students

The employed

Homemakers

The unemployed

The self-employed

Armed forces

Retired people

2 Read an extract from an economics textbook and check your answer in 1.

> A country with a strong economy usually has high employment and low unemployment. As a result, economists often compare the working population of a country with the dependent population. The working population is all the people of a working age; in other words, employed, self-employed, people in the armed forces, and unemployed people who are looking for work. The dependent population includes students in education, retired people, or unemployed people who do not want to work. They are 'dependent' on the working population to produce the goods and services they need.
>
> SOURCE: Adapted from Moynihan, D. and Titley, B. 2012. p.347. *Complete Economics for Cambridge IGCSE and O Level* 2nd ed. Oxford: Oxford University Press.

3 Work in pairs and discuss the questions.

1 How strong is your country's economy at the moment?
2 Do you think the percentage of the working population is higher or lower than the dependent population?

TASK 2 Listening for the language of trends

1 ▶6.2 Watch part of an economics lecture about working population and dependent population. Which graph shows Brazil? Which graph shows Spain?

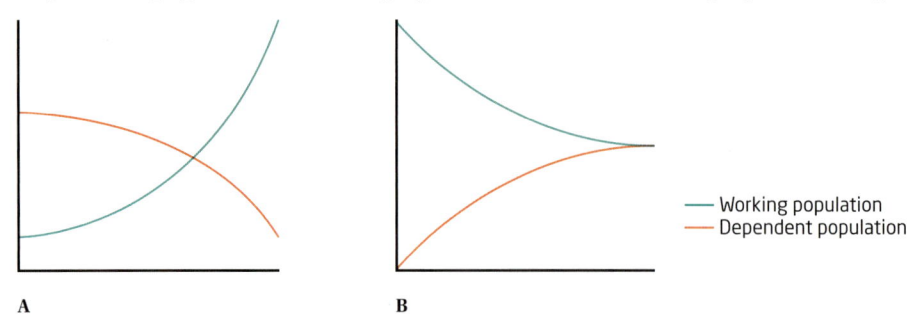

A

B

— Working population
— Dependent population

What is a trend?
A trend refers to the general direction of changes over a period of time, e.g. *an economic trend*. A change is when one thing becomes different, e.g. *a change in the population*.

2 Look at the verbs the lecturer uses to describe economic trends. Write up (↑) or down (↓).

increase ↑   fall ....   go up ....
decrease ....   rise ....   go down ....

3 ▶6.3 Watch part of the lecture again and complete the text with the correct form of the verbs in 2.

In a country like Brazil, ... the working population ¹ __is__ currently *increasing* and at the same time, the dependent population ² .... That's because the number of younger people in work ³ .... and, especially, more and more women these days are going to work instead of staying at home.

In a country such as Spain, the dependent population is increasing because the number of older and retired people ⁴ .... In addition, the number of younger people in Spain ⁵ .... That's because they're leaving Spain for new jobs in other countries. So at the moment the working population ⁶ ....

ACADEMIC LANGUAGE ▶ Language reference page 152

Changes and trends (1) Present progressive, present simple

Use the present progressive to describe a change or a trend which is in progress now or at the time of speaking:

	be	+ verb + -ing
The working population	is	*increasing*.
Prices	are	*falling*.
The dependent population	isn't	*rising*.
Government taxes	aren't	*going down*.

Remember, use the present simple (<u>not</u> the present progressive) to describe states or situations which are not changing:

   All governments **want** high employment.

Verbs that describe a state or condition, e.g. *believe, know, understand, have, mean, say*, are also usually in the present simple:

   Countries always **have** a dependent population (NOT Countries ~~are always having~~ ...).

Time references
Time references, e.g. *at the moment, currently, now, these days*, often appear with the present progressive:

   The working population is **currently** increasing.
   Prices are falling **at the moment**.

🔊 6.4 Listen and repeat the present progressive sentences.

080 UNIT 6A LISTENING & SPEAKING

TASK 3 Practising the present progressive

1 Complete the paragraph with the verbs in brackets in the present progressive.

Globally, more females ¹ *are working* (work) outside the home than ever before. The cost of living ² _____ (rise) in many countries, so many mothers ³ _____ (return) to work after having children. In addition, younger women ⁴ _____ (not start) families when they leave school; more and more ⁵ _____ (continue) their education at university or starting a career. The number of men in work, on the other hand, ⁶ _____ (fall) around the world. That's because the types of jobs in many parts of the world ⁷ _____ (change); for example, industries in developed countries ⁸ _____ (not offer) so many manual jobs in areas such as manufacturing, and men, not women, traditionally did these jobs.

2 Underline the correct form of the verb in italics.
1 At the moment, employment *increases / is increasing* in my country.
2 Overall, the cost of living usually *rises / is rising* by 4% every year.
3 The number of pensioners *goes up / is going up* again this year.
4 Employers in my region *don't offer / aren't offering* any manual jobs these days; everything is in IT and service industries now.
5 More employment *doesn't always mean / isn't always meaning* a stronger economy if those jobs are mainly part-time.
6 In the past, people went to work in other countries, but they *return / are returning* again now because the economy is strong.
7 I *don't understand / 'm not understanding* the term 'dependent population'.
8 Why *does / is* the cost of housing *go up / going up* at the moment?
9 How often *do / are* governments *increase / increasing* taxes?

TASK 4 Talking about your country's economy

1 Work in pairs. Choose an economic topic on the left and a verb on the right. Make three sentences about changes and trends in your country's economy. Think of reasons.

Example: *Unemployment is rising at the moment because …*

Topic	Verb
unemployment the birth rate (= number of babies per year) the cost of housing / food the number of university students / retired people … the number of manufacturing jobs / service jobs … other: _____	increase / rise / go up decrease / fall / go down

2 ◄)) 6.5 Listen to a short conversation. Write the missing words.
Student A ¹ _____ in my country is rising at the moment.
Student B ² _____ is it rising?
Student A ³ _____ is increasing and there aren't any new jobs for young people.

3 Work in pairs. Have similar conversations about the topics in 1.
A Start with a sentence from 1.
B Ask a question with *Why …?*
A Give your reason with *Because …*

4 If you are from the same country, do you agree with each other? If you are from different countries, compare your countries' economic situations.

> **INDEPENDENT STUDY**
>
> It is useful to personalize what you learn, i.e. relate the language to information about your own country or experience.
>
> ▶ Research online some information about the economy in your country. Describe the situation using the language of trends.

6B Reading Textbooks (6)

This module covers:
- Understanding the main trend in a graph
- Understanding changes and trends described in a text

TASK 1 Understanding the main trend in a graph

1 Think about the population of your town or city. Is it currently increasing or decreasing? Why?

2 Read Text 1 and look at the graph. Answer the questions.
   1 What information is on the X-axis (horizontal) and Y-axis (vertical) of the graph?
   2 Is the world's population going up or down at the moment?
   3 In recent years, is the rate of population growth faster or slower?

TEXT 1

The population explosion

In 1804, the world population was one billion. By 1927, there were two billion people. Then, from the 1930s to the 1960s, it increased by another billion. Now the world population is around seven billion and experts think it will increase to 9 billion by the middle of this century.

SOURCE: Adapted from Moynihan, D. and Titley, B. 2012. p.400. *Complete Economics for Cambridge IGCSE and O Level* 2nd ed. Oxford: Oxford University Press.

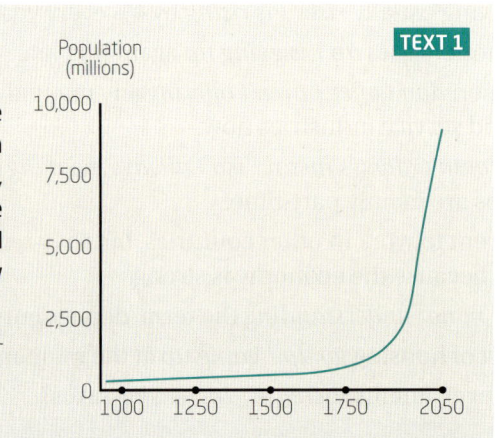

GLOSSARY

population explosion (n) a sudden, large increase in the number of people

---

ACADEMIC LANGUAGE ▸ Language reference page 153

Time, place, and quantity Prepositional phrases

Use a **prepositional phrase** to refer to time, place, and quantity / amount:

Time
- **In** 1400, the global population was around half a billion.
- The population increased **from** the 1820s **to** the 1880s. (start date = 1820s, end date = 1880s)
- **By** 1800, the world's population was one billion people.

Place
- The largest population was **in** Europe.

Quantity
- The population increased **by** half a billion.
- Overall, the population increased **from** half a billion **to** one billion.

TASK 2 Practising time, place, and quantity phrases

1 Read Text 1 again. Circle the prepositional phrases. Do they refer to time, place, or quantity?

2 Match 1–6 with a–f to make prepositional phrases.
   1 by _c_
   2 from ....
   3 in the ....
   4 by the middle ....
   5 in ....
   6 from 1.3 ....

   a the USA
   b 20th century
   c ~~20%~~
   d 1800 to 1900
   e of the 18th century
   f billion to 2.3 billion

3 Complete the paragraph with the prepositions in the list.

   in (x2)   from   to   by (x2)

   ¹........ 1950, 8% of the world's population was aged 60 years and over. ²........ the end of 2010, the figure was 11%. Experts think it will rise ³........ 11% ⁴........ 22% in the next 40 years and ⁵........ 2050 one in every five people ⁶........ developing countries will be over 65 years.

TASK 3 Understanding changes and trends described in a text

1 Read Text 2. Are statements 1–8 true (T) or false (F)?
   1 The global population started to rise in the 18th century. ....
   2 The population explosion started in Asia. ....
   3 Housing and medicine in Europe improved in the 18th century. ....
   4 Nowadays, the birth rate is going up in every European country. ....
   5 Nearly two thirds of the world's population lives in Asia. ....
   6 China and India have over a third of the world's population. ....
   7 Africa has a smaller population than Europe. ....
   8 Experts think the population of every continent will increase in the future. ....

2 Underline the words in Text 2 that are important for your answers.

TEXT 2

The global population

In the 18th century, the world's population started to grow and it is still increasing now. In fact, the global population is increasing by over 70 million people each year. The population explosion started in Europe after the Industrial Revolution in the 18th century. The quality of housing and medicine went up, so the number of deaths
5 decreased and the number of births rose. The population of Europe rose by over 300% from 1750 to 1910. In the 20th century, the population of Europe stayed the same and now, in some European countries, people are moving to other parts of the world and birth rates are falling.

The new population explosion is in Asia and Africa. Around 4 billion people, over 60%
10 of the world's population, currently live in Asia and this number grows every year. The two largest countries by population, China and India, together have about 37% of the world's population. Africa follows with 1 billion people, 15% of the world's population, while Europe has about 750 million people, about 11% of the world's population.

In the future, experts believe the populations of Asia and Africa will grow from around
15 5 billion people in 2010 to over 7 billion by 2050 - an increase of 60%. In contrast, the population of Europe will probably go down from 750 million to about 690 million people. So by 2050, the world population will reach 9 billion in total.

SOURCE: Adapted from Moynihan, D. and Titley, B. 2012. pp.399–400. *Complete Economics for Cambridge IGCSE and O Level* 2nd ed. Oxford: Oxford University Press.

GLOSSARY
the Industrial Revolution *(n)* the period in Europe when machines began to be used to do work and industry grew

ACADEMIC LANGUAGE
▶ Language reference page 153

Changes and trends (2) Past and present tenses, *will*

Use the **past simple** for events in the past:
  The population **rose** in Europe.
  It **stayed** the same in the 20th century.

Use the **present simple** to express states, situations, and repeated actions:
  China and India **have** about 37% of the world's population.
  The population **increases** every year.

Use the **present progressive** for changes and trends now or in progress:
  The population of the world **is increasing**.
  The birth rate **is falling**.

Use **will + infinitive** to talk about changes and trends in the future and make predictions:
  Many people **will move** to other countries.
  The populations of Asia and Africa **will grow**.

> **What is a prediction?**
> A prediction is a statement about what will happen in the future. In academic subjects (e.g. economics) a prediction is based on evidence from past and present trends.

TASK 4 Practising the language of trends

1 Find verbs 1–9 in Text 2 and write the form(s). Then look at Academic Language and note down how each verb form is used.

1 increase	*is increasing*	*present progressive – a change in progress*
2 go up		
3 rise		
4 stay the same		
5 fall		
6 grow		
7 grow		
8 go down		
9 reach		

2 Look at the graphs and the text about population growth in China. Complete the text with the verbs in brackets in the correct form.

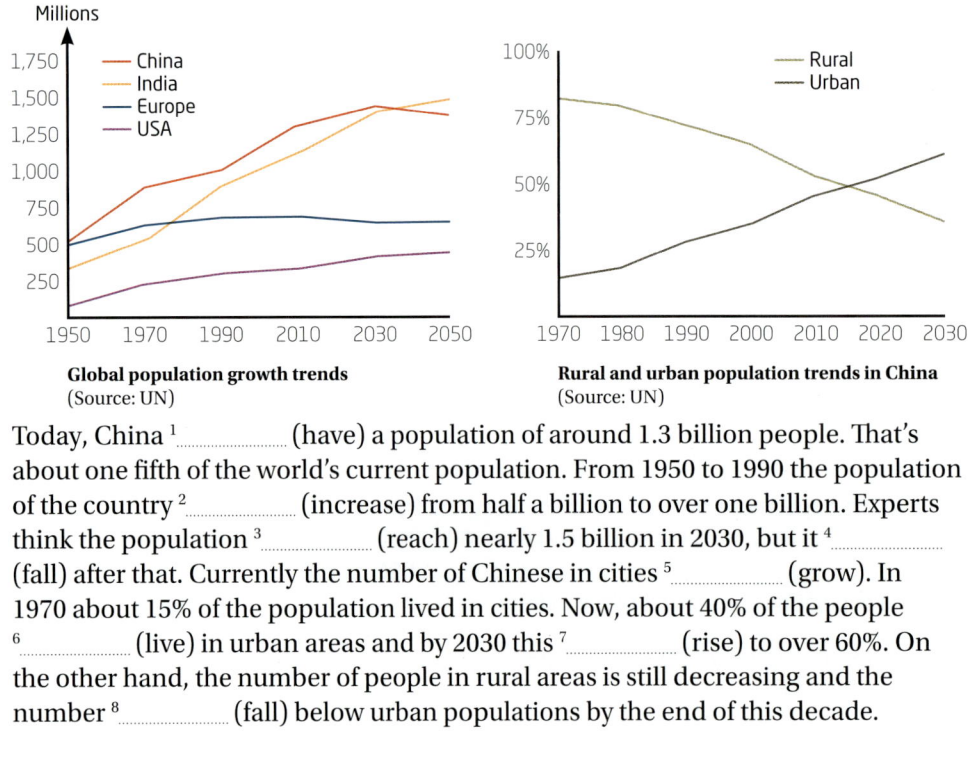

Global population growth trends
(Source: UN)

Rural and urban population trends in China
(Source: UN)

Today, China [1]_____ (have) a population of around 1.3 billion people. That's about one fifth of the world's current population. From 1950 to 1990 the population of the country [2]_____ (increase) from half a billion to over one billion. Experts think the population [3]_____ (reach) nearly 1.5 billion in 2030, but it [4]_____ (fall) after that. Currently the number of Chinese in cities [5]_____ (grow). In 1970 about 15% of the population lived in cities. Now, about 40% of the people [6]_____ (live) in urban areas and by 2030 this [7]_____ (rise) to over 60%. On the other hand, the number of people in rural areas is still decreasing and the number [8]_____ (fall) below urban populations by the end of this decade.

3 Work in pairs. Look at the population trends of India, Europe, and the USA in the graph in Task 4.2. Complete six sentences about these regions.
   1 Today, the population of India _____.
   2 From 1950 to the end of the century, the population of India _____.
   3 By 2050, India's population _____.
   4 In 1950, Europe's population _____.
   5 At the moment, Europe's population _____.
   6 By 2030, the population of the USA _____.

TASK 5 Critical thinking – predicting the future

1 Work in groups and discuss the question. Think about past and present trends relating to the items in the diagram. Write some predictions.

   Example: *In the future, we will need more food, so everyone will grow fruit and vegetables. Also, our free time will increase because …*

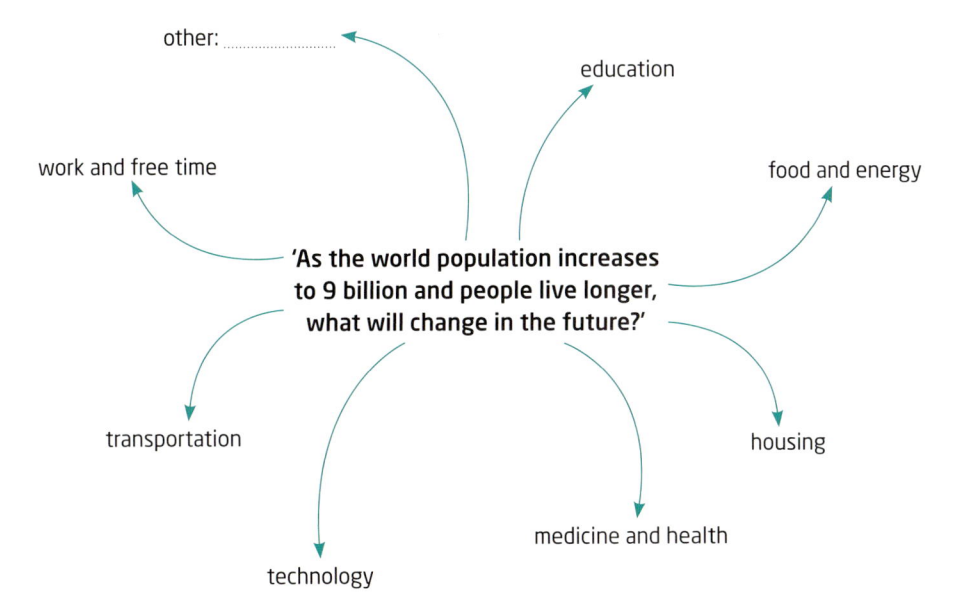

   'As the world population increases to 9 billion and people live longer, what will change in the future?'

   - other:
   - education
   - work and free time
   - food and energy
   - transportation
   - housing
   - technology
   - medicine and health

INDEPENDENT STUDY

Look for trend language when you read.
▶ Read part of an article in English about economics and finance in a newspaper or textbook. Underline any trend language. Find things that increased, decreased, or stayed the same.

2 Present your predictions to the class. Are your predictions similar?

6C Writing (1) Sentences about trends

This module covers:
- Writing sentences about trends using adverbs

TASK 1 Understanding sentences about trends

1 **Match the economic terms in the list with definitions a–e. Use a dictionary to help you.**

exchange rate   inflation   population   tax   unemployment

a the general rise in the price of goods and services in a country ....
b the number of people in a country ....
c money that you pay to the government ....
d the amount of money you need to buy the money of another country ....
e the number of working age people with no paid job ....

2 **Read sentences 1–5. Which economic terms in 1 do they refer to?**

1 The number of people living in the countryside goes down slightly every year.
2 The overall cost of living is increasing rapidly, so people are spending less on shopping.
3 The euro is rising steadily against the dollar and one euro equals about one dollar thirty today.
4 The number of people without work will fall quickly next year, according to many experts.
5 The government didn't add anything to cigarettes last year, so the price stayed the same.

ACADEMIC LANGUAGE   ▶ Language reference page 153

Describing trends (1) Adverbs

You can use a **verb** + **adverb** combination to write a sentence about a trend. The verb refers to the trend. The adverb describes how the trend happens.

	trend		
The average temperature	increased / went up	rapidly / quickly	from June to September.
Unemployment will	decrease / fall	slightly / steadily	next year.

Common **verbs** to refer to trends:
  increase / decrease
  rise / fall
  go up / go down
  climb
  reach
  grow
  continue to + verb

Common **adverbs** to describe trends:
  rapidly, quickly
  steadily, slowly
  slightly

To form an adverb, you can often add *-ly* to an adjective:
  rapid – rapidly   steady – steadily

You do not use an adverb with 'stay the same' because it means 'there is no change'.

---

086   UNIT 6C WRITING (1)

TASK 2 Practising verb + adverb to describe trends

1 Look at sentences 1–5 in Task 1.2 and underline the five verb + adverb phrases. Then match sentences 1–5 with graphs a–e.

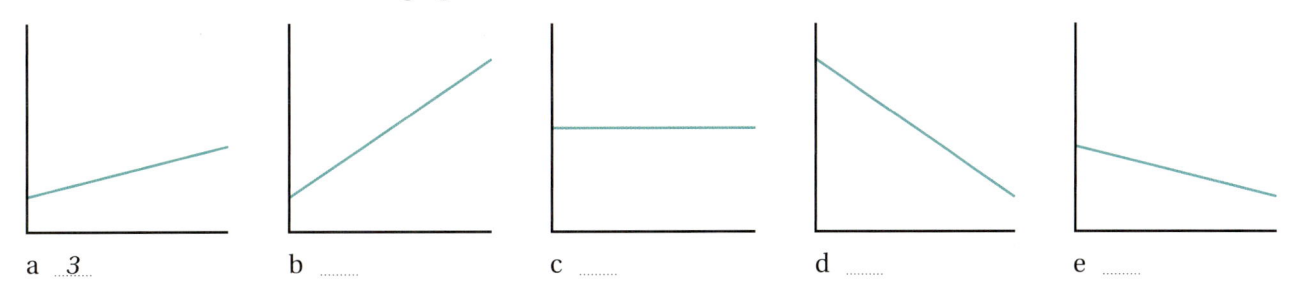

a *3*   b ....   c ....   d ....   e ....

2 Look at four graphs of economic data for the United Kingdom. Match the titles to graphs a–d.

Exchange rate   Population growth   ~~Rate of inflation~~   Unemployment rate

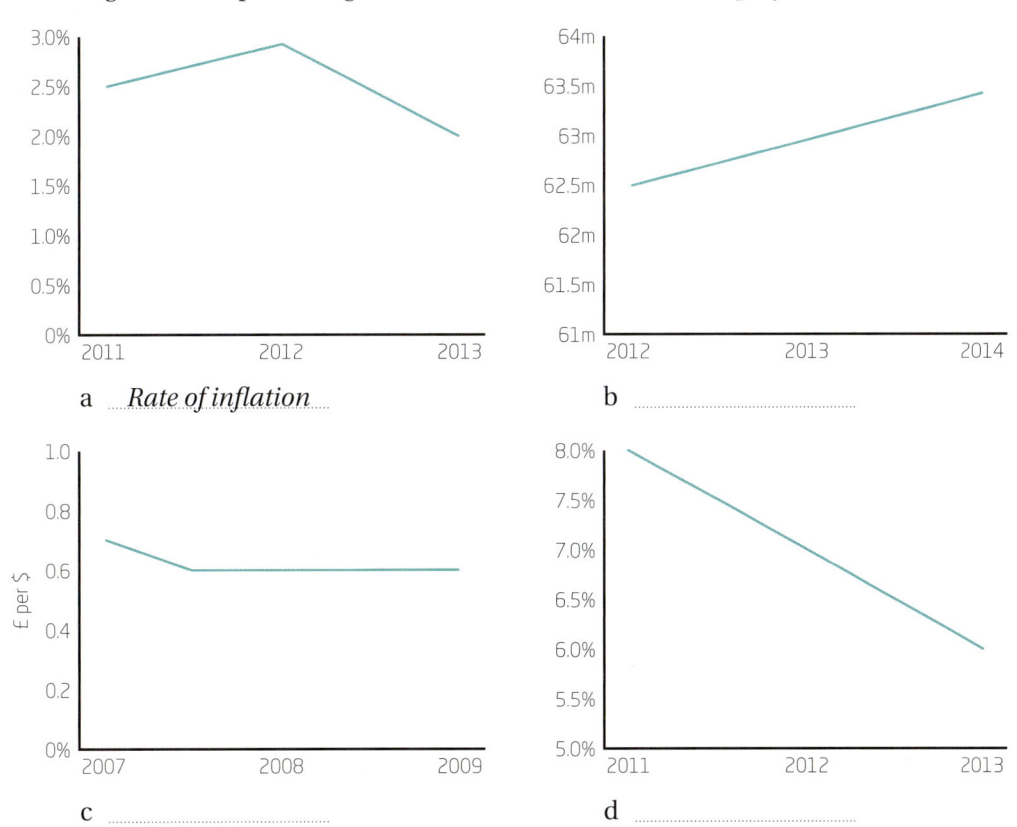

a *Rate of inflation*

b ....

c ....

d ....

3 Look at the graphs again. Complete the sentences with the phrases in the list.

decreased steadily   rose, and then fell   stayed the same
went down slightly   went up slowly

Graph a: In the first 12 months, inflation [1] .... in the next year.
Graph b: From 2012 to 2014, the UK population [2] .... by a million people.
Graph c: In 2007, the average rate for the pound per dollar [3] .... and then it [4] .... for two years.
Graph d: Over the two years, unemployment [5] ....

TASK 3 Writing sentences to describe trends

1 Turn to page 162 and draw trend lines on each graph.

2 Write four sentences, one to describe each graph.

3 Work in pairs. Exchange your graphs. Check your partner's sentences about their graphs. Do the sentences describe the trends accurately?

6C Writing (2) A description of a graph

This module covers:
- Analysing a description of a graph
- Describing trends in a graph using adverbs and adjectives

TASK 1 Analysing a description of a graph

1 Work in pairs. Look at the graph from the UK Office of National Statistics and complete the notes.

Title of graph: ....
Number of years: ....
Number for each year: ....
Overall trend for self-employment in the UK: ....
Possible reasons for this trend: ....

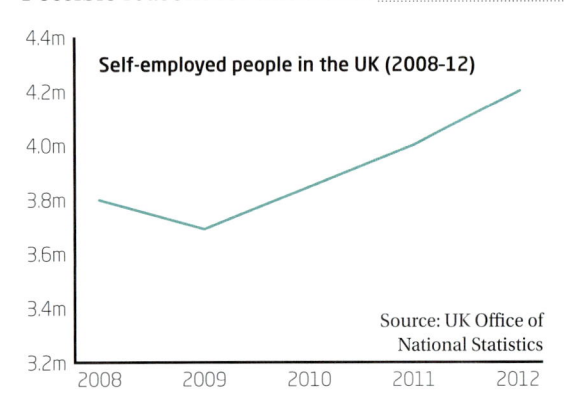

Self-employed people in the UK (2008-12)

4.4m
4.2m
4.0m
3.8m
3.6m
3.4m
3.2m
    2008   2009   2010   2011   2012

Source: UK Office of National Statistics

2 Read a paragraph about the graph. Which sentence (1–5) …?

a gives information about trends in the first two years ....
b introduces the topic of the graph ....
c introduces the main trend in the graph ....
d contrasts and adds information about trends in later years ....
e gives a future prediction based on the past evidence ....

> [1]The graph shows the number of self-employed people in the UK between 2008 and 2012. [2]Overall, there was a large growth in the number of self-employed people. [3]In 2008 there were 3.8 million self-employed people and this figure fell slightly in 2009. [4]However, there was a steady increase in 2010 and the number rose steadily in 2011 and again in 2012. [5]Experts think the trend for self-employment will continue to go up as more people work from home and start their own business.

ACADEMIC LANGUAGE   ▸ Language reference page 154

Describing trends (2) Adjectives and adverbs

You can write about the same trend with a **verb** + **adverb** or an **adjective** + **noun**. The two sentences mean the same and you can use a combination in your writing:

Employment *rose quickly*. / There was a *quick rise* in employment.
The population *fell slowly* for two years. / There was a *slow fall* in the population for two years.

Common nouns to refer to trends:
 increase / decrease   rise / fall   climb   growth

Common adjectives to describe trends:
 large / small   rapid / steady   quick / slow   slight

088 UNIT 6C WRITING (2)

TASK 2 Practising adjectives and adverbs to describe trends

1 Read the paragraph in Task 1 again. Underline trend language with a verb + adverb and with an adjective + noun.

2 Tick (✓) the words in the list which can be verbs or nouns. Use a dictionary.
   Example: *to increase (v), an increase (n)*
   increase ✓   decrease ☐   fall ☐   go down ☐
   climb ☐   reach ☐   rise ☐   stay the same ☐

3 Underline the correct forms of the words in italics.
   1 There was a slight *decrease / decreased* in Japanese inflation from 1990.
   2 Japanese inflation went down *slow / slowly* in the early 1990s.
   3 The rate of inflation in Japan started to go up *rapid / rapidly* in 1972.
   4 There was a *steady / steadily* fall in Japanese inflation during the 1980s.
   5 Inflation in Japan *fall / fell* quickly after 1975.
   6 Last year, there was a small *rise / rose* in inflation.

4 Rewrite the sentences using adjective + noun.
   1 Income tax fell steadily between 1992 and 1995.
      There was a _____ in income tax between 1992 and 1995.
   2 Unemployment decreased rapidly from 8% in 2010 to below 5% in 2012.
      Between 2010 and 2012 there was a _____ in unemployment.
   3 From 1978 to 1980 inflation rose slightly.
      From 1978 to 1980 there was a _____ in inflation.

TASK 3 Writing a description of a graph

1 Look at another graph from the UK Office of National Statistics. Write a paragraph about the graph. Use the paragraph in Task 1 as a model. Use the notes to order your paragraph and remember to use trend language.
   - The graph shows ...
   - Overall, ...
   - 2008 / 2009
   - 2010–2012
   - Experts think that employment will ...

   Employed workers in the UK (2008-12)
   Source: UK Office of National Statistics

2 Use this checklist to check your paragraph. Then exchange with a partner and give feedback. Did you:
   - introduce the topic of the graph? ☐
   - introduce the main trend in the graph? ☐
   - give information about trends in the first two years? ☐
   - add information about trends in later years? ☐
   - give a future prediction? ☐
   - describe the trends with verbs + adverbs and adjectives + nouns? ☐

INDEPENDENT STUDY
Evaluate your writing regularly using the checklists in this course.
▶ Choose a graph with trends from a textbook or website. Write a description of the graph and check it.

Sample answer:
page 160

6D Vocabulary

TASK 1 Vocabulary-building: Word forms

1 Complete the sentences with a form of *employ*.

1 This university .... over 100 lecturers.
2 The company has about 300 ....
3 Many .... say they can't find the right people for the job because they don't have the qualifications and experience.
4 .... people have jobs.
5 .... people don't have jobs.
6 People who work for themselves are self-............... .
7 .... is very high; 60% of young people now have no full-time or part-time job.
8 The number of people in full-time .... is staying the same.

TASK 2 Trends

1 Complete the table with the trend verbs in the list.

climb   decrease   fall   go down   go up   grow   increase   ~~rise~~   stay the same

↑	↓	→
rise		

2 Which trend verbs in 1 can also be nouns? Write the noun form.

Example: rise (v) – *a rise (n)*

TASK 3 Economic terms

1 Complete the sentences with the economic terms in the list.

exchange rate   inflation   population   tax   unemployment

1 As prices in supermarkets are rising, many people think the government should do more to keep .... lower.
2 The .... of the dollar to the pound is about 1.53.
3 By training more young people with the right job skills, the government hopes to reduce .... in the future.
4 By 2050, the global .... will be around nine billion.
5 People who earn over £40,000 will pay about 40% of that in .... to the government.

2 Write five sentences with economic terms and a trend verb or noun.

Example: *In my country, the population is rising.*

> **INDEPENDENT STUDY**
>
> It is useful to learn new words in context. You can use a sentence which is personal to you, e.g. a sentence about your country.
>
> ▶ Choose five new words from this unit and write personal sentences.

6E Academic Language Check

TASK 1 Present progressive, present simple, past simple, *will*

1 Complete sentences 1–8 with the verbs in brackets in the present progressive or the present simple.
   1 This month, the price of petrol _____ (fall).
   2 Every year, driving a car _____ (get) more and more expensive.
   3 These days, more and more young people _____ (stay) in education until they are in their twenties.
   4 A strong economy _____ (mean) more jobs.
   5 The rate of the euro against the dollar _____ (go up) again this week.
   6 The students _____ (not / understand) the word 'tax'.
   7 Why _____ unemployment _____ (rise) at the moment?
   8 How often _____ you _____ (pay) tax?

2 Choose the correct form of the verbs in italics.

Investing in new countries and markets is always risky. In the 1990s, many people ¹*invest / invested* money in countries such as Thailand and Indonesia. But by 1997, those countries ²*have / had* currency problems and some people ³*lose / lost* a lot of money. Nowadays, many investors ⁴*are putting / will put* their money into the BRIC countries (Brazil, Russia, India, and China). At the moment, these countries' economies ⁵*grow / are growing* and most investors expect that they ⁶*continue / will continue* to grow; in particular, China ⁷*has / will have* a large population and natural resources, so it ⁸*became / will become* more and more attractive for new businesses.

TASK 2 Prepositional phrases

1 Complete the short texts with the prepositions in the lists.

by   from   in   to
¹_____ 2000, the rate of inflation was at around 3%. However, ²_____ 2001
³_____ 2003 it rose ⁴_____ 5%.

by   from   in   to
⁵_____ Europe, the currency exchange rate for the US dollar two months ago was 1.5 dollars to the euro. However, the exchange rate increased ⁶_____ 1.5
⁷_____ 1.9 in only four weeks and ⁸_____ the end of last month it was 2.1.

2 Do prepositions 1–8 in 1 refer to time (T), place (P), or quantity (Q)?
   1 ___   2 ___   3 ___   4 ___   5 ___   6 ___   7 ___   8 ___

TASK 3 Adverbs and adjectives

1 Rewrite the first sentence using verb + adverb or adjective + noun.
   1 Unemployment decreased slightly last month.
      There was _____ in unemployment last month.
   2 The pound rose slowly against the dollar.
      There was _____ in the pound against the dollar.
   3 There was a rapid growth in the number of retired people.
      The number of retired people _____ .
   4 There is a slight increase every year in the number of international students at UK universities.
      Every year, the number of international students at UK universities _____ .
   5 The price of petrol climbed steadily this month.
      There was _____ in the price of petrol this month.

UNIT 7 Resources

ACADEMIC FOCUS: UNDERSTANDING FACT AND OPINION

LEARNING OBJECTIVES

This unit covers:

Listening and Speaking
- Reading to prepare for a seminar
- Understanding facts and opinions in a seminar
- Discussing an issue

Reading
- Understanding factual information in a text
- Noticing features of text types
- Distinguishing between fact and opinion

Writing
- Writing passive sentences about steps in a process
- Writing an evaluative sentence
- Analysing a description of a process
- Describing a diagram using linking language

Vocabulary
- Resources
- Vocabulary-building: Adjectives

Academic Language Check
- Giving and supporting opinions, agreeing / disagreeing
- Describing facts and processes
- Describing steps in a process

Discussion

1 Work in pairs. Look at the picture. What is the energy resource? How does it work?

2 Match the energy resources in the list with pictures 1–8.

biofuel   coal   hydroelectric power   natural gas
oil   wave power   solar power   wood

1 ....   2 ....   3 ....   4 ....

5 ....   6 ....   7 ....   8 ....

3 Read two definitions. Put the energy resources in 1 and 2 in two groups, 'renewable' and 'non-renewable'.

> **renewable energy resources**
> resources you can use again and again
> **non-renewable energy resources**
> resources that will not last forever

4 Which energy resources are important in your country at the moment? Will this change in the future?

   Example: *The main energy sources in Qatar are oil and natural gas. In the future, we will also produce solar energy.*

7A Listening & Speaking Seminars (1)

This module covers:
- Reading to prepare for a seminar
- Understanding facts and opinions in a seminar
- Discussing an issue

TASK 1 Reading to prepare for a seminar

> **What is a seminar?**
> A seminar is a group class at university. Students prepare before the class. In class, the students and the tutor study and discuss a topic.

1 Look at the extract from a textbook, which is the preparation for a seminar on nuclear power. What does the diagram show?

2 Read the text. Which paragraph (1, 2, or 3):
- gives information about nuclear energy? ………
- describes how a nuclear power station works? ………
- gives information about nuclear waste? ………

Is nuclear power the best choice?

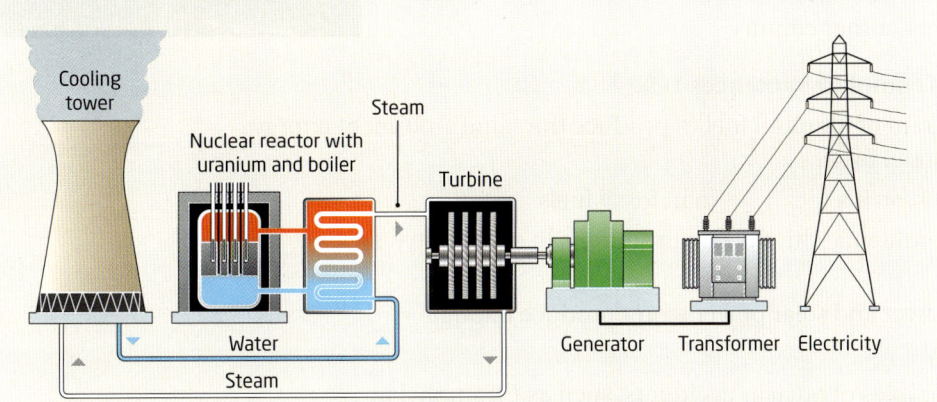

[Diagram showing: Cooling tower, Nuclear reactor with uranium and boiler, Steam, Turbine, Water, Steam, Generator, Transformer, Electricity]

1 Nuclear power stations use solid fuel that contains uranium. The nuclear reactor splits the uranium atoms and this produces heat. The heat boils water, which produces steam, and this drives turbines, producing electricity.
2 Nuclear power stations are an effective alternative to non-renewable fossil fuels; for example, one gram of uranium fuel produces as much energy as eight kilograms of fossil fuel. In addition, a nuclear power station doesn't produce carbon dioxide (CO_2).
3 However, when the fuel from the uranium becomes solid nuclear waste, it is radioactive. Some nuclear waste will be radioactive for thousands of years. Nuclear waste sites store the radioactive material in concrete under the ground, but if there's an accident, the waste can contaminate the local land and water.

SOURCE: Adapted from Fullick, A. et al. 2011. pp.272-3. *GCSE Science Higher*. Oxford: Oxford University Press.

GLOSSARY
contaminate *(v)* to make sth dirty or not pure by adding a dangerous material
fossil fuel *(n)* a fuel such as coal or oil that was formed over millions of years under the ground from plants and animals

3 Read the text again and complete the student's notes.

> **How nuclear power stations work:**
> Nuclear power stations use solid fuel + [1] ………
> The fuel heats the water → the steam drives the turbines → produces [2] ………
>
> **Positive points:**
> Energy production: 1 g of uranium = 8 kg of [3] ………
> Nuclear power doesn't produce [4] ………
>
> **Negative points:**
> It produces [5] ……… waste
> The waste can contaminate local [6] ………

UNIT 7A LISTENING & SPEAKING 093

TASK 2 Understanding facts and opinions in a seminar

1 ▶7.1 **Watch part of a seminar about nuclear power. Choose two correct answers for each question.**
   1 In the seminar last week, what did they talk about?
      a non-renewable energy resources
      b renewable energy resources
      c nuclear energy
   2 What did the tutor ask the students to do before the seminar?
      a attend a lecture
      b read part of a textbook
      c do online research about nuclear power
   3 How does Adam support his opinion?
      a with information from the textbook
      b with the example of his own country
      c with information from a newspaper
   4 How does Travis support his opinion?
      a with information from the textbook
      b with examples of real nuclear accidents
      c with the example of another country

> **What is a fact?**
> A fact is information that can be checked and shown to be true. In contrast, an opinion is information that people agree or disagree about. In academic discussions, opinion is supported with facts.

2 ▶7.1 **Watch again and complete sentences 1–9.**
   1 You need .... gram of uranium fuel to produce the same amount of energy as .... kilos of fossil fuels.
   2 It doesn't produce CO_2, so it's .... than fossil fuels.
   3 There are never any problems with the power stations in my country, so it's ....
   4 In the future, wind power and solar power won't produce enough ....
   5 Nuclear power is very ....
   6 There are famous examples of nuclear accidents, such as Chernobyl in .... and Fukushima in ....
   7 In Germany the government plans to close all of the nuclear power stations over the next .... years.
   8 Only 15% of the UK's energy comes from ....
   9 The UK .... live without nuclear power.

3 **Which sentences in 2 give a fact (F)? Which sentences give an opinion (O)?**
   Example: 1 *F*

094 UNIT 7A LISTENING & SPEAKING

ACADEMIC LANGUAGE   ▶ Language reference page 154

Expressing opinions Giving and supporting opinions, agreeing / disagreeing

You can use a variety of expressions to discuss a topic and give opinions.

Asking for opinions
What's your opinion? / What do you think? / Do you agree?

Giving your opinion
I think ... / I don't think ... / In my opinion ...

Supporting your opinion with facts
The textbook says ...   In my experience ...   There are famous / good examples of ...

Agreeing and disagreeing
I agree (with you).   Yes, but ...   (Sorry,) I don't agree.

🔊 **7.2** Listen and repeat the expressions.

TASK 3 Practising the language of discussion

1 ▶7.1 Watch the seminar again. Tick (✓) the person who uses each expression.

	Tutor	Adam	Travis
What's your opinion?	✓		
The textbook says ...			
I agree.			
I also think ...			
What do you think?			

	Tutor	Adam	Travis
Do you agree with ...?			
In my opinion ...			
Yes, but ...			
I don't agree that ...			
There are famous examples of ...			

2 Read statements 1–5 about energy. Do you agree (✓) or disagree (✗)?
   1 Nuclear energy is very dangerous.
   2 People will use more energy in the future.
   3 Everyone should use less energy.
   4 We should build more nuclear power stations.
   5 The best energy resources are renewables like the Sun, wind, and water.

3 Think of a fact to support each statement in 2. Use information from the text, the seminar, or your own knowledge or experience.

4 Work in pairs and give your opinion about the statements in 2. Use some of the expressions in 1 and support your opinion with a fact.
   Example: In my opinion, nuclear energy is dangerous. The waste is radioactive.

TASK 4 Discussing an issue

1 Work in groups. Discuss the question below.

   > Is nuclear power the best choice?

   Compare your ideas on nuclear energy. Do you agree or disagree?
   Example: **A** *I agree that people will use more energy in the future because of the world's population. What do you think?*
   B *I agree with you. In my opinion, ...*
   C *Yes, but ...*

> **INDEPENDENT STUDY**
>
> It's easier to give your opinion on an academic topic if you have reliable facts to support your ideas.
>
> ▶ Research another type of energy such as wind power or solar power. Make a list of facts.

7B Reading Textbooks (7)

This module covers:
- Understanding factual information in a text
- Noticing features of text types
- Distinguishing between fact and opinion

TASK 1 Understanding factual information in a text

1 Work in pairs. What do you know about these energy resources?
a biofuels
b hydroelectric power
c power from waves and tides
d solar power
e wind power

2 Read Text 1 and complete subheadings 1–5 with the resources in 1.

TEXT 1

Renewables – how do they work?

A renewable energy resource will never run out, so many countries are using more and more renewable energy sources.

1 ....
The Sun provides an average of about 100 watts of solar power per square metre of ground. The Sun's radiation is used by solar panels to heat water and buildings. Other types of solar panels can also generate electricity; these are called photovoltaic (PV) panels. Spain and Germany currently use more PV panels than any other country.

2 ....
Water is heated by the Sun, then it evaporates, and finally it falls as rain. On high ground, this rainwater is stored behind a dam and it is used to turn turbines in hydroelectric power stations. In countries with mountains and rivers, hydroelectric power stations are common; for example, the majority of electricity in Norway is from hydroelectricity and in Iceland, it's 70%.

3 ....
Wind energy is also used to turn turbines, which drive electricity generators. Currently, wind farms with large numbers of turbines produce an average 2W per square metre. More than 5% of the UK's electricity is now produced by wind farms and this figure will grow in the future, because, as a country with long coastlines, the UK can build more and more offshore wind farms.

4 ....
Gravity between the Earth and the Moon changes the movement of the oceans and the ocean tides rise and fall. The water movement of the tides and waves can drive turbines. Again, countries with long coastlines and surrounded by the sea can use tidal power to provide around 11 kWh per person per day.

5 ....
In countries with large areas of farmland, certain plants are grown for energy, not food. For example, the USA now produces more than 50% of its corn for biofuels such as ethanol and biodiesel. Increasingly, these biofuels are used in transportation and some plants are also burned in thermal power stations.

SOURCE: Adapted from Fullick, A. et al. 2011. pp.274–5. *GCSE Science Higher*. Oxford: Oxford University Press.

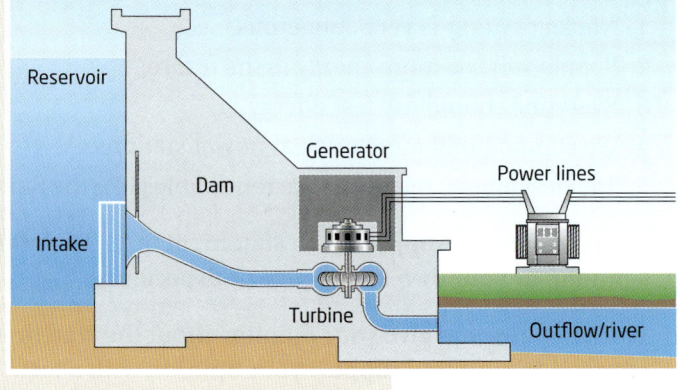

GLOSSARY

offshore *(adj)* at sea, not far from the land

watt *(n)* a unit of power; abbreviations include W (watt), kWh (kilowatt-hour)

3 **Match energy-related words 1–5 with their meanings a–e.**
   1 solar   _d_   a light
   2 hydro   ____   b life
   3 bio   ____   c heat
   4 photo   ____   d ~~Sun~~
   5 thermal   ____   e water

4 **Work in pairs. Find these numbers in Text 1 and say what they refer to.**
   100   70   2   5   11   50

ACADEMIC LANGUAGE   ▸ Language reference page 154

Present simple passive (1) Describing facts and processes

Academic texts often describe facts and processes with the present simple tense in the passive form:
  Water is heated by the Sun.
Use the verb *be* + past participle:
  Water is heated by the Sun.
  Plants are grown for biofuels.
The passive form emphasizes the action or the object of the action. The object of a sentence in the active form becomes the subject of the sentence in the passive form:

Active	Passive
The Sun heats water.	Water is heated by the Sun.
People grow plants for biofuels.	Plants are grown for biofuels.

Some past participles are irregular. Check the correct form in your dictionary.

TASK 2 Practising the present simple passive

1 **Find the passive form in Text 1 of active sentences 1–5.**

   Example: Solar panels use the Sun's radiation to heat water and buildings.
   The Sun's radiation is used by solar panels to heat water and buildings.

   1 People store rainwater behind a dam.

   2 People use it to turn turbines.

   3 Wind farms now produce more than 5% of the UK's electricity.

   4 Transportation uses biofuels.

   5 People also burn some plants in thermal power stations.

2 **Underline the correct form of the verbs in italics, active or passive.**

   Nowadays, wind energy ¹*is used / uses* in many countries. First, the wind ²*is turned / turns* a turbine and this ³*generates / is generated* electricity. Some wind turbines ⁴*locate / are located* on land and others ⁵*build / are built* at sea. In Northern Ireland, a tidal power station ⁶*is provided / provides* energy to the town of Strangford. The station ⁷*is called / calls* SeaGen and it ⁸*produces / is produced* enough energy for over 1,000 homes. SeaGen ⁹*is fixed / fixes* to the bottom of the sea and its turbines ¹⁰*are driven / drive* by the strong tides and waves.

TASK 3 Noticing features of text types

1 Read and compare two texts, Texts 2 and 3, about the same topic. Which text:
   a is from a textbook?
   b is a personal blog?
   c includes facts?
   d gives a personal opinion?

TEXT 2

A fossil fuel is formed over millions of years from plant and animal remains. Coal, petroleum, and natural gas are all examples of fossil fuels. Currently, humans are using them more quickly than they can form. The table
5 shows how long the world's petroleum supplies will last in the ten countries where most of the world's petroleum is found (from 2010).
   In addition to the future shortage of fossil fuels, when they are burned, they produce carbon dioxide
10 (CO_2) gases. As a result, the Earth's climate is changing, so alternative fuels are needed. Like fossil fuels, biofuels produce CO_2 when they are burned, but unlike fossil fuels (which take millions of years to form), they are produced quickly. Nuclear fuel, on the other hand,
15 does not make CO_2, but it produces radioactive waste.

Country	Years
Saudi Arabia	70
Canada	147
Iran	93
Iraq	148
Kuwait	108
United Arab Emirates	91
Venezuela	86
Russia	15
Libya	64
Nigeria	39

SOURCE: Adapted from Fullick, A. et al. 2011. p.257. *GCSE Science Higher*. Oxford: Oxford University Press.

TEXT 3

In the future, the world will have a bigger population and people will use more and more energy. So where do we get it from? Only a few countries will have fossil fuels and eventually they'll run out. In addition, fossil fuels are dangerous because they produce CO_2 and cause climate change. Biofuels are a good alternative, but I don't think we can produce enough energy with them, because people also need plants for food. In my opinion, the best answer is nuclear energy, because it's cleaner, safer, and produces lots more energy than other renewables. Our government should build more nuclear power stations before it's too late!

2 Which text (Text 2, Text 3, or both):
   • gives a strong opinion about the use of nuclear energy?
   • gives more facts about different fuels?
   • would you use to support your opinion in a seminar discussion?

3 Read Texts 2 and 3 again. Tick (✓) the language features in the table for each text.

This text uses ...	Text 2	Text 3
a definition with an example	✓	
several passive forms		
all active forms		
accurate names, dates, and figures		
personal opinions (e.g. *I think*)		
contracted forms (e.g. *don't*)		
more adjectives		
informal punctuation (e.g. question marks, exclamation marks)		

TASK 4 Distinguishing between fact and opinion

1 Look at the sentences from two different texts about wind farms. Complete with the words and numbers in the list.

aren't   beautiful   I think   is   reliable   ugly   6 out of 10   20   1994

1 Wind power _____ a type of renewable energy.
2 Wind power isn't always _____, because often, the wind doesn't blow.
3 Denmark built the world's first offshore wind farm in _____.
4 Wind farms provide _____ kWh per person per day.
5 _____ governments should develop more wind farms in the future.
6 Some people say wind turbines are noisy and _____, but to me they're clean and _____!
7 According to one survey, _____ people in the UK support wind farms.
8 Why _____ there more wind farms?

2 Which sentences in 1 give a fact (F)? Which sentences give an opinion (O)?
Example: 1 *F*

TASK 5 Critical thinking – expressing facts and opinions

1 Choose one of the topics and prepare two sentences. One sentence must express a fact about the topic and one sentence must express an opinion.
- fossil fuels / renewable energy
- nuclear power / solar energy and wind power
- biofuels / oil
- world population now / in the future

2 Work in pairs. Listen to your partner read their two sentences aloud. Say which sentence expresses a fact and which expresses an opinion. Say which words in the sentence make it a fact or an opinion.

3 Choose another topic in 1 and repeat the activity.

INDEPENDENT STUDY

When you read, think about what kind of text it is. Are there more facts or more opinions?

▶ Look back at texts in the previous units of this book. Look for a) examples of language for presenting factual information, and b) examples of sentences with the writer's opinion.

7C Writing (1) Sentences about processes

This module covers:
- Writing passive sentences about steps in a process
- Writing an evaluative sentence

TASK 1 Describing steps in a process

1 Match the process verbs in the list with pictures 1–8.

build   burn   combine   connect   drive   grow   ~~heat~~   transform

1 *heat*
2 .... 
3 .... 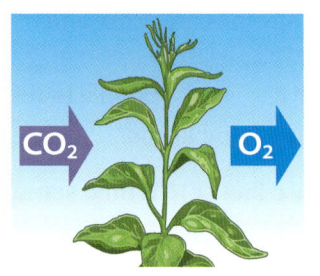
4 .... 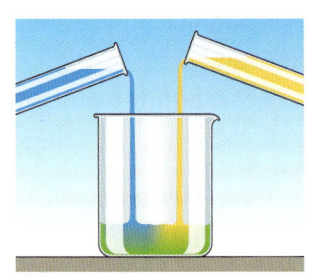
5 .... 
6 .... 
7 .... 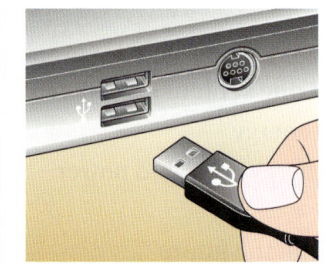
8 .... 

ACADEMIC LANGUAGE   ▶ Language reference page 154

Present simple passive (2) Describing a process

When you write about facts and processes, you can use the present simple passive form.
Use *by* + agent when it's important to write what (or who) is responsible for the action:

	be	+ past participle	+ by + agent
The water	is	heated	by energy in the nuclear reactor.
The panels	are	heated	by the sun.

Don't write *by* + agent after the passive form if the agent is not necessary / important:
  Food is heated in the microwave oven ~~by a person~~.
  Wind turbines are designed ~~by engineers~~ to produce electricity.

TASK 2 Practising passive sentences

1 Complete the sentences with the verbs in Task 1 in the passive form.
  1 Food *is heated* in a microwave oven with radiation.
  2 When the two chemicals ...., they produce a gas.
  3 In hydroelectric power stations, the turbines .... by water.
  4 The internet .... to our homes by fibre-optic cables.
  5 Off-shore wind turbines .... at sea on large concrete blocks.
  6 Cocoa beans .... in the Ivory Coast and exported to make chocolate.
  7 When coal ...., it produces waste gases.
  8 In photosynthesis, carbon dioxide .... into oxygen by plants.

2 Rewrite sentences 1-8 using the passive form.

1 When you heat water to 100°C, it boils.
   When water ____is heated____ to 100°C, it boils.
2 Strong winds drive the turbines to produce energy.
   The turbines _____ by strong winds to produce energy.
3 You combine hydrogen and oxygen to make water.
   Hydrogen and oxygen _____ to make water.
4 Many people in developing countries burn wood for heat and cooking.
   Wood _____ by many people in developing countries.
5 Companies build hydroelectric power stations next to mountains and rivers.
   Hydroelectric power stations _____ by companies.
6 In the UK, the National Grid connects homes to power stations.
   In the UK, homes _____ by the National Grid.
7 A nuclear reactor transforms uranium into energy.
   Uranium _____ by a nuclear reactor.
8 Farmers grow miscanthus grass for fuel.
   Miscanthus grass _____ by farmers.

Miscanthus grass

3 Look at the diagram and the notes about using a wind turbine to produce electricity. Write three sentences about the process using the passive form.

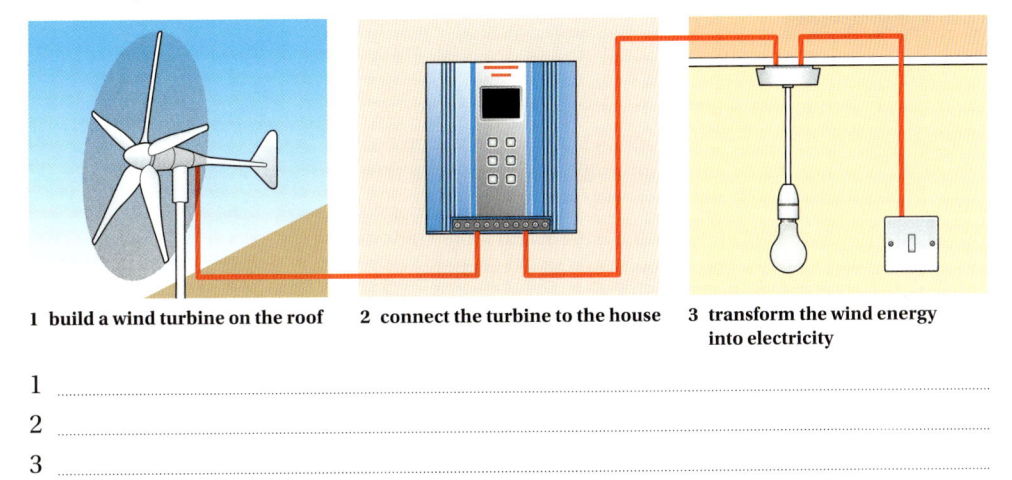

1 build a wind turbine on the roof   2 connect the turbine to the house   3 transform the wind energy into electricity

1 ....
2 ....
3 ....

TASK 3 Evaluating a process

1 Look at sentences a–h. Underline the evaluative adjectives.

a This is an <u>effective</u> way to deliver large amounts of data.
b It's a very easy way to cook.
c This type of energy is cheap in countries with many rivers and lakes.
d They are more expensive than turbines on land.
e This process is a complex part of the lifecycle of the natural world.
f The gas smells, but it is a safe process.
g Carbon dioxide is one of the most dangerous of these.
h They are probably the country's most important product.

2 Match the evaluative sentences in 1 to the factual sentences (1-8) in Task 2.1.

Example: 1 – b *Food is heated in a microwave oven with radiation. It's a very easy way to cook.*

3 Look at your sentences from Task 2.3. Write another sentence about the process using an evaluative adjective.

> **What is evaluation?**
> Evaluation is giving an opinion or comment on something. When you evaluate something you ask questions such as 'Is this useful / safe / effective?'

UNIT 7C WRITING (1) **101**

7C Writing (2) A description of a process

This module covers:
- Analysing a description of a process
- Describing a diagram using linking language

TASK 1 Analysing a paragraph about a process

1 Look at the picture of a solar water tank on the roof of a house. How do you think it works?

2 Look at the diagram and read the paragraph. Answer the questions.
   1 Where do people use these water tanks?
   2 What heats the water?
   3 When does the water rise?

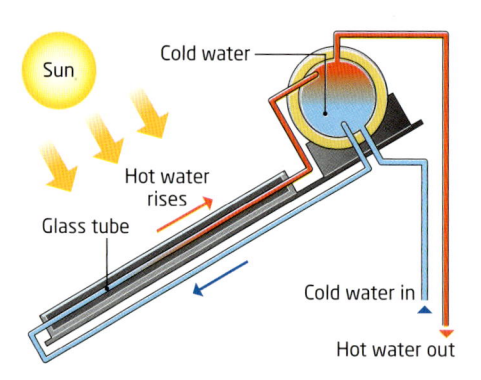

¹A large amount of electricity is needed to heat water in houses, so in hot countries, water tanks with solar thermal panels are used. ²This diagram shows how the process works. ³First of all, the tank and panel are fixed to the roof of the house and the tank is filled with cold water. ⁴Then, during the day, the Sun heats the cold water in the glass tubes. ⁵When the water is hot, it rises, and flows back into the tank and more cold water flows into the glass tubes until, finally, all the water is hot. ⁶Overall, it's a cheap and efficient way to heat water.

3 Match sentences 1-6 in the paragraph with their purpose a-d.
   Sentence 1: ......   a to introduce the diagram
   Sentence 2: ......   b to give an evaluation
   Sentences 3, 4, and 5: ......   c to introduce the topic of the paragraph
   Sentence 6: ......   d to describe the steps in the process

ACADEMIC LANGUAGE   ▶ Language reference page 154

Linking language (6) Describing steps in a process

We often use sequencing words and phrases such as *first of all, secondly, then, after that, next, finally,* etc. to describe the order of facts in a process:

   First of all, uranium is put into the nuclear reactor.
   Then, the nuclear reactor produces heat.
   Next, steam is produced and **finally**, this drives the turbines.

You can use a sentence pattern with *When ...* to describe the result of an action in the process:

   The fuel becomes very hot. → The fuel boils the water.
   When the fuel becomes very hot, it boils the water.

The final sentence in a paragraph often uses linking language to evaluate the process, such as *Overall, To sum up, In general, On the whole,* etc.:

   Overall, it's a very effective process.
   In general, the process is cheap but reliable.

TASK 2 Practising describing a process

1 Look at six sentences about the diagram of a hydroelectric power station (Text 1, page 096). Number them in the correct order 1 to 6.

Then, it is used to turn the turbines. ....

Hydroelectric power stations are often built in regions with high mountains, rivers, and lakes. _1_

First of all, rainwater is stored behind a dam. ....

This diagram shows how the process works. ....

Overall, hydroelectric power stations are expensive to build, but the energy is renewable and cleaner than fossil fuels. ....

When the turbines turn, electricity is generated and, finally, it is transferred to power lines. ....

2 Complete the paragraph with the words in the list.

finally   first of all   in general   then   when

Sunflowers are often grown for oil and used in cooking, but they are also used as biofuel. ¹............., the sunflowers are planted in early spring. ².............. the seeds are ready (normally in the early autumn), they are picked and ³.............. they are taken for processing. The seeds are pressed to produce oil and ⁴.............. the oil is transformed into biofuel for transportation. ⁵.............., biofuel from sunflowers is more expensive than other types of biofuels, but it offers an environmentally-friendly alternative to petrol.

TASK 3 Writing a description of a diagram

1 Look at the stages in a diagram for using solar energy to produce electricity. Answer the questions.
   1 What generates the electricity from the Sun?
   2 What stores the electricity?
   3 What converts the power to use in a house?

| The sun heats | solar PV panel generates electricity | battery stores electricity | inverter converts power | use in house |

2 Write a paragraph about the diagram in 1. Use the paragraph in Task 1 as a model. Remember to:
   • introduce the topic and the diagram
   • describe the steps in the process
   • end with an evaluative sentence about this type of energy.

3 Use this checklist to check your paragraph. Then exchange with a partner and give feedback. Did you:
   • introduce the topic of the paragraph? ☐
   • introduce the diagram? ☐
   • describe the steps in the process? ☐
   • use verbs in the active and passive form? ☐
   • use sequencing words and phrases? ☐
   • give an evaluation at the end? ☐

INDEPENDENT STUDY

Writing about processes is a good way to learn sequencing language.
▶ Find another process diagram from a textbook (in English or in your language). Write a description of the process.

Sample answer:
page 160

UNIT 7C WRITING (2) 103

7D Vocabulary

TASK 1 Resources

1 Complete sentences 1–10 with the words in the list.

biofuel   coal   gas   hydroelectric   nuclear   oil   solar   wave   wind   wood

1 You can produce .... from plants such as corn.
2 .... power is generated with large turbines either on land or offshore.
3 In countries such as Norway, ... power stations are built near lakes and rivers in the mountains.
4 A large amount of .... comes from the Middle East and is used for petrol in vehicles.
5 .... from trees is probably the most traditional form of energy and heat.
6 Countries surrounded by the sea can produce their energy with .... power.
7 Russia is one of the largest producers of natural .... It exports a lot of this clean fuel through pipes to countries in Europe and Asia.
8 .... power stations use solid fuel that contains uranium.
9 .... energy is produced by photovoltaic panels; these convert the Sun's radiation into electricity.
10 .... is a non-renewable fossil fuel which comes from under the ground – people burn it on fires.

TASK 2 Vocabulary-building: Adjectives

1 Complete sentences 1–6 with the adjective form of the words in brackets.

Example: A USB stick is an *effective* way to store and transfer computer data. (effect)

1 In general, nuclear energy is safe; it's only .... if you don't control it properly. (danger)
2 Wind power is clean energy, but it's .... to build turbines. (expense)
3 Wind power isn't .... because the wind doesn't always blow. (rely)
4 This .... part of the countryside will be spoilt if they build wind farms on it. (beauty)
5 The power station is about a kilometre away, but it's very ....! (noise)
6 Water tanks with solar panels are very .... in hot climates. (use)

2 Write antonyms for the adjectives in 1. Use prefixes, suffixes, or new words.

1 effect   *effective   ineffective*
2 danger
3 expense
4 rely
5 beauty
6 noise
7 use

> **INDEPENDENT STUDY**
>
> Some adjectives use a prefix (e.g. *un-, in-*) or a suffix (e.g. *-less*) to make the antonym. The antonyms of some adjectives are new words, e.g. *expensive / cheap*.
>
> ▶ Find and note down more adjectives which use prefixes and suffixes to make antonyms.

7E Academic Language Check

TASK 1 Giving and supporting opinions, agreeing / disagreeing

1 **Complete the conversation.**

   A In my ¹o_____, we need to build more nuclear power stations because we won't have enough energy by 2030. And there are good ²e_____ of countries which use and control their nuclear energy, for example, France. Do you ³a_____?

   B Well, I agree ⁴w_____ you that we need more energy by 2030; in fact, I ⁵t_____ we'll need alternative energy resources before then. But ⁶w_____ do you think about wind power? It's clean and renewable.

   A ⁷Y_____, but the textbook ⁸s_____ it isn't as efficient and reliable as nuclear power, so I ⁹d_____ think wind turbines can produce all the energy we need and certainly not in the next few years.

2 Write a similar conversation between two people discussing solar energy and hydroelectric power. Use some of the expressions in the conversation in 1.

TASK 2 Describing facts and processes

1 **Match the nouns with the verbs. Complete sentences 1–5 using the passive form.**

   Nouns: hydroelectricity   turbines   plants   sea water   solar panels   ~~water~~

   Verbs: ~~boil~~   design   generate   grow   heat   move

   Example: _Water is boiled_ by the heat from a nuclear reactor.

   1 _____ by the Sun.
   2 _____ by rainwater behind a dam.
   3 _____ to convert wind into electricity.
   4 _____ up and down because of the gravity between the Earth and the Moon.
   5 _____ for food but also for biofuel.

2 **Rewrite the sentences in 1 in the active form.**

   1 _The heat from a nuclear reactor boils water._
   2 The Sun _____.
   3 When rainwater behind a dam turns turbines in a power station, it _____.
   4 To convert wind into electricity, engineers _____.
   5 The gravity between the Earth and the Moon _____.
   6 Farmers _____.

TASK 3 Describing steps in a process

1 **Choose the correct expression from the words in italics.**

   ¹*First of all / Finally*, the water container is placed near a wall of the house. ²*Then / When*, a pipe is attached to a drainpipe down the wall. ³*Next / When* it rains, water flows down the gutter. ⁴*Finally / Next of all* the water runs into the container. ⁵*General / Overall*, it's a very simple process for saving rainwater and saving money.

UNIT 8 Impact

ACADEMIC FOCUS: UNDERSTANDING CAUSE AND EFFECT

LEARNING OBJECTIVES

This unit covers:

Listening and Speaking
- Reading to prepare for a seminar
- Taking notes in a seminar
- Discussing cause and effect in a seminar

Reading
- Identifying the purpose of a paragraph
- Taking notes on cause and effect in a text
- Organizing information with a flowchart

Writing
- Writing cause and effect sentences in a variety of patterns
- Analysing a cause and effect paragraph
- Writing a paragraph describing positive and negative impacts

Vocabulary
- Noun phrases
- Prepositions

Academic Language Check
- Cause and effect: Verbs and prepositions
- Modals: *could*, *might*, and *may*

Discussion

1 Look at the picture of a holiday destination. Describe this type of holiday with three adjectives from the list. Compare with a partner and give reasons.

boring busy clean crowded exciting healthy
interesting noisy peaceful polluted quiet
refreshing relaxing stressful unhealthy

2 Which adjectives in 1 have a positive or negative meaning, or both? Complete the diagram. Use a dictionary to help you.

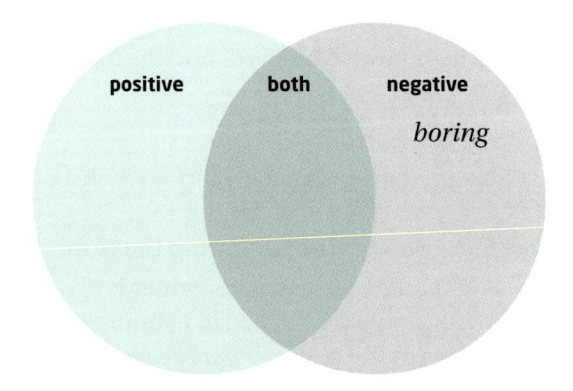

positive — both — negative

boring

3 Look at the list. Is tourism positive or negative for these people? Why?

a bus driver   a hotel owner   a local resident
a shop owner   an unemployed person

Example: *It's negative for a bus driver because the roads are busy and crowded.*

106

8A Listening & Speaking Seminars (2)

This module covers:
- Reading to prepare for a seminar
- Taking notes in a seminar
- Discussing cause and effect in a seminar

TASK 1 Reading a text to prepare for a seminar

1 Read the text, which is the preparation for a seminar on tourism. Answer the questions.
   1 Are the impacts of tourism positive, negative, or both?
   2 What three types of impact does tourism have?

Impacts of tourism

When tourists visit a destination they change it in some way. In other words, they have an impact on the local area. Some of the changes can be positive for the environment, or good for local people. Other impacts of tourism are negative for the local economy, society, or the environment. In summary, tourism has three types of impact:
- **economic** the impact on jobs, business, and income
- **social** the impact on local people, their way of life, and their facilities
- **environmental** the impact on nature and also the global environment

SOURCE: Adapted from Rickerby, S. 2009. p.83. *Leisure and Tourism GCSE*. Cheltenham: Nelson Thornes.

GLOSSARY

impact *(n)* the positive or negative effect that sth has on sth else, e.g. the impact of tourism on the environment

2 Work in groups. Read six comments about a new holiday destination. What types of impact do they refer to? Tick (✓) the table.

Comment	Economic	Social	Environmental
1 'Unemployment always goes down in the summer months.'	✓	✓	
2 'The town is always crowded and the shops are more expensive.'			
3 'When I was a child there was a beautiful forest next to the sea. Now it's all concrete.'			
4 'I left the town years ago, but I'm moving back here to open a restaurant.'			
5 'It's expensive for the local council to clean up the rubbish on the beach.'			
6 'Nowadays you can get a bus late at night, so I don't have to pay for a taxi home.'			

TASK 2 Taking notes in a seminar

1 ▶ 8.1 Watch a seminar and complete the notes.

Impact	Positive	Negative
Economic	Tourists spend [1]............. . Tourism creates more local [2]............. . Business owners employ more [3]............. . This produces more jobs.	Tourism is seasonal. Tourists come in the summer, so there are no [4]............. in the winter.
Social	New facilities for tourists lead to better leisure [5]............. for local people.	Leisure facilities may be too [6]............. for local people.
Environmental	Local people plant trees and build [7]............. .	Air travel causes global [8]............. .

UNIT 8A LISTENING & SPEAKING 107

ACADEMIC LANGUAGE ▶ Language reference page 155

Cause and effect (1) Verbs

To describe cause and effect, we can use the verbs *cause*, *create*, *lead to*, and *produce* with the pattern **cause** + **verb** + **effect**. The verb is followed by a noun or noun phrase.

cause	+ verb	+ effect
Air travel	**causes**	pollution.
Tourism	**creates**	more local business.
More advertising	**leads to**	more visitors.
More business	**produces**	more jobs.

In a series of cause–effect events, the effect of one thing can be the cause of the next:
more advertising → more visitors → more business → more jobs
More advertising leads to more visitors to the town. More visitors create more local business. More business produces more jobs.

You can use *this* to refer back to a cause and effect:
More advertising leads to more visitors. **This** creates more local business.
This refers to 'more visitors' / to the idea that 'More advertising leads to more visitors'.

🔊 **8.2** Listen and repeat the cause and effect sentences.

> **What is cause and effect?**
> Academic texts about change often discuss the relationship between a cause and an effect, i.e. how one action (the cause) makes something else happen (the effect).

TASK 3 Practising describing cause and effect

1 Read sentences 1–6. Circle the causes and underline the effects.
   Example: (Tourism) creates *more local business*.
   1 Business owners employ more people and this produces more jobs.
   2 New facilities for tourists lead to better leisure facilities for local people.
   3 Millions of tourists travelling by air causes global pollution.
   4 Trees and parks for tourists also create a better environment for locals.
   5 Many tourists drive to the coast. This leads to traffic problems.
   6 Tourists want hotels on the beaches. This produces an ugly coast.

2 Work in pairs. Look at the cause and effect diagram. Complete the text.

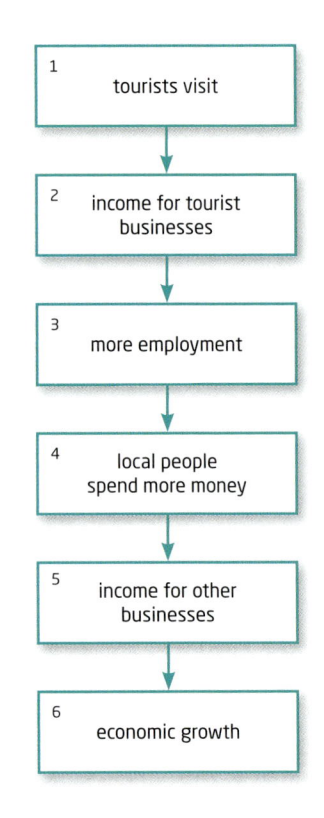

   The economic impact of tourism on the local economy

   When ¹ *tourists* visit a city, they spend money. This creates more ² .... for tourist ³ .... More business leads to ⁴ .... ⁵ .... and local people ⁶ .... more ⁷ .... This produces ⁸ .... for other businesses. More income causes ⁹ .... ¹⁰ ....

3 Underline the cause and effect verbs in 2.

4 Work in pairs. Cover the text. Describe the diagram with cause and effect verbs.

TASK 4 Expressing possibility

1 🔊 **8.3** Listen to three extracts from the seminar. Complete the sentences with *could*, *may*, or *might*.
   1 One negative point is seasonal employment. Tourism .... lead to higher employment in the summer, but it .... not create new jobs in the winter.
   2 Local people .... want better leisure facilities. But the facilities for tourists .... be too expensive for local people.
   3 Local people .... plant trees and build parks. And that .... create a better environment for tourists and locals.

2 What verb form comes after the modal verb in sentences 1–3?

---

1 tourists visit
2 income for tourist businesses
3 more employment
4 local people spend more money
5 income for other businesses
6 economic growth

108 UNIT 8A LISTENING & SPEAKING

ACADEMIC LANGUAGE
▶ Language reference page 155

Expressing possibility Modals *could, might,* and *may*

When you are not 100% certain, you can use the modal verbs *could, might,* or *may* to make present simple statements less certain.

Present simple	Modal verb + infinitive
New facilities **lead to** more tourists. →	New facilities **could lead to** more tourists.
More business **creates** jobs in the summer. →	More business **might create** jobs in the summer.
Busy roads **cause** traffic problems. →	Busy roads **may cause** traffic problems.

Use *might not* or *may not* (NOT *could not*) when you are less certain about a negative effect:

New facilities **may not lead to** more tourists. NOT *New facilities could not lead to* ...

🔊 **8.4** Listen and repeat the sentences without and with modal verbs.

TASK 5 Practising modal verbs

1 Look at Task 3.1. Make the sentences less certain.

   Example: *Tourism **could create** more local business.*

2 Look at Task 3.2. Make the description less certain.

   Example: *When tourists visit a city, they **might spend** money. This ...*

TASK 6 Participating in a seminar

1 Work in groups. Read a case study about a tourist destination. Make notes about:
   - the positive points of Seathorpe as a tourist destination
   - its problems as a tourist destination.

   Case study
   The medium-sized town of Seathorpe is on the east coast of Britain. It has beautiful beaches, so in the summer months a lot of UK tourists spend their holidays here. There are some good hotels, restaurants, and leisure facilities; however, most of these are closed for at least six months of the year, during the colder winter months. The town is three hours by train to London or to an airport. The local Council wants to help the local economy by attracting more visitors all year round. There are three options:

   Option 1: Build a business conference centre.
   Option 2: Develop the small local college into a large university.
   Option 3: Build an airport near the town.

2 Discuss the options for the Council. Draw a cause and effect diagram for each option.

   Example: *build a business conference centre → businesses come during the winter → more employment and income for local area*

3 For each option, make a list of positive and negative impacts on the local area.

4 Choose the best option. Present your choice to the class. Give reasons.

> **INDEPENDENT STUDY**
>
> It is easier to discuss a topic in a seminar if you have read a lot about it.
>
> ▶ When you prepare for a seminar discussion, read two or three texts about the subject of the seminar. Make a list of any positive and negative points related to the topic.

8B Reading Textbooks (8)

This module covers:
- Identifying the purpose of a paragraph
- Taking notes on cause and effect in a text
- Organizing information with a flowchart

TASK 1 Critical thinking – evaluating your impact

1 Look at the holiday activities. Which do you prefer? Rank them 1–5 (1 = like best, 5 = don't like).
   - Visiting ancient places, monuments, or museums ......
   - Doing organized sporting and leisure activities (e.g. skiing, snorkelling) ......
   - Watching cultural events (e.g. festivals, religious ceremonies) ......
   - Visiting local shops or markets ......
   - Relaxing (e.g. reading, swimming, watching TV or films) ......

2 Work in pairs. Compare your answers in 1. Explain your preferences.
   Example: *I like visiting ancient places because I can learn about history.*

3 Work in pairs. For each activity in 1, decide if it has any positive or negative impact on the local destination.

TASK 2 Identifying the purpose of a paragraph

1 Read Text 1 about the social impacts of tourism. Which sentence (a–c) summarizes the purpose of each paragraph (1–3)?
   a describes negative social impacts ......
   b describes positive social impacts ......
   c gives an example of a real destination with positive and negative impacts ......

TEXT 1

The social impacts of tourism

1 Tourism can often have a positive social impact. Because of [1]new leisure facilities for tourists, for example, [2]local people may have new opportunities for sport and entertainment. [3]These kinds of facilities also create [4]more jobs and improve the quality of life for local people. In addition, [5]tourists and locals can meet and learn from each other. So, as a result of [6]tourism, [7]people from different places and cultures understand each other's views and attitudes better.

2 However, tourism can also lead to the disruption of the traditional way of life. Due to the growth of tourism in some countries, many local people have left farming in the countryside. These have often been younger adults, who have moved to cities or tourist resorts to work and have left the older population behind. Traditional communities in the countryside may disappear because of tourism.

3 Many long-haul tourist destinations are in the less economically developed world (LEDW) and the traditional ways of life of the people who live there are interesting to many visitors from countries in the more economically developed world (MEDW). In places such as the Maldives (photo A), for example, tour companies organise excursions to local villages. Tourists spend a lot of money to watch local people perform traditional dances and religious ceremonies (photo B). Local people have more money as a result of these visits. However, some people think this kind of tourism produces a negative social impact, due to a devaluation of the local culture and its religious beliefs.

SOURCE: Adapted from Rickerby, S. 2009. pp.86-7. *Leisure and Tourism GCSE.* Cheltenham: Nelson Thornes.

A The Maldives

B A visit to a local village

2 **Match dictionary definitions 1–8 with nouns / noun phrases a–h from the text.**
   1 a public or religious event with traditional actions _f_
   2 making something seem less important than it really is ....
   3 how a person or group of people lives ....
   4 the level or standard of living ....
   5 something you think or feel is true ....
   6 the beliefs and lifestyle of a particular country or group ....
   7 the way you think or feel about somebody / something ....
   8 making it difficult for somebody to continue in the normal way ....

   a quality of life
   b culture
   c attitude
   d disruption
   e way of life
   f ~~ceremony~~
   g devaluation
   h belief

3 **Look at the highlighted sections 1–7 in Text 1, Paragraph 1. Which refer to a cause? Which refer to an effect?**

4 **Read Paragraphs 2 and 3 of Text 1. Circle the causes and underline the effects.**

ACADEMIC LANGUAGE   ▸ Language reference page 155

Cause and effect (2) Introducing cause with prepositions

As well as cause and effect verbs such as *create*, *cause*, *produce*, and *lead to*, prepositions can also introduce the cause.
Use *because of*, *due to*, and *as a result of* before the cause:
   Because of new leisure facilities for tourists, local people may have new opportunities.
   As a result of tourism, people from different cultures understand each other's attitudes better.
   Due to the growth of tourism, many local people have left farming in the countryside.
The preposition + cause can also come after the effect:
   Local people may have new opportunities **because of** new leisure facilities for tourists.
   People from different cultures understand each other's attitudes better **as a result of** tourism.
A preposition can be one word (e.g. *of*, *with*) or more than one word (e.g. *as a result of*).

TASK 3 Practising identifying the cause

1 **Read sentences 1–9. Underline the causes in each sentence.**
   Example: *Because of <u>the growing population</u>, we have fewer natural resources.*
   1 There is more overseas tourism due to cheaper air travel.
   2 Because of more people having cars, there is less public transport.
   3 More aeroplanes cause noise pollution for people living near the airport.
   4 There are fewer tourists in winter as a result of the cold weather.
   5 Tourists meeting local people leads to sharing cultural ideas.
   6 Due to mobile phone technology, communication has become faster.
   7 There is more air pollution because of more industrialization.
   8 An increase in overseas visitors creates a need for foreign language training.
   9 As a result of colder summers, there are fewer tourists.

2 Which sentences in 1 introduce the cause with a preposition? Circle the effect in each sentence.

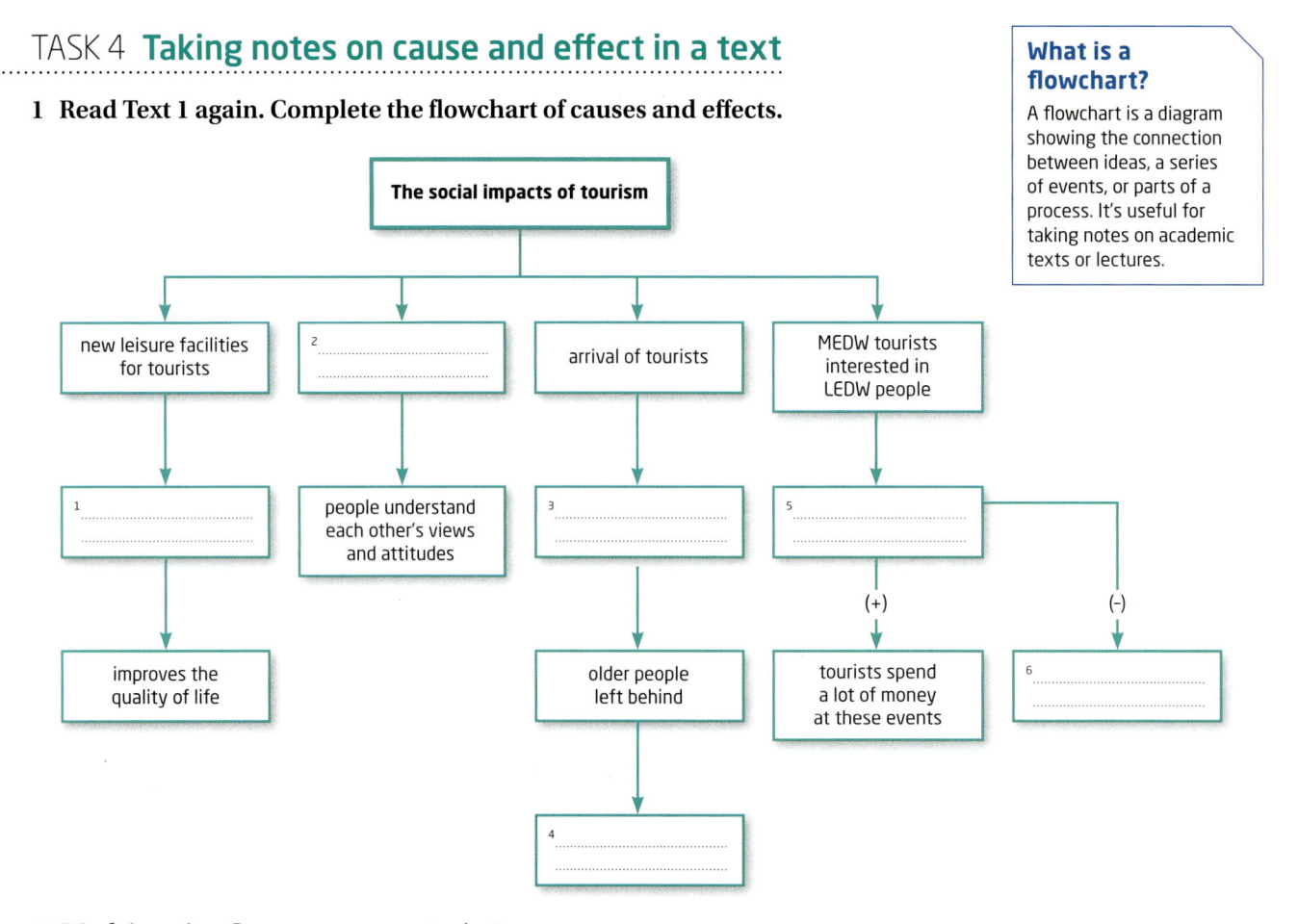

TASK 4 Taking notes on cause and effect in a text

1 Read Text 1 again. Complete the flowchart of causes and effects.

What is a flowchart?
A flowchart is a diagram showing the connection between ideas, a series of events, or parts of a process. It's useful for taking notes on academic texts or lectures.

Flowchart:
- The social impacts of tourism
  - new leisure facilities for tourists → 1 _____ → improves the quality of life
  - 2 _____ → people understand each other's views and attitudes
  - arrival of tourists → 3 _____ → older people left behind → 4 _____
  - MEDW tourists interested in LEDW people → 5 _____
    - (+) tourists spend a lot of money at these events
    - (−) 6 _____

2 Work in pairs. Compare your notes in 1.

TASK 5 Recognizing cause and effect in a text

1 Read Text 2 about the environmental impact of tourism. List the different types of impact. Are they positive or negative?

The environmental impact of tourism   TEXT 2

1 Travel and tourism can change the environment in two ways: through the impact of pollution and through the impact on resources. Air travel, for example, causes both air and noise pollution. Air pollution is created by plane emissions, which add carbon into the air. The amount of carbon per traveller is known as their carbon footprint. Noise pollution is another negative impact of travel; typically, it's produced by planes landing and taking off. An increase in tourism can also mean an increase in other types of pollution such as water pollution, land pollution, and the visual impact of tourism such as building in areas of natural beauty.

2 Local resources are also affected by tourism. The impact on water, land, and energy is often caused by increased numbers of visitors to an area. The Maldives is a good example; it consists of over 1,000 small islands and receives 600,000 tourists a year. Because of this, there should be economic benefits for local people, but many tourist resorts are built on islands away from local people. Locally-produced food, such as fresh fruit and vegetables, goes directly to these tourist islands. As a result of this, there is a shortage of food on some islands and, according to one United Nations report, 30% of Maldivian children under the age of five suffer from malnutrition.

SOURCE: Adapted from Rickerby, S. 2009. pp.86–9. *Leisure and Tourism GCSE*. Cheltenham: Nelson Thornes.

GLOSSARY
benefit *(n)* a helpful, useful effect that sth has
emission *(n)* gas, etc. that is sent out into the air
malnutrition *(n)* poor health caused by a lack of the right type of food

2 **Look at two sentences from Text 2. Answer questions a and b for each sentence.**
   1 **Air travel** causes both **air and noise pollution**.
   2 **Air pollution** is created by **plane emissions**.

   a Is the subject of the sentence the cause or the effect?
   b Is the verb in the active or passive form?

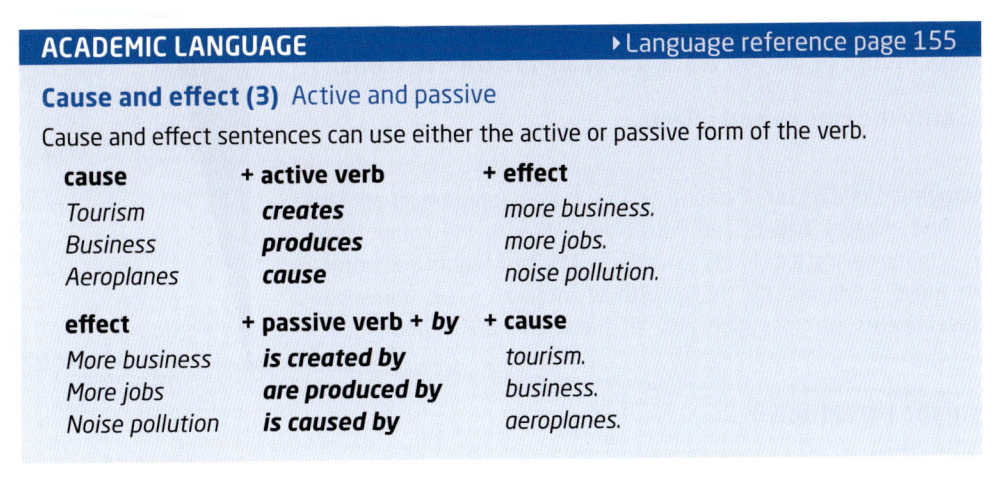

ACADEMIC LANGUAGE ▶ Language reference page 155

Cause and effect (3) Active and passive
Cause and effect sentences can use either the active or passive form of the verb.

cause	+ active verb	+ effect
Tourism	creates	more business.
Business	produces	more jobs.
Aeroplanes	cause	noise pollution.

effect	+ passive verb + by	+ cause
More business	is created by	tourism.
More jobs	are produced by	business.
Noise pollution	is caused by	aeroplanes.

TASK 6 Practising active and passive forms

1 Look at pairs of phrases from Text 2. Identify:
   a the cause (C) and effect (E) in each pair
   b the verb (active or passive) or preposition in the text that connects them.

   Example: *air travel* _C_ / *air and noise pollution* _E_ – *causes* = *active verb*
               air pollution _E_ / *plane emissions* _C_ – *is created* = *passive verb*

   1 noise pollution _____ / planes landing and taking off _____
   2 increase in tourism _____ / other types of pollution _____
   3 local resources _____ / tourism _____
   4 impact on water, land, and energy _____ / increased number of visitors _____
   5 locally-produced food goes to tourist islands _____ / a shortage of food on some islands _____

TASK 7 Organizing information with a flowchart

1 Work in pairs. Organize the information in Text 2 as a flowchart. Start like this and add the causes and effects in Task 6.

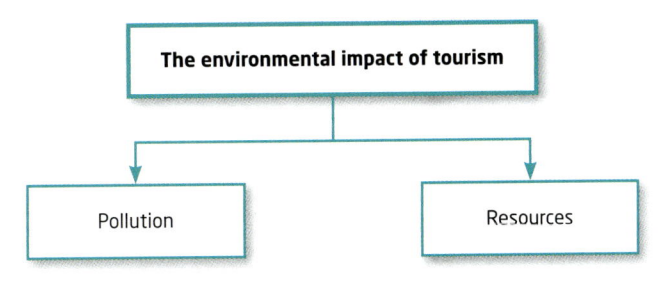

```
        The environmental impact of tourism
              /                \
        Pollution            Resources
```

2 Do you think using a flowchart is a good way to take notes? Will you use it again in the future?

INDEPENDENT STUDY

Many academic subjects discuss causes and effects and positive and negative impacts.
▶ Think of a cause and effect relationship in a subject you study, or find a cause and effect text. Draw the causes and effects as a flowchart.

8C Writing (1) Cause and effect sentences

This module covers:
- Writing cause and effect sentences in a variety of patterns

TASK 1 Comparing cause and effect sentences

1 Do you book your holidays online or do you use a travel agent? Give reasons.

2 Read the paragraph. Identify the causes and effects.

> The travel industry is changing. ¹As a result of online selling, more people travel abroad. ²Nowadays tourists may find cheaper tickets and better deals due to the competition between travel websites. ³Online selling also leads to easier booking of flights and hotels. ⁴Overall, the increase in travel is caused by the growth of internet sales. ⁵However, traditional high street travel agents are closing because of many more online bookings.

3 Which sentences (1–5) in the paragraph in 2:
   1 have a preposition before the cause? ......, ..., ...
   2 has the verb before the cause? ......
   3 has the verb after the cause? ......

ACADEMIC LANGUAGE
▶ Language reference page 155

Sentences (3) Writing about cause and effect
When we write about cause and effect, we can use a variety of sentence patterns.

Active form
Use *create, cause, lead to, produce*:
   Tourism **creates** more local jobs. (cause + verb + effect)

Passive form
Use *create, cause, produce*:
   Local jobs **are created by** tourism. (effect + verb + *by* + cause)

Preposition before the cause
Use *because of, as a result of, due to*:
   Because of tourism, there are more local jobs.
   There are more local jobs **because of** tourism.
   Due to tourism, there are more local jobs.
   There are more local jobs **as a result of** tourism.

TASK 2 Practising cause and effect sentence patterns

1 Write five sentences you agree with. Use the verbs in the active or passive + *by*. Use *not* to make a negative sentence if necessary.

   Example: Local jobs ... (an increase in tourism / create)
   Local jobs are created by an increase in tourism. OR
   Local jobs are not created by an increase in tourism.

   1 Cheap travel websites ... (more tourists / produce)
   2 Air pollution ... (better transport links / cause)
   3 Train travel ... (a smaller carbon footprint / create)
   4 Noise pollution ... (tourist facilities such as bars and nightclubs / produce)
   5 New employment opportunities ... (tourism / create)

2 Work in pairs and compare your sentences.

3 Rewrite the sentences in 1.
1 More tourists _____.
2 Better transport links _____.
3 A smaller carbon footprint _____.
4 Tourist facilities such as bars and nightclubs _____.
5 Tourism _____.

4 Complete sentences 1–5 using prepositions.

Example: online booking → fewer high street travel agents
    Because of online booking, there are fewer high street travel agents.

1 better cycle paths → more cyclists on the road
    Due to _____.
2 the high price of fuel → more people using public transport
    As a result of _____.
3 more campsites → the warmer summers
    There _____.
4 more tourism in our city → the new airport
    There is _____.
5 more visitors from the USA → a strong dollar
    There are _____.

TASK 3 Writing cause and effect sentences

1 Match the causes of recent changes in a small town (1–5) with effects (a–e).

1 more public transportation ____   a less waste
2 less traffic ____   b more people going to the gym
3 building the new park ____   c fewer traffic problems
4 recycling bins ____   d more children playing outside
5 the new sports centre ____   e cleaner air

2 Write sentences about the causes and effects in 1. Use verbs or prepositions.

Example: *More public transportation leads to fewer traffic problems. / Due to more public transportation, there are fewer traffic problems.*

3 Think about recent changes in your local area. Note down the cause of each change. Write three sentences about the changes using cause and effect language. Work in pairs and compare your sentences.

> **INDEPENDENT STUDY**
> Memorizing cause and effect sentence patterns helps you use the language accurately.
> ▶ Write your own sentences on a topic using all the patterns in this module. Read them every day for a week. Then write a short cause and effect text about the topic, using the patterns.

UNIT 8C WRITING (1) 115

8C Writing (2) A cause and effect paragraph

This module covers:
- Analysing a cause and effect paragraph
- Writing a paragraph describing positive and negative impacts

TASK 1 Analysing a cause and effect paragraph

1 Look at the picture of a tourist destination in a National Park in Thailand. What positive or negative impacts of tourism could there be on the local area?

Khao Sok National Park, Thailand

2 Read about Khao Sok National Park. Does the paragraph include your ideas in 1?

> [1]Eco-tourism is a type of environmentally friendly tourism. [2]It is when people visit an environmentally important destination without changing that environment. [3]A good example of eco-tourism is the Khao Sok National Park in Thailand. [4]There are hundreds of visitors every year due to the Park's beautiful mountains and rainforest. [5]Tourism leads to jobs for the local people in the Park's shops and hotels. [6]In addition, the Park restaurants create local business because they buy food grown by the farmers in the area. [7]The only negative impact is that environmental problems in the Park are caused by too many tourists. [8]As a result of these problems, the Park limits the number of visitors per day. [9]Overall, the Khao Sok National Park is a good example of how eco-tourism can have a positive impact.

3 Match sentences 1–9 in the paragraph with their purpose a–f.

Sentence 1: _d_
Sentence 2: ____
Sentence 3: ____
Sentences 4, 5, and 6: ____
Sentences 7 and 8: ____
Sentence 9: ____

a to give a definition
b to conclude the paragraph
c to explain the positive impacts
d ~~to introduce the term~~
e to explain a negative impact
f to introduce an example

4 Underline verbs and prepositions in the text that refer to cause and effect.

TASK 2 Writing a cause and effect paragraph

1 Look at the picture of a type of tourism called agri-tourism. Why do you think people choose this type of holiday?

Agri-tourism in California

2 Read the notes about agri-tourism in California.

> **Type of tourism:** agri-tourism
> **Definition:** people stay on a farm or a ranch
> **Example:** many agri-tourists visit Californian farms and ranches
> **Positive impacts:** 2.5 million agri-tourists per year / tourists learn about the countryside and agriculture / extra income for Californian farmers / employment for local people
> **Negative impact:** increase in traffic in the countryside because of tourists

3 Use the notes to complete the sentences.
  1 Agri-tourism is
  2 It is when
  3 For example,
  4 2.5 million agri-tourists per year creates
  5 Tourists learn about
  6 The only negative impact is

4 Use the information in the notes and write a paragraph about agri-tourism. Use the paragraph in Task 1 as a model.

5 Use this checklist to check your paragraph. Then exchange with a partner and give feedback. Did you:
  - introduce the term? ☐
  - give a definition and an example? ☐
  - explain positive impacts? ☐
  - explain a negative impact? ☐
  - conclude the paragraph? ☐
  - use cause and effect language? ☐

Sample answer:
page 160

UNIT 8C WRITING (2) 117

8D Vocabulary

TASK 1 Noun phrases

1 Complete the noun phrases in sentences 1–10 with the words in the list.

beliefs   communities   economic   footprint
global   holiday   impact   leisure   local   travel

1 Tourism can have a negative **environmental** ...., such as increased carbon emissions.
2 **Air** .... is so cheap these days that more and more people are flying.
3 .... **people** often benefit because tourists bring money and jobs to an area.
4 Building new .... **facilities** such as swimming pools and gyms is good for everyone.
5 Some **traditional** .... are worried that their young people are affected by modern culture.
6 More travelling has an effect on the .... **environment**, not just the local area. It affects the whole world.
7 Many countries have **religious** .... which are different from those of the tourists.
8 A **carbon** .... is the amount of carbon dioxide produced by an event, product, or person.
9 New jobs and money create .... **benefits** for a town or region.
10 This company offers many different .... **destinations** in Africa.

2 Look at the noun phrases in 1. Write adjective + noun (AN) or noun + noun (NN).

1 *AN*
2 ....
3 ....
4 ....
5 ....
6 ....
7 ....
8 ....
9 ....
10 ....

TASK 2 Prepositions

1 Complete sentences 1–10 with the prepositions in the list.

at   for   from   in   of   on (x2)   to (x3)

1 Some of the changes are good .... the environment.
2 There is an impact .... the lives of local people.
3 It leads .... more visitors and crowded beaches.
4 Many local people rely .... tourism for their living.
5 Younger people are moving .... the cities.
6 The quality .... life often improves.
7 Look .... this flowchart.
8 The increase .... tourism causes different types of pollution.
9 The term 'impact' refers .... the positive or negative effect that something has on something else.
10 Tourists and locals can meet and learn .... each other.

> **INDEPENDENT STUDY**
>
> Some prepositions often come after certain verbs, adjectives, or nouns, e.g. lead **to**, good **at**.
>
> ▶ Find and note down prepositions which come after verbs, adjectives, or nouns.

8E Academic Language Check

TASK 1 Cause and effect: Verbs and prepositions

1 Write cause → effect sentences in the active form. Use the verbs *cause*, *create*, or *produce*.
   Example: *TV advertising → more business*
   TV advertising creates more business.
   1 online booking → cheaper holidays

   2 more aeroplanes → noise pollution

   3 more business → more local jobs

   4 more tourism → more litter

2 Rewrite the sentences in 1 as effect → cause sentences. Use the passive form.
   Example: *More business is created by TV advertising.*
   1 Cheaper holidays _____.
   2 Noise pollution _____.
   3 More local jobs _____.
   4 More litter _____.

3 Now rewrite the sentences with a preposition + *there is / are*.
   Example: *Because of TV advertising, there is more business.*
   1 Due to _____.
   2 _____ as a result of _____.
   3 _____ because of _____.
   4 _____.

TASK 2 Modals: *could*, *might*, and *may*

1 Correct one mistake in each sentence.
   1 New leisure facilities could leads to better health.

   2 The plan might to create an increase in employment.

   3 More police on the street may could lead to fewer crimes.

   4 Crowded beaches not might create a good atmosphere in the town.

   5 Improved public transport could not guarantee more tourists, but it's possible.

UNIT 9 Invention

ACADEMIC FOCUS: RECOGNIZING PERSPECTIVE

LEARNING OBJECTIVES

This unit covers:

Listening and Speaking
- Understanding evidence in a presentation
- Giving evidence in a discussion
- Using evidence in a discussion

Reading
- Evaluating text types for academic study
- Evaluating different texts on one topic
- Noticing perspective in texts

Writing
- Using active and passive sentence patterns
- Analysing paragraph structure
- Writing a cohesive paragraph about an inventor

Vocabulary
- Vocabulary-building: Adjectives and nouns
- Vocabulary-building: Verbs and nouns
- Prepositional phrases

Academic Language Check
- Past simple and present perfect
- Describing discoveries and inventions
- Using pronouns and determiners for cohesion

Discussion

1 Look at the picture. The Standard of Ur is about 4,500 years old. What invention does it show?

2 Match the type of discovery or invention with 1–5.

~~astronomical~~   engineering   linguistic
mathematical   medical   scientific

Example: Galileo Galilei (1564–1642) discovered Jupiter's moons.   *astronomical*

1 Ludwik Zamenhof invented the international language of Esperanto in 1887.
2 Over 5,000 years ago, the Chinese used the first abacus for counting.
3 Ignaz Semmelweis (1818–65) discovered that hand-washing can save lives in hospitals.
4 Ibn al-Haytham (965–1040) studied light and optics and made the first type of camera.
5 No one knows the inventor of the wheel but the Sumerians of Mesopotamia used it in around 4,500 BC.

3 Work in pairs. Think of a discovery or invention. Note down information about:
- the type of discovery or invention (e.g. medical)
- the period or date in history
- the person or people who discovered or invented it.

4 Work with another pair. Take turns to describe your discovery or invention.

9A Listening & Speaking Seminars (3)

This module covers:
- Understanding evidence in a presentation
- Giving evidence in a discussion
- Using evidence in a discussion

TASK 1 Understanding evidence in a presentation

1 Work in pairs. Do you use social networking sites such as Facebook and Twitter? If so, how many people do you communicate with?

2 ▶9.1 Watch the introduction to a presentation. What is the main topic of the presentation? What is Professor Dunbar's main argument?

3 ▶9.2 Now watch the presenter explaining the evidence for Professor Dunbar's theory. Tick (✓) the types of evidence he mentions.

business ☐   educational ☐   historical ☐
medical ☐   political ☐   social media ☐

4 ▶9.2 Watch again and complete the notes.

(1) ¹_____ **evidence**
  - groups of ²_____ often lived in communities of about 150
  - the number of ³_____ in a typical military unit was around 150

(2) ⁴_____ **evidence**
  - Bill Gore (of Gore-Tex® clothing) decided that 150 was the maximum number of ⁵_____ in one factory
  - whenever the number in a factory has reached 150, Gore-Tex has ⁶_____

(3) ⁷_____ **evidence**
  - in a study published in the *Proceedings of the National Academy of Sciences* Dunbar studied the ⁸_____ of 24 ⁹_____
  - when a student made a new close ¹⁰_____, they spent less time communicating with ¹¹_____; they ¹²_____ increase the communication, but they limited ¹³_____ to around 150

5 Look at the verb forms in the notes in 4. Which two tenses are used?

ACADEMIC LANGUAGE ▶Language reference page 156

Past events Past simple and present perfect
When we describe an academic theory and the evidence for it, we use different tenses to explain what happened and when.
Use the **past simple** to talk about discoveries and events from a finished period of time.
  *In ancient times groups of people often **lived** in communities of about 150 individuals.*
  *In 1958, a man called Bill Gore **started** the clothing company Gore-Tex.*
Use the **present perfect** (has / have + past participle) to connect events in the past to the present, i.e. the events still have some significance in the present.
  *Over the last 20 years, Dunbar **has discovered** groups of humans with approximately 150 members.*
  *More recently, anthropologists **have researched** human relationships on social networking sites.*

🔊 9.3 Listen and repeat the sentences.

TASK 2 Practising talking about discoveries and evidence

1 **Underline the correct form of the verbs in italics.**
  1 In the 11th century, about 150 people *lived* / *have lived* in the average English village.
  2 Ten years ago, Dunbar *studied* / *has studied* how many greetings cards a typical English family sent. He discovered that the average figure *was* / *has been* 153.5.
  3 Programmers at social network companies like Facebook *became* / *have become* interested in Dunbar's work, because it helps them understand their users.
  4 The size of human social networks *didn't change* / *hasn't changed* for hundreds of years, according to Dunbar. It is the same now as it was 250,000 years ago.
  5 In 2011, another research paper *found* / *has found* that the average person regularly interacts with between 100 and 200 followers.
  6 More recently, other anthropologists *disagreed* / *have disagreed* with Dunbar. For example, the anthropologist Russell Bernard and network scientist Peter Killworth *also studied* / *have also studied* numbers of average social networks. They say the number is 291.

2 **Work in pairs. Take turns to talk about Dunbar's life and work. Use the past simple or present perfect.**

  Example: in 1969 / graduate / from Oxford University
  In 1969, Robin Dunbar graduated from Oxford University.
  1 over the last 40 years / teach / in Sweden and the UK
  2 in 2007 / start / working at Oxford University
  3 recently / study / human relationships on social networking sites
  4 in 2010 / write / book called *How many friends does one person need?*
  5 lots of people / become / interested in his theories

TASK 3 Giving evidence in a discussion

1 🔊 9.4 **Read the statement about the Dunbar number. Then listen to a seminar discussion and tick (✓) the evidence that the students refer to.**

> Dunbar believes that 150 is the number of people we can have meaningful relationships with at one time.

  1 evidence from military history ☐
  2 evidence from the company Gore-Tex ☐
  3 evidence from Dunbar's research ☐
  4 evidence from personal experience ☐
  5 evidence from a study by Bernard and Killworth ☐
  6 evidence from a study in the *Proceedings of the National Academy of Sciences* ☐
  7 evidence in the *Journal of the American Statistical Association* ☐

2 🔊 9.4 **Listen again and tick (✓) the table.**

	Male	Female
1 This student agrees with the Dunbar number.		
2 This student gives evidence from personal experience.		
3 This student doesn't agree with everything.		
4 This student gives evidence from other academic sources.		

122 UNIT 9A LISTENING & SPEAKING

ACADEMIC LANGUAGE
▶ Language reference page 156

Referring to evidence Reporting verbs

In a seminar discussion, it is useful to talk about evidence from published texts and research. Refer to evidence using reporting verbs such as *believe, report, say, show, suggest, state* (+ *that*):

Dunbar **states that** humans communicate with a maximum of 150 people.
Dunbar's study **shows that** people talk to an average of 150 friends on Facebook.
Their research **suggests that** Dunbar's theory is wrong.

You can also use the verb *support* + noun:

Other research **doesn't support** this **theory**.

🔊 9.5 Listen and repeat the sentences.

TASK 4 Practising reporting verbs

1 🔊 9.4 Listen again to the seminar discussion. Complete the sentences with the reporting verbs in the list.

believes   reports   shows   states   suggests   supports

1 Dunbar .... that 150 is the number of people we can have meaningful relationships with at one time.
2 The evidence from Gore-Tex .... that you can't work with more than 150 employees in one place.
3 Dunbar's research .... that people communicate with an average of 150 friends on social media.
4 His evidence .... the theory.
5 One study by the anthropologist Russell Bernard and a scientist called Peter Killworth .... that the average number for a social network is 291.
6 Another study in the *Journal of the American Statistical Association* .... that it's 611.

TASK 5 Using evidence in a discussion

1 Work in pairs. Look at the evidence from the Pew Research Center in the USA. Answer the questions.
  1 What has the Pew Research Center studied in its research?
  2 Do you think any of the evidence is surprising?

  - 74% of online adults use social networking sites. 71% used Facebook.
  - 49% of people over the age of 65 use social networking sites.
  - 74% of women use social network sites compared with 62% of men.
  - Around 70% of people under 50 use social networking to keep in contact with friends.
  - The research shows that Facebook users have closer relationships with friends.

  SOURCE: Pew Research Internet Project, 2014, pewinternet.org/fact-sheets/social-networking-fact-sheet

2 Work in groups. Discuss three statements about social networking. Say if you agree or disagree and refer to evidence from the Pew Research Center, your own evidence, or personal experience.

'Social networking is mainly for young people.'
'Women spend a lot more time online and social networking than men.'
'People who spend a lot of time online don't see other people much.'

INDEPENDENT STUDY

It's important to know about the evidence for something before you agree or disagree with a statement.

▶ When you hear or read an opinion on a topic, find out more and make notes about the evidence.

9B Reading Textbooks (9)

This module covers:
- Evaluating text types for academic study
- Evaluating different texts on one topic
- Noticing perspective in texts

TASK 1 Evaluating text types for academic study

1 When you want to find out information about a topic in your language, what kind of texts do you read?

2 How reliable do you think these types of text are for academic study? Mark the texts from 1 to 3.
   1 = It isn't reliable.
   2 = It might be reliable, but I need to check the information in another text.
   3 = It's very reliable.

   an academic journal ....
   a daily newspaper ....
   a personal blog ....
   a science magazine ....
   a textbook in your library ....
   a web page on the university website ....

3 Work in pairs and compare your opinions about the texts in 2.

> **What is a reliable text?**
> A reliable text is a text written by experts that gives true, accurate information. For academic research, it's important to read reliable texts.

TASK 2 Evaluating different texts on one topic

1 Look at the picture of a printer. What is the difference between a 2D and a 3D printer?

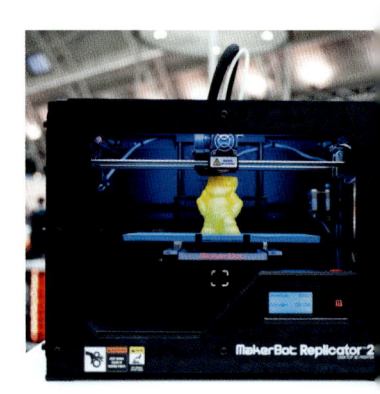

2 A student is researching 3D printers for a presentation. Read Texts 1–4. Match each text with the type of information (a–d) in the text.

   Text 1, a textbook ....   a medical evidence
   Text 2, a scientific journal .... b mainly financial information
   Text 3, a technology magazine .... c mainly personal evidence
   Text 4, a blog ....   d a technical description

A 3D printer

3 Which of the text types in 2 are academic? Which are reliable for student research? Why? / Why not?

TEXT 1

With a normal 2D printer, ink is printed onto paper that has length and width. With a 3D printer, a third dimension is added, which is height. The height is increased by adding one layer at a time. And unlike a 2D printer, a 3D printer doesn't print with ink. Instead a polymer material is used in 3D printing for:
- dental products such as false teeth
- quick prototypes of products for designers
- 3D components designed using CAD software.

TEXT 2

Historically, the first working 3D printer was invented by Charles W. Hull in 1984. However, until the end of the 20th century, 3D printing was very expensive and was used only in specialist industries. In more recent years, the costs have dropped and 3D printers have become much more affordable. A few years ago a standard 3D printer cost around $20,000. Surprisingly, the same printer is sold nowadays for less than $1,000. The economics of modern 3D printing means they are about to become part of everyday business.

TEXT 3

From a medical perspective, 3D printing has already had a huge impact on areas such as dentistry and artificial limbs. Now, bio-engineers at Cornell University in New York have developed a 3D bio-printer. A research report on the *Public Library of Science* website describes how a human ear was printed with a special type of 3D printer. A material containing living cells was sprayed in layers instead of using normal plastic polymers and these cells were grown into an ear. At the moment, these ears are prototypes, but in three years the bio-engineers plan to test them on real humans.

TEXT 4

From an industrial point of view, 3D printing has transformed modern engineering. For example, you've probably flown on an aeroplane with parts made on a 3D printer. However, the next question is whether it will ever take off in the home? To test this question I bought the cheapest 3D printer on the market. It costs around $1,000 dollars. You connect it to your computer, download a design, and press print. The printer can only create plastic models such as toy frogs or action figures, so the choice is limited at the moment. However, as the technology improves, I think 3D printers will eventually change the way we live by delivering everything from cakes to car parts, clothing to kitchenware, and we won't have to leave the house.

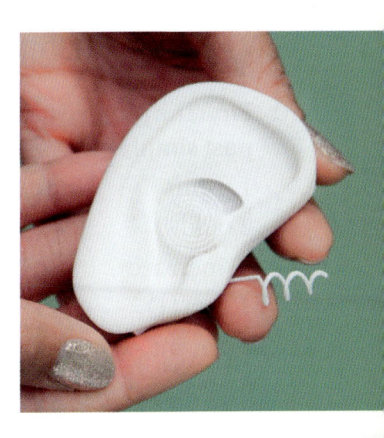

GLOSSARY
component *(n)* a part of something
prototype *(n)* the first design of something
take off *(phr v)* become successful

4 Read Texts 1–4 again. Decide which text:
 a explains the differences between 2D printing and 3D printing. *1*
 b describes how we might use 3D printers in the future. ......
 c gives an example of how 3D printing helps in the building of transportation. ......
 d refers to the inventor of 3D printing. ......
 e describes an experiment with 3D printers. ......
 f gives three examples of how 3D printing is used now. ......
 g looks at the costs of 3D printers in the last 30 years. ......
 h lists four things we might make with 3D printers in the future. ......

ACADEMIC LANGUAGE ▸ Language reference page 156

Past simple passive Describing discoveries and inventions

The passive form of the past simple is common in descriptions of past discoveries and inventions.
Use *was / were* + past participle:
 Esperanto **was invented** in 1887.
 X-rays **were discovered** in 1895.
The past simple passive can also be used to describe stages in a process in the past:
 The first printed pages were made with pieces of wood. A flat piece **was carved** with words and pictures. This **was brushed** with ink. Then the wood blocks **were pressed** onto paper.

+ *by* for emphasis
If who or what did the action is important, then *by* + the name is given before (or after) the date / year:
 The first working 3D printer was invented **by Charles W. Hull** in 1984.

TASK 3 Practising identifying passive and active forms

1 Find the passive forms of verbs 1–10 in Texts 1–4. Which verbs are in the past simple?

1 print   *is printed*
2 add   ....
3 increase   ....
4 use (1)   ....
5 invent   ....
6 use (2)   ....
7 sell   ....
8 print   ....
9 spray   ....
10 grow   ....

2 Work in pairs and answer the questions.
  1 Which of the four texts has the most passive forms?
  2 Which text has no passive forms?
  3 Do the academic texts have more passive forms?

TASK 4 Noticing perspective in texts

1 Text 2 has several perspectives. Read the text again and tick (✓) the correct perspectives in the table.

	Historical	Financial	Medical	Industrial	Sociological
Text 2					

2 Which words or phrases in Text 2 helped you to decide the perspective?

> **What is perspective?**
> A perspective is how a topic is linked to its academic context, e.g. an educational perspective refers to information from an educational point of view. Different texts about one topic often have different perspectives.

ACADEMIC LANGUAGE ▸ Language reference page 156

Perspective Expressions and vocabulary

Academic texts often describe and analyse topics from different perspectives. When you read a text, it's important to identify the perspective.
Sometimes the perspective is clear in the text. Look for these expressions:

   From an economic perspective, online business is highly profitable.

   However, **from a sociological point of view**, the impact of online businesses could result in fewer job opportunities.

   Technologically, nothing has had the same impact as the internet in recent years.

Sometimes the perspective is more difficult to identify, so look at the type of vocabulary and its meaning:

   The first 3D printer was invented **in 1984**. (= historical perspective)

   The impact of the internet on **human behaviour** is both positive and negative. (= sociological perspective)

   Teachers and parents are still unsure about how much technology affects **the classroom**. (= educational perspective)

126 UNIT 9B READING

TASK 5 Practising identifying perspective

1 Read extracts from six different texts about the internet. Decide the main perspective (a–f) of each text. Underline the words which help you to decide.

a economic
b educational
c historical
d medical
e political
f sociological

1 Doctors report that more and more patients have read about their illness online before they arrive at the hospital. ......
2 The rise of the internet could result in the end of face-to-face contact and a change in human relationships. ......
3 Governments have tried to control how people use the internet, but their attempts have often failed. ......
4 One study estimates that the internet is worth approximately £100 billion a year to the UK economy. ......
5 There is concern that children are spending too many hours a day on the internet and this badly affects their ability to concentrate in the classroom. ......
6 Tim Berners-Lee invented the world wide web in 1989. ......

2 Read Texts 3 and 4 again. Tick (✓) the perspectives in the table. Underline the words or phrases in the texts which helped you to decide.

	Historical	Financial	Medical	Industrial	Sociological
Text 3					
Text 4					

TASK 6 Critical thinking – applying different perspectives

1 Look at the notes from Texts 1–4 on 3D printers. The information is organized according to different perspectives. Think of one more perspective that a student could research and make notes on.

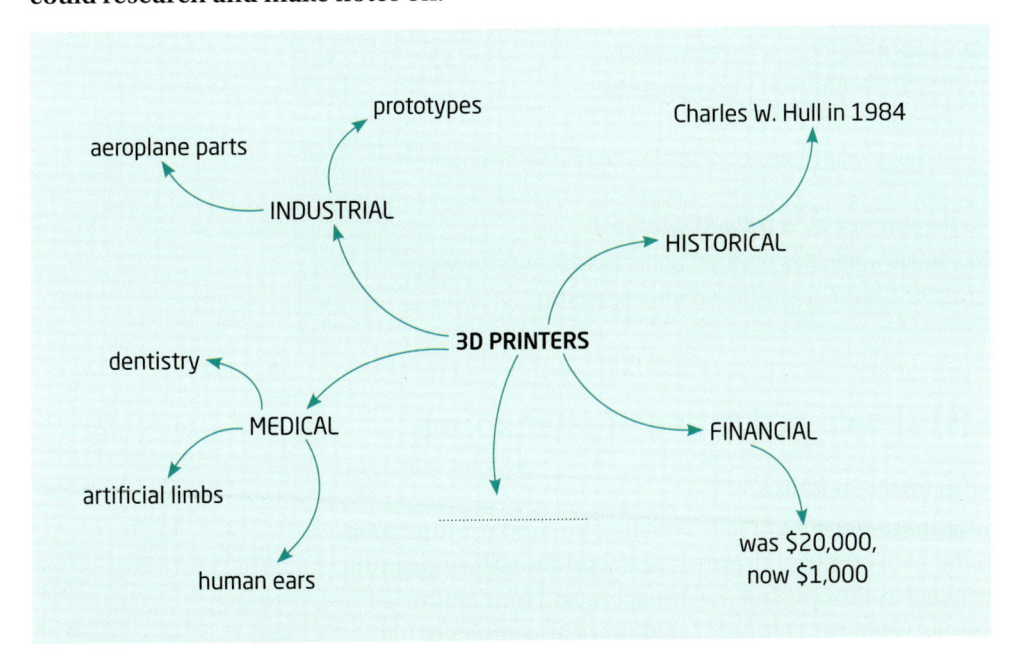

3D PRINTERS

- INDUSTRIAL
  - prototypes
  - aeroplane parts
- HISTORICAL
  - Charles W. Hull in 1984
- MEDICAL
  - dentistry
  - artificial limbs
  - human ears
- FINANCIAL
  - was $20,000, now $1,000

2 Work in pairs. Choose another invention or discovery, for example:

air travel   antibiotics   the internet   satellite communication   television

What different perspectives could you research for your topic? Make notes similar to those in 1 for each perspective.

INDEPENDENT STUDY

The perspective of the texts you read is very important in academic study.

▶ Look at different types of texts, e.g. in other units from this book or in other textbooks. Try to identify the perspective(s).

UNIT 9B READING 127

9C Writing (1) Sentences about invention

This module covers:
- Using active and passive sentence patterns

TASK 1 Recognizing sentence patterns

1 Read the text. Which paragraph has a historical perspective? Which paragraph has a scientific perspective?

> 1 Samuel Morse graduated from Yale in 1810 and then studied painting in England, where he became a portrait painter. However, later in life he became increasingly interested in electricity and in 1844 he invented his first telegraph machine, which he demonstrated to the US Congress.
>
> 2 The messages from the machine were sent using electricity. Each letter of the alphabet was represented by a special code, a series of dots and dashes. These were tapped into the machine by a trained operator and transmitted over telegraph wires. Finally, the message was received at the other end in the form of dots and dashes on paper tape. 'Morse code' was eventually recognized around the world as a universal form of communication.

2 Look at the verbs in the text in 1. Complete the information.

Paragraph .... is about the inventor. The verbs are in the .... form.
Paragraph .... is about the invention. The verbs are in the .... form.

ACADEMIC LANGUAGE ▶ Language reference page 156

Sentences (4) Changing emphasis with active / passive / *by*

When we write about past discoveries and inventions, we can use the past simple active or passive. Try to use both forms in your writing.
Use the **past simple active form** to focus on the inventor:
  Samuel Morse **graduated** *from Yale in 1810 and then studied painting in England.*
Use the **past simple passive form** to focus on the invention:
  The messages from the machine **were sent** *using electricity.*

by + agent
In the active form you know who or what caused the action. In the passive form, use *by* + agent:
  These were tapped into the machine **by a trained operator***.*
You do not have to use *by* + agent when it is obvious, unnecessary, or unknown:
  The message was received at the other end (by another operator).

TASK 2 Practising past simple active and passive forms

1 Underline the correct verb forms in italics.

In the west, Johannes Gutenberg ¹*invented* / *was invented* the first printing press with moveable letters in the 15th century. However, the world's earliest printing press ²*invent* / *wasn't invented* in Europe, but in China, around four centuries earlier. The inventor Bi Sheng (990–1051) ³*made* / *was made* the letters of his printing press from clay. The clay ⁴*put* / *was put* on an iron plate. This ⁵*heated* / *was heated* before ink ⁶*put on* / *was put on*. Paper ⁷*then applied* / *was then applied*. Bi Sheng's clay letters were not strong enough for large-scale printing, but later, in the 12th and 13th centuries, new types of printing presses ⁸*also developed* / *were also developed* in China. These ⁹*made* / *were made* from wood and metal.

2 Rewrite the second sentence to mean the same as the first. For passive sentences, add *by* + agent if necessary.

1 The wheel was used over 7,000 years ago.
   Humans _____ over 7,000 years ago.
2 Archimedes calculated the number π.
   The number π _____ .
3 Galileo Galilei (1564–1642) discovered Jupiter's moons.
   Jupiter's moons _____ .
4 Chess was played in ancient India before it spread across the world.
   People _____ in ancient India before it spread across the world.
5 Paper was produced in China by the inventor Cai Lun.
   The inventor Cai Lun _____ .
6 Antonie van Leeuwenhoek observed bacteria with a microscope in the early 18th century.
   Bacteria _____
   with a microscope in the early 18th century.
7 Persians invented the earliest windmills around the seventh century.
   The earliest windmills _____ in Persia.
8 The first satellite in space was launched by the Soviet Union in 1957.
   The Soviet Union _____ .

TASK 3 Writing about inventors and inventions

1 Use the notes to write sentences about Benjamin Franklin and his invention. Use the past simple in the active and passive form.

> Benjamin Franklin - **be** - an author, printer, scientist, politician, and inventor
> in 1741 - **invent** - a stove
> it - **be made from** - a metal box with a door and - **connect** - to a chimney
> the new type of stove - **produce** - more heat than a normal fireplace
> unfortunately - the early Franklin stoves - **not sell** - very well
> later, the design - **develop** and **improve** - and it - **become** - popular

2 Work in pairs. Exchange your sentences and check your partner's use of active and passive forms.

Benjamin Franklin

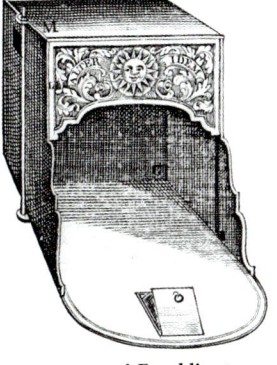

A Franklin stove

9C Writing (2) A description of an inventor

This module covers:
- Analysing paragraph structure
- Writing a cohesive paragraph about an inventor

TASK 1 Analysing paragraph structure

1 Read Paragraph 1. In what order (1–3) does it give this information?
   a the inventor's main invention ....
   b the inventor's biographical information ....
   c the impact of the invention on people's lives ....

> **Paragraph 1**
>
> Johannes Gutenberg was a printer and publisher in the 15th century. Gutenberg also became famous for his inventions; his inventions included a printing press with moveable wooden or metal letters in 1448. Before 1448, books were written and copied by hand. As a result of Gutenberg's printing press, books could be printed in large numbers and for the first time the average person could buy a book and read a book.

TASK 2 Understanding cohesion

1 Compare Paragraph 2 with Paragraph 1. How are they different?

> **Paragraph 2**
>
> Johannes Gutenberg was a printer and publisher in the 15th century. He also became famous for his inventions; these included a printing press with moveable wooden or metal letters in 1448. Before this, books were written and copied by hand. As a result of Gutenberg's printing press, they could be printed in large numbers and for the first time the average person could buy a book and read it.

What is cohesion?
Cohesion in a text means that information and ideas are clearly connected together using linking language such as pronouns and determiners.

2 Find these words in Paragraph 2. What do they refer to?
   1 He _Gutenberg_   4 this ....
   2 his ....   5 they ....
   3 these ....   6 it ....

> ### ACADEMIC LANGUAGE   ▶ Language reference page 156
>
> **Linking language (7)** Using pronouns and determiners for cohesion
>
> We often use cohesive language such as subject / object pronouns and determiners (*his / this*, etc.) to avoid repetition. This makes a paragraph easier to read.
>
> **Pronouns**
> Subject pronouns *he / she / it / they*:
>   Gutenberg was a printer and publisher. **He** (Gutenberg) was also an inventor.
> Object pronouns *him / her / it / them*:
>   Johannes Gutenberg printed books and sold **them** (books).
>
> **Determiners**
> Possessives *his / her / its / their*:
>   Gutenberg was a printer. **His** (Gutenberg's) most famous invention was the printing press.
> Demonstratives *this / that / these / those*:
>   He is famous for his inventions; **these** (his inventions) include the printing press.

TASK 3 Practising cohesion

1 **Complete the text with the words in the list.**

~~he~~   him   his (x2)   it   them

Percy Spencer (1894–1970) was an engineer and inventor. During the Second World War, ¹__he__ specialized in radar technology and worked for the US army. He is remembered for ²_____ invention of the microwave oven. Spencer accidentally discovered that microwaves could cook food. One day he was near a radar which melted a chocolate bar in ³_____ pocket. This interested ⁴_____, so he put popcorn near the machine and cooked ⁵_____. Over the next two years, Spencer developed the invention and sold the first microwave oven in 1947. As a result of Spencer's discovery, microwave ovens have become common in kitchens, because more families can afford ⁶_____.

2 **Replace the words in italics with pronouns or determiners.**

Stephanie Kwolek (1923–2014) was an American inventor and scientist. ¹*Kwolek* studied chemistry at university in the 1940s. ²*Kwolek's* first job was with DuPont in 1946. At first ³*the job* was a temporary position, but the work interested ⁴*Kwolek*, so she took a full-time post. ⁵*Kwolek's* research into polymers led to the invention of Kevlar, a kind of very strong material. Due to ⁶*Kevlar's* incredible strength, ⁷*Kevlar* is now used in products such as car tyres, helmets, and bulletproof vests; ⁸*car tyres, helmets, and bulletproof vests* are products which save many lives.

TASK 4 Writing a paragraph about an inventor

1 **Look at the notes about Ajay Bhatt. Which of your computer devices use USB technology?**

> **Ajay Bhatt**
> - inventor and computer architect – born in India in 1957 – studied in the USA – joined Intel in 1990
> - at Intel invented different computer technologies – became famous for co-inventing USB technology in the mid-nineties
> - before the mid-nineties, computer devices connected in different ways
> - Bhatt's invention → all computer devices now connected with USB technology

2 **Write a paragraph about Ajay Bhatt using the notes in 1. Use Paragraph 2 in Task 2 as a model.**

3 **Use this checklist to check your paragraph. Then exchange with a partner and give feedback. Did you:**
- include biographical information about the inventor? ☐
- give an explanation of their main invention? ☐
- talk about the impact of the invention on modern life? ☐
- use a range of verb forms and tenses (active, passive, present simple, past simple, present perfect)? ☐
- use cohesive language (pronouns and determiners)? ☐

Sample answer:
page 160

UNIT 9C WRITING (2) **131**

9D Vocabulary

TASK 1 Vocabulary-building: Adjectives and nouns

1 **Choose the correct adjective or noun in italics.**
   1 The *economic / economy* of the country is improving at the moment.
   2 From an *educational / education* perspective, businesses need to invest more money in local schools and colleges.
   3 The invention of the aeroplane has great *historical / history* significance.
   4 Penicillin was one of the great *medical / medicine* discoveries of the 20th century.
   5 Many people are not interested in *political / politics* and the work of politicians.
   6 From a *sociological / sociology* point of view, the internet has changed the way people communicate with each other.
   7 My favourite piece of *technological / technology* is my smartphone.
   8 In the past this country had a lot of manufacturing and *industrial / industry*, but now it imports more products than it exports.
   9 The abacus was one of the first inventions designed for *mathematical / mathematics*.
   10 What do you think is the most important *scientific / science* discovery of this century?

> **INDEPENDENT STUDY**
>
> Adjectives ending with the suffix *-ic* or *-al* are classifying adjectives. Classifying adjectives are very common in academic writing. They usually come before the noun, e.g. *a medical discovery*.
> ▶ Find and note down examples of classifying adjectives. Does the adjective also have a noun form, e.g. *medical* (adj) - *medicine* (n)? Use a dictionary to check.

TASK 2 Vocabulary-building: Verbs and nouns

1 **Look at the words in bold. Write verb (V) or noun (N).**
   1 Dunbar **believes** (____) that 150 is the number of people we have close relationships with at one time. However, there is another **belief** (____) that the number is closer to 300.
   2 This is a **report** (____) of the findings from the study. Interestingly, the researchers don't **report** (____) all the findings.
   3 My lecturer **suggested** (____) this textbook, but I don't think it has the information I need. Do you have a different **suggestion** (____)?
   4 Gutenberg **invented** (____) the printing press in the 15th century. His **invention** (____) changed printing in Europe forever.
   5 There is quite a lot of **disagreement** (____) about the theory because some scientists **disagree** (____) with the way the research was carried out.

TASK 3 Prepositional phrases

1 **Complete sentences 1–4 with the prepositions in the list. Circle the prepositional phrase in each sentence.**

   at   by   from   ~~in~~   with

   Example: The first working 3D printer was invented by Charles W. Hull (in) 1984.
   1 Humans communicate _____ a maximum of 150 people.
   2 Zamenhof developed the language of Esperanto _____ the end of the 19th century.
   3 The study was published last month _____ a group of scientists.
   4 Samuel Morse graduated _____ Yale.

9E Academic Language Check

TASK 1 Past simple and present perfect

1 Complete the text with the verbs in brackets in the past simple or the present perfect.

American linguist Carmel O'Shannessy ¹_____ (discover) a new language in the town of Lajamanu in Australia. Around 350 people speak the language and they are all under the age of 35. O'Shannessy ²_____ (make) the discovery while she was at a local school and she ³_____ (recently / publish) her research in *Language*, the journal of the Linguistic Society of America. She believes that local people ⁴_____ (invent) the language in the 1970s and 1980s when they ⁵_____ (switch) between three languages: English and two Aboriginal languages called Warlpiri and Kriol. Over time, it ⁶_____ (develop) into a new language called *Light Warlpiri*. Now, a new generation of children ⁷_____ (grow) up with *Light Warlpiri*.

TASK 2 Describing discoveries and inventions

1 Complete sentences 1–7 with the verbs in the list in the past simple passive.

discover   fly   invent   make   reach   send   write

1 The moons of Jupiter _____ by Galileo Galilei in the 17th century.
2 The printing press in Europe _____ by Gutenberg.
3 Egyptian hieroglyphs _____ on papyrus, an ancient form of paper.
4 The first aeroplane _____ by the Wright brothers on 3 December 1903.
5 The South Pole _____ by the Norwegian explorer Roald Amundsen in 1911.
6 On 12 December 1901 the first radio signal _____ across the Atlantic.
7 The Franklin Stove _____ from metal with a door and a chimney.

TASK 3 Using pronouns and determiners for cohesion

1 Complete the table.

Subject pronouns	Object pronouns	Possessive (determiners)
I	¹ *me*	my
you	you	² _____
he	³ _____	his
⁴ _____	her	⁵ _____
it	⁶ _____	its
we	us	⁷ _____
they	⁸ _____	their

2 Replace the words in bold with a pronoun or determiner in the list.

he   ~~his~~   it   its   them   these

Example: Gutenberg was an inventor. **Gutenberg's** most famous invention was the printing press.   *His*

1 Paper was produced in China. Cai Lun invented **paper**. _____
2 Ajay Bhatt invented computer technologies. He invented **computer technologies** for the company Intel. _____
3 Steve Jobs died in 2011. **Steve Jobs** invented Apple computers. _____
4 The machine produces a series of dots and dashes. **The dots and dashes** represent a special code or message. _____
5 Google is a famous search engine. **Google's** head office is in California. _____

UNIT 10 Research

ACADEMIC FOCUS: QUESTIONING

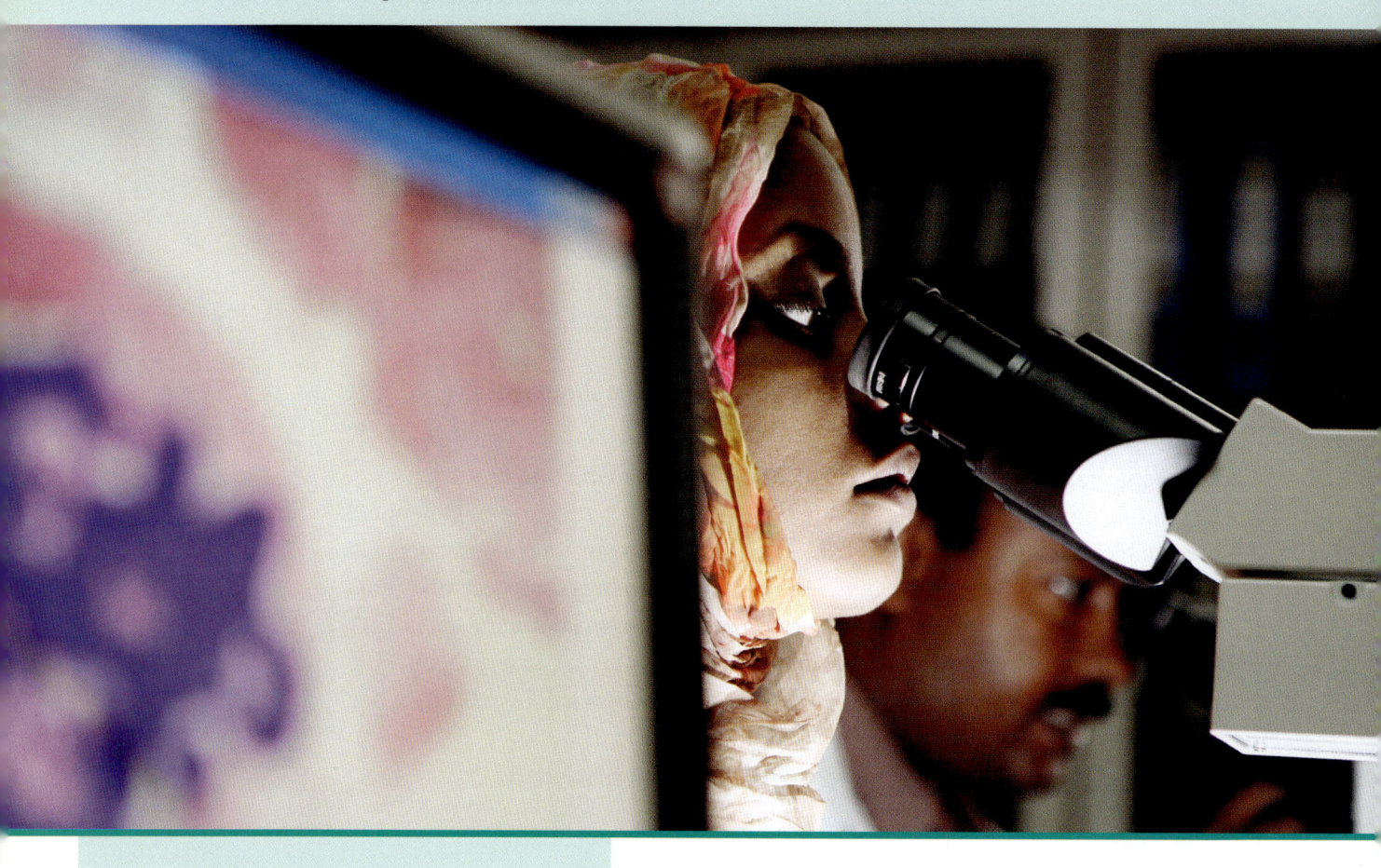

LEARNING OBJECTIVES

Listening and Speaking
- Taking notes on a topic
- Recognizing the purpose of questions

Reading
- Identifying relevant information in a text
- Taking notes about reasons
- Applying information from a text

Writing
- Writing a questionnaire using different question forms
- Analysing a paragraph about survey results
- Writing a paragraph about the results of research

Vocabulary
- Research
- Collocation: Verb + noun

Academic Language Check
- Open and closed questions
- Questions: Form and tense
- The language of reports

Discussion

1 **Complete definitions 1-5 with the words in the list.**

an interview   online research   a questionnaire
research   respondents

1 *Research* is a careful study of a subject in order to find out information or discover new facts.
2 _____ is a research method using the internet.
3 _____ involves asking people questions about a subject – it can be done face-to-face, by phone, or by video chat.
4 A list of questions that you answer is _____.
5 The people who answer research questions are called _____.

2 **Work in pairs and discuss the questions.**
  1 Which jobs involve research? Make a list.
  2 Why is research important in the following areas?
     academic study   business   medicine   politics
     technology
  3 Do you do research in your studies? If so, what research methods do you use?

3 **Work in groups and compare your answers in 2.**

10A Listening & Speaking Questions

This module covers
- Taking notes on a topic
- Recognizing the purpose of questions

TASK 1 Understanding a topic

1 Work in pairs. Read about the business in the pictures. Answer the questions.

> The Good & Proper Tea Company sells cups of high-quality tea. The company was set up in 2012 by Emilie Holmes. The business is based in the City of London and sells the tea from a 1974 Citroën van. The main customers are people going to work.

1 What kind of research do you think Emilie Holmes did before she set up her business?
2 How can you get the money you need to start a business like this?
3 Why is it important to do research before you set up a business?

2 Read about three sources of finance (a–c). Which would be best for the business in 1? Give reasons.
  a **Crowdfunding** is financing a new business with money from lots of different people, via the internet, in return for a reward.
  b A **grant** is money from the government or another organization.
  c A **loan** is money you borrow from a bank or another source, which you pay back over a period of time. This usually includes interest, i.e. extra money you pay back as part of the loan.

TASK 2 Taking notes on a topic

1 ▶10.1, 10.2, 10.3 Watch extracts from a lecture, a student presentation, and a seminar. Complete the table with notes on the topic of each extract and the sources of finance the speakers mention.

	Topic(s)	Sources of finance
Extract 1 (lecture)	the importance of doing research before you set up a business	
Extract 2 (presentation)		crowdfunding, bank loan
Extract 3 (seminar)		

2 Work in pairs and compare your notes.

TASK 3 Identifying key information

1 ▶10.1 Watch Extract 1 again and answer questions 1–3.
   1 According to the lecturer, what does doing research mean?
   2 What are the important questions to ask when starting a business?
   3 What does the student ask the lecturer to explain?
      a why new businesses fail
      b what a government grant is

2 ▶10.2 Watch Extract 2 again and choose the correct answer, a or b.
   1 The main purpose of the presentation is to explain:
      a how crowdfunding works.
      b arguments for and against crowdfunding.
   2 Emilie didn't use a bank loan because:
      a the bank wouldn't give her one.
      b the interest rate was too high.

3 ▶10.3 Watch Extract 3 again and choose the correct answer, a or b.
   1 The students have to choose the best:
      a source of finance.
      b type of loan.
   2 One student thinks the company will not receive a grant because:
      a it's not an educational business.
      b it doesn't sell educational equipment.

TASK 4 Recognizing the purpose of questions

1 Match questions 1–6 from the video extracts to a purpose a–c.
   1 Can you explain how that works? ......
   2 Is a government grant like an interest-free loan? ......
   3 Why does the government give away the money? ......
   4 Why didn't she take out a bank loan? ......
   5 What do you think? ......
   6 Do you think the government will give them money? ......

   a asking for an explanation or to check information
   b asking for the other person's view
   c asking for a reason

> **What is critical questioning?**
> Critical questioning is when you ask questions to find out the reasons for something. It helps you to understand the arguments around a topic in more detail.

136 UNIT 10A LISTENING & SPEAKING

ACADEMIC LANGUAGE
▶ Language reference page 157

Questions (1) Open and closed questions

Open questions

Open questions start with words such as *What, Why, How,* or a modal verb like *Can.* Use open questions to ask for explanations and more detailed information.

What are the advantages of doing proper research?
Why do governments not give loans to some businesses?
How do you start a business with crowdfunding?
Can you explain what you mean by a grant?

Closed questions

Closed questions often start with *Do / Does* or *Is / Are.* Use closed questions to ask for specific information to check meaning.

Does the government give grants for free?
Is it difficult to get a loan?
Are they expensive?

You can use a closed question after an open question to ask for more information:

Can you explain what you mean by a grant? **Do you mean** it's like a loan?

You can answer a closed question with *Yes* or *No,* but we often add information.

Q: Does the government give grants for free?
A: **Yes**, it does because new businesses create jobs and help the economy.

◀)) **10.4** Listen and repeat the questions.

TASK 5 Practising questions

1 Complete questions 1–8 with the words in the list.

Are   Can   Do   How   Is   What (x2)   Why

1 .... are the benefits of using an investor?
2 .... government grants easy to apply for?
3 .... you mean a family loan is better than a bank loan?
4 .... you explain the term 'interest'?
5 .... do governments give grants to new businesses?
6 .... there any disadvantage with a bank loan?
7 .... do you think about crowdfunding?
8 .... does an investor make money?

2 Which questions in 2 are (a) closed and (b) open?

3 Work in pairs. Practise closed and open questions.
   Student A: go to page 161.
   Student B: go to page 163.

TASK 6 Critical thinking – using questions critically

1 Work in pairs. Read the statements about different kinds of research. Choose one statement and note down three questions to ask about it.
   - 'When a person or a company is starting a new business, perhaps the most important thing is to do proper research.'
   - 'To have a successful career in science, you must understand the methodology behind any research and know the correct procedures to follow.'
   - 'Research must begin with a clearly defined goal.'

2 Work with another pair and explain your questions.

> **INDEPENDENT STUDY**
>
> It's useful to prepare questions before you attend a presentation or seminar in English.
>
> ▶ Before your next presentation or seminar, make a list of questions about the topic you are going to study. If a question is not answered by the tutor, presenter, or other students, then ask it.

10B Reading Textbooks (10)

This module covers
- Identifying relevant information in a text
- Taking notes about reasons
- Applying information from a text

TASK 1 Identifying relevant information in a text

1 Work in groups. Look at the title of Text 1 and read questions 1–5. How many can you answer?
   1 What types of *market research* are there?
   2 What is *marketing*?
   3 Why is market research important for a business?
   4 What are *primary research* and *secondary research*?
   5 Is market research reliable?

2 Read Text 1 quickly and note down answers to questions 1–5.

> **What is relevance?**
> Relevance means that information is closely connected with the subject you are researching. When you read, think about what you hope to learn from the text and read for information that is relevant.

Market research in business   TEXT 1

1 **Marketing** describes the different activities used by a business in its relationship with its customers. These activities can include:
   - finding out what people want from the business's products or services
   - receiving feedback from customers on existing products and services
   - pricing the products at the correct level
   - promoting the products in the best way
   - selling products to customers in the most effective way.

   Marketing can be expensive, so small companies have to be careful. However, it is important to do some research before starting your business.

2 There are two types of market research: primary research and secondary research. **Primary research** is information that has not existed before; to get this information, a business can interview people face-to-face and carry out surveys with questionnaires. **Secondary research** means analysing information that already exists. For example, older companies can look back at their sales information from previous years, or study data from government or business organizations.

3 Primary research is often the most useful because it is more up-to-date and specific. It allows new businesses to define their aims and their target market. In addition, existing businesses also need market research to set objectives for the future because customers change. The main benefits to a small business of market research include:
   - understanding customers' needs, so that the company avoids spending money on products that will not sell
   - estimating the demand, so that the company avoids making too few or too many products
   - finding out about competitors' location, products, and prices.

4 It is also important to note that market research is sometimes unreliable. With primary research, it is important to ask for customers' opinions; however, if you interview too many people of a particular age group or income level, then you may draw conclusions about your whole market which are not correct. With secondary research, the information can be out-of-date and imprecise; for example, texts on a website can over-emphasize a particular view or report incorrect data.

SOURCE: Adapted from Hammond, A. et al. 2009. pp.35-6. *AQA Applied Business GCSE*. Cheltenham: Nelson Thorne.

GLOSSARY

conclusion *(n)* something you decide when you have thought about all the information

demand *(n)* customers' need for products or services

existing *(adj)* the ones that are there now

over-emphasize *(v)* to make something seem more important than it is

target market *(n)* the customers a business wants to sell to

3 **Read Text 1 again and answer the questions. Choose *Yes, No,* or *Not given* (if the information is not in the text).**
   1 Is marketing one specific type of activity? Yes / No / Not given
   2 Do businesses use market research to decide on the price of a new product or service? Yes / No / Not given
   3 Can marketing cost a lot of money for a small business? Yes / No / Not given
   4 Do larger companies do the most market research? Yes / No / Not given
   5 Is primary research usually more accurate than secondary research? Yes / No / Not given
   6 Can secondary research include using information in libraries? Yes / No / Not given
   7 Is it important to know about your competitors? Yes / No / Not given
   8 Is primary research always reliable and accurate? Yes / No / Not given
   9 Are online questionnaires more effective than interviewing people face-to-face? Yes / No / Not given

TASK 2 Taking notes about reasons

1 **Look at Text 1 again. Answer the questions.**
   1 Which paragraph gives reasons for using market research? ....
   2 Which two paragraphs mainly explain what market research is? ....
   3 Which paragraph gives reasons against using market research? ....

2 **Work in pairs. Use information from Text 1 to make notes. Give reasons why the research is important (advantages) and why it can be unreliable (disadvantages).**

	Advantages	Disadvantages
Primary research		
Secondary research		

ACADEMIC LANGUAGE ▸ Language reference page 157

Collocation Verb + noun

Verbs in academic texts often combine with certain nouns. These combinations are called collocations. Examples of common **verb** + noun collocations:
   do *research*   **discuss** *an idea*   **examine** *the evidence*
   give *a presentation*   **list** *the main points*
Many verbs can form collocations with more than one noun. For example:
   analyse *data / feedback / results*
   ask for *information / feedback / an opinion*
   carry out *research / a study / an experiment*

TASK 3 Practising collocations

1 **Find the verbs in A in Text 1. Note down how they collocate with the nouns in B.**
   Example: *analyse information*
   A ~~analyse~~   ask for   carry out   define   do   draw   interview   receive   set   study
   B aims   conclusions   data   feedback   ~~information~~   objectives   opinions   people   research   a survey

2 Cross out the word that does <u>not</u> form a collocation with the word in bold. Use a dictionary to help you.

Example: *After a company has done / ~~made~~ / completed* **research**, *they develop the product.*

1 At the end of a presentation, it's usual to **ask for** *questions / opinions / objectives* from the audience.
2 Because of unreliable data, we were not able to *draw / reach / set* any final **conclusions**.
3 Over 90% of the **feedback** *received / obtained / defined* from the survey was positive.
4 We should **define** the *objectives / research / aims* of the report more clearly.
5 The *data / experiment / survey* was **carried out** over a period of eight weeks.
6 **Results** from two different age groups were *analysed / interviewed / compared* to see if there was a clear difference.
7 64% of the **people** we *interviewed / talked to / completed* answered all the questions.

TASK 4 Applying information from a text

1 Work in pairs and discuss.

Have you ever …?
- completed a questionnaire for market research ➜ How long was the questionnaire? How easy was it to complete?
- given feedback on a product or service ➜ What was it? What did you say?

2 Read Text 2. Choose the main purpose of the text, a, b, or c.

a to explain how to design and write a questionnaire
b to explain how to analyse the answers and data from a questionnaire
c to explain how to encourage customers to complete a questionnaire

---

TEXT 2

1 The easiest and cheapest way to discover information on how to improve your business is by getting feedback from existing customers. However, knowing why some people have never bought your product, or why a past customer has stopped using your business, can also help to identify issues with the product and to increase customer numbers.

2 Often businesses will get this information with a questionnaire. The key features of an effective questionnaire are as follows:

- Most questions should be closed questions or questions with single word answers. This means that there will only be a few possible answers to each question. This allows the company doing the research to analyse the results more easily. For example, 'Which brand of ice cream do you buy most frequently?'
- A good questionnaire should be as short as possible. This will encourage people to take part in the research and it will make it easier to study their responses.
- Before constructing the questionnaire, the business should set the research objectives. In other words, the business must define its aims for the survey. So, if it is important to find out the age range of people who most often buy takeaway pizzas, include a question about age.
- Usually the first question on the questionnaire will find out about the person answering (e.g. age, gender, etc.). This allows researchers to stop the questionnaire if the person does not fit the profile.
- Other questions are often used to find out about buying habits and opinions of the type of products and services that the company wants to sell.

SOURCE: Adapted from Hammond, A. et al. 2009. pp.38–9. *AQA Applied Business GCSE.* Cheltenham: Nelson Thornes.

GLOSSARY

age range *(n)* the ages in a group, from the lowest to the highest
construct *(v)* make, create
gender *(n)* male or female
issue *(n)* a problem or worry about something
profile *(n)* a description of somebody that gives useful information

3 Read Paragraph 1 of Text 2 again and answer the questions.
   1 What is the advantage of gaining feedback from existing customers?
   2 Why is it important to talk to customers who don't use your product or service?

4 Read Paragraph 2 of Text 2 again and make notes in the table about the features of a questionnaire.

Item	Key point	Reason / Example
Question types		
Length of questionnaire		
What to do before creating the questionnaire		
The first question		
Other questions		

5 Work in pairs. Use the information in Text 2 and your notes in 4. Make a list of tips on how to write a questionnaire. Include any ideas of your own.
   Example: *Tip 1 – Keep the questionnaire as short as possible.*

TASK 5 Critical thinking – improving a questionnaire

1 Work in pairs. Read the business idea and the questionnaire. Answer the questions.
   1 Which parts of the questionnaire follow the advice in Text 2 and your tips in Task 4.5?
   2 Which parts of the questionnaire would you change? Why?

> A young business person plans to open a vegetarian café in his local town. The town has many fast food outlets selling burgers, pizzas, and kebabs. However, there is nowhere selling fresh, healthy, inexpensive vegetarian food. He believes there is a market for this kind of café, especially among people aged 18–40. He wants to do primary market research with a questionnaire.

1 How old are you? ....
2 Are you male or female?   ○ Male   ○ Female
3 Why do you like vegetarian food?
4 Do you only eat vegetarian food or do you sometimes eat meat?
5 What was the name of the last vegetarian café or restaurant that you ate at?
6 How good was the food there? Explain why.
7 How many times last month did you eat out?
8 How much, on average, do you pay for a vegetarian meal?
9 Do you have any suggestions about what makes a good vegetarian restaurant?

2 Work with another pair. Compare your feedback on the questionnaire. Give reasons for your changes.

> **INDEPENDENT STUDY**
>
> Collocations are common in academic texts. They make writing and speaking sound more natural.
>
> ▶ Choose some texts from this book and find verb + noun collocations. Practise using the collocations in your writing, or when you speak in presentations or seminars.

10C Writing (1) Questions

This module covers:

- Writing a questionnaire using different question forms

TASK 1 Identifying question forms

1 Work in pairs. Note down five famous brands, e.g. Microsoft, Samsung, Gucci. What brands do you buy?

2 Read part of an online survey. Is it for new customers or existing customers?

> 1 How often do you use this brand?
>   ○ every week   ○ once every two weeks   ○ once a month
>
> 2 Are you currently using other similar products from our competitors?
>   ○ yes   ○ no   Please give details: _____
>
> 3 How did you first hear about this brand?
>   ○ friends / colleagues   ○ in the media   ○ on the internet   ○ in a shop
>
> 4 How long have you used this brand?
>   ○ less than six months   ○ less than one year   ○ more than two years
>
> 5 Will you recommend this brand to family and friends in the future?
>   ○ yes   ○ no   Please give details: _____
>
> 6 Would you be interested in receiving emails about our other products?
>   ○ yes   ○ no

What is a survey?
A survey is questionnaire-based research into the behaviour or opinions of a group of people. It is used to gather facts which can be used as evidence.

3 Answer the questions.
  1 Which questions in **2** are open questions? Which are closed questions?
  2 How does the questionnaire ask for additional information in the response?
  3 How does the questionnaire limit the response?

ACADEMIC LANGUAGE   ▶ Language reference page 157

Questions (2) Form and tense

When you write questions for research, e.g. as part of a survey, use a variety of closed questions and open questions in different tenses and with different verb forms.

	Closed	Open
Present simple	**Are** you **interested** in our products? **Do** you **use** our hotels?	**Why are** you **interested** in our products? **How often do** you **use** our hotels?
Present progressive	**Are** you currently **studying** at this university?	**Where are** you currently **studying**?
Past simple	**Was** our representative **polite**? **Did** our representative **call** you back within 24 hours?	**How polite was** our representative? **When did** our representative **call** you back?
Present perfect	**Have** you ever **eaten** at our restaurants?	**How many times have** you **eaten** at our restaurants?
Modal verbs	**Will** you **travel** overseas in the next six months? **Would** you **recommend** this product?	**Where will** you **travel** overseas in the next six months? (NOT ~~to travel~~) **Who would** you **recommend** this product to? (NOT ~~to recommend~~)

142   UNIT 10C WRITING (1)

TASK 2 Practising questions

1 Match the six questions in the questionnaire in Task 1.2 with the correct tense in Academic Language.

   Example: 1 How often do you use this brand?   *present simple*

2 Correct the mistakes in questions 1–7.

   Are you
   Example: ~~Do you~~ interested in receiving further information from us?
   1 How often are you buying this brand?
   2 Which supplier of our products do you currently using?
   3 How would you to describe the service you received?
   4 How long has the treatment take?
   5 How many times are you been ill in the last six months?
   6 Did our staff helpful in solving your problem?
   7 When you will next travel by plane?

3 Read part of a survey about student accommodation. Complete the questions with the correct form of the verb in brackets.

   1 _____ (be) you aged between 18 and 25?   ◯ yes   ◯ no

   2 _____ (currently / study) full-time at university?   ◯ yes   ◯ no

   3 How long _____ (study) at your university?   ◯ 1 year   ◯ 2 years   ◯ 3 years

   4 Where _____ (live)?
     ◯ in university accommodation   ◯ in rented accommodation   ◯ with your parents

   5 If you live in rented accommodation, how _____ (find) it?
     ◯ on a website   ◯ in a newspaper   ◯ from other students   ◯ other

   6 How many times _____ (move) accommodation while at university?

   7 _____ (be) interested in using an agency specializing in student accommodation?
     ◯ yes   ◯ no

TASK 3 Writing a questionnaire

1 Work in pairs. Read the list of research objectives about students' use of mobile devices. Then write six questions for a questionnaire. Remember to:
   - keep your questionnaire short
   - use both open and closed questions
   - include a question for all the research objectives.

   Research objectives – to find out:
   - what mobile devices (e.g. smartphone, tablet, smartwatch) students aged 18–25 own
   - how long they have owned them
   - how they use them in their studies (e.g. for writing assignments, for doing research)
   - where they use them (e.g. in class, in the library, travelling to university, at home)
   - how they use them outside university (e.g. to send and receive texts and email, to make video calls, to use social media, to watch films)
   - if they would be interested in free online courses to help them study more effectively.

2 Interview other students with your questionnaire. Note down their answers.

INDEPENDENT STUDY

When you write questions, check your accuracy.

▶ Look at your questions in Task 3. Which tenses and verb forms have you used? Are the question forms correct?

10C Writing (2) A description of results

This module covers:
- Analysing a paragraph about survey results
- Writing a paragraph about the results of research

TASK 1 Analysing a report paragraph

> **What is a report?**
> A report is a description and explanation of the results of research into a situation, problem, or academic area. It often includes data.

1 Read a paragraph reporting the results of a survey. Complete the notes.
1 Type of survey: .... survey
2 Researchers wanted to analyse ....
3 Students completed the survey ....
4 Percentage of students that completed the survey: ....
5 Students spend most of their money on ....

> ¹The aim of this report is to summarize the results of a financial survey. ²The purpose of the survey was to analyse the spending habits of students aged between 18 and 21 years. ³The research was carried out by inviting 200 students at a university to complete an online survey. ⁴The response rate was 33.5% with answers received from 67 students. ⁵With reference to the question of living costs, 63 respondents said that they spent most of their money on accommodation and 58 stated that heating and food were also a main expense. ⁶The responses show that a typical student spends about 75% of their budget on accommodation, heating, and food. ⁷According to three-quarters of the respondents, the cost of books was also too high, and only two respondents said that they were able to save money during the term. ⁸Overall, the results suggest that living costs are the biggest expense for most students and that this is a serious problem in cities where the cost of living is particularly high.

2 Match sentences 1–8 in the paragraph with the four main reporting stages a–d.

Sentences 1 and 2: ....   a describing the research method(s) and the response rate
Sentences 3 and 4: ....   b explaining the aim of the report and the purpose of the research
Sentences 5, 6, and 7: .... c discussing the results of the research
Sentence 8: ....   d presenting the results of the research

---

ACADEMIC LANGUAGE   ▸ Language reference page 158

Sentences (5) The language of reports

When we write a report, we often use key phrases to show the main stages.

Stating aims and purpose
   The aim of this report is to …
   The purpose of the survey was to …

Explaining research methods and response rate
   The research was carried out by …
   The response rate was …

Presenting results
   With reference to the question of …
   According to three-quarters of the respondents, …
   X respondents said that …
   The responses show that …

Discussing results
   (Overall,) the results suggest that …

---

144   UNIT 10C WRITING (2)

TASK 2 Practising report language

1 Complete the report with phrases from Academic Language.

The ¹ *aim of this report* is to summarize the results of a customer survey. The ² _____ was to receive feedback on the new website for clients registered with our 'Gold Customer' programme. The research was ³ _____ by inviting 4,325 registered members of the programme to complete an online survey. The ⁴ _____ was 19%, with answers received from 826 respondents. ⁵ _____ the question of booking online, 81% of respondents rated the website as *very good* or *good*. ⁶ _____ show that the website is easy to use and has improved the booking experience. ⁷ _____ two thirds of the respondents, website registration also provides financial benefits by saving them money. The ⁸ _____ the new website was very positive and that the cost of the website upgrade was worthwhile.

TASK 3 Writing a paragraph about research results

1 Work in pairs. Look at the research data from an online survey by a mobile technologies company. Answer questions 1–6.

1. Who was the survey designed for?
2. What did the company want to analyse?
3. What was the response rate?
4. What are some of the main findings of the survey?
5. What overall conclusions do you think the company might draw from the results?
6. Do you think any of the results are surprising? Why? / Why not?

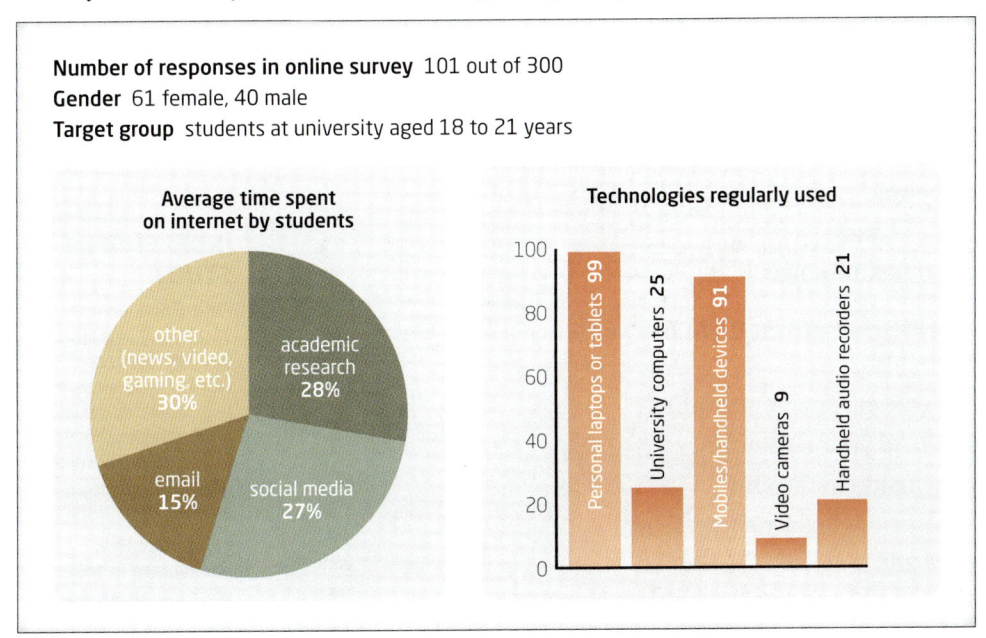

Number of responses in online survey 101 out of 300
Gender 61 female, 40 male
Target group students at university aged 18 to 21 years

Average time spent on internet by students:
- other (news, video, gaming, etc.) 30%
- academic research 28%
- social media 27%
- email 15%

Technologies regularly used:
- Personal laptops or tablets 99
- University computers 25
- Mobiles/handheld devices 91
- Video cameras 9
- Handheld audio recorders 21

2 Write a paragraph reporting the research data in 1. Use the paragraph in Task 1 as a model.

3 Use this checklist to check your paragraph. Then exchange with a partner and give feedback. Did you:
- state the aim of the report and the purpose of the research? ☐
- describe the research method and response rate? ☐
- present the results of the research? ☐
- discuss the results in your final sentence? ☐
- use reporting language? ☐

Sample answer:
page 160

10D Vocabulary

TASK 1 Research

1 Complete sentences 1–9 with the words in the list.

interviews   market   questionnaire   research   respondents   results   surveys
objectives   online

1 As part of the research we carried out face-to-face .... with 50 people.
2 After the interviews, we also asked people to fill in a short ....
3 It's cheaper to put a questionnaire .... and let people access it via the internet.
4 Out of 200 .... , 2% completed the survey.
5 Overall, the .... of the survey suggest living costs are too high.
6 .... can include interviews, questionnaires, and surveys.
7 Online .... are not always accurate because the same person can complete them more than once.
8 .... research can include asking customers questions or looking at websites of competitors.
9 What are the main .... of your current research?

TASK 2 Collocation: Verb + noun

1 Cross out the verb in each group that does not collocate with the noun in bold.

Example: do / ~~make~~ / carry out **research**

1 discuss / have / set **an idea**
2 define / ask / list **aims**
3 draw / do / reach **conclusions**
4 give / ask for / set **feedback**
5 carry out / analyse / compare **results**
6 interview / set / talk to **people**
7 collect / interview / analyse **data**
8 complete / fill in / ask **a questionnaire**

2 Complete sentences 1–8 with a verb from 1. (In two sentences, both verbs are possible.)

1 Does anyone .... an idea for a new product?
2 Can you .... the aim of your research?
3 Did you .... a conclusion in the end?
4 Can you .... me some feedback on my essay?
5 Let's .... the last result.
6 I plan to .... 20 people with these questions.
7 Did you .... the data with a survey?
8 Please .... the questionnaire by ticking the boxes.

> **INDEPENDENT STUDY**
>
> Record and learn vocabulary in groups. You can record new words / phrases by topic (e.g. *websites, research*), or by academic focus (e.g. *comparison, data, defining and explaining, questioning*).
>
> ▶ **Organize new vocabulary in topic or study areas. Add to each area when you read a new text or study a new topic.**

10E Academic Language Check

TASK 1 Open and closed questions

1 Complete the interview with the question words in the list.

can   do   does   how often   is   what   why

A Hello. ¹_____ I ask you some questions?
B Sure, go ahead.
A ² _____ do you use the university library?
B About once a week.
A ³ _____ it easy to find what you need?
B Yes, it is. Usually. Everyone is very helpful.
A Good. ⁴ _____ time of day do you normally come here?
B In the morning.
A So ⁵ _____ the opening hours suit you?
B In general. Sometimes I'd like to come in the evenings though.
A ⁶ _____ do you need to use the library in the evening?
B Because during periods when we have exams, I need to study late.
A I see. And finally, ⁷ _____ the library always have the books you need?
B Yes, it does.

TASK 2 Questions: Form and tense

1 Correct one mistake in each question.
   1 Is you interested in our products? _____
   2 Does the university helps you to find accommodation? _____
   3 How often do you using our hotels? _____
   4 Where is you currently studying? _____
   5 Was the exam questions difficult? _____
   6 When does Alexander Fleming discover penicillin? _____
   7 Did our representative called you back last week? _____
   8 Have you ever use our online library? _____
   9 How many times have she taken this exam? _____
  10 Will you to apply to university next year? _____

2 Write eight questions for another student in your class. Start with these words:

Are   Do   Have you ever   How often   Was   When   Why   Will

TASK 3 The language of reports

1 Match the sentence halves.
   1 The aim of this report ... _____
   2 The purpose of the survey ... _____
   3 The research was carried out ... _____
   4 With reference to the question of current opening times, ... _____
   5 9% of the respondents said that ... _____
   6 Overall, the results ... _____

   a they wanted later evening opening times.
   b was to analyse use of the university library.
   c by online surveys.
   d suggest that students are very satisfied.
   e is to summarise the results of a survey.
   f 91% of the respondents were satisfied.

Language reference

Unit 1

1.1 Present simple: Talking about now

Verb *be*

Positive (+)

I'm	I'm from Turkey.
you're	You're good at French.
he / she / it's	It's wrong.
we / you / they're	They're psychologists.

Negative (-)

I'm not	I'm not an engineer.
you aren't	You aren't in our class.
he / she / it isn't	She isn't an economist.
we / you / they aren't	You aren't from Spain.

Question (?)

Am I	Am I in class 2?
Are you	Are you free now?
Is he / she / it	Is he in our group?
Are we / you / they	Are we in the lab today?

Contractions: I am → I'm, you are → you're, he is → he's, she is → she's, it is → it's, we are → we're, they are → they're

Other verbs

Positive (+)

I / you / we / they **like** he / she / it **likes**	I like geography. You study hard. We design websites. They plan to work hard. She manages a company.

Negative (-)

I / you / we / they **don't like** he / she / it **doesn't like**	I don't work at night. You don't need an A. We don't like maths. They don't like videos. He doesn't study biology.

Question (?)

Do I / you / we / they **like** Does he / she / it **like**	Do I have your textbook? Do you use the gym? Do we have a project? Do they study here? Does it look interesting?

Contractions: do not → don't, does not → doesn't

Spelling of *he / she / it* form

Add -s after the verb → She likes maths.

Verbs ending -y → -ies (*studies*), -ch / -s / -sh / -z / -x → -es (*watches*), consonant -o → -es (*does, goes*).

Contractions

We often use contractions in spoken English. We usually use full forms in written English.
I'm a maths student. It's really interesting. (spoken English)
The internet is an important technological development. (written English)

Uses of the present simple

Use the present simple with *be* and most other verbs to talk about things that are generally true.
I'm from Spain. He's from Turkey. The university is in Canberra.

Use the present simple for habits and repeated actions.
I work with computers. We go to the other campus every Wednesday.

After *like* and *enjoy*, use a noun or the *-ing* form of the verb.
I like Arabic. I like learning Arabic.
She enjoys learning English. She doesn't enjoy media studies.

1.2 Present simple + *to* infinitive: Talking about future plans

Verbs *plan, hope, want, would like*

Use the verbs *plan, hope, want* plus another verb in the *to* infinitive form to talk about future plans. We use the present simple because the subject (*I / She*) knows now about the plans.
I want to study engineering at university. I hope to become an engineer. She plans to do her Master's degree in the USA.

You can also use *would like* + *to* infinitive.
I'd like to study medicine. (= I want to study medicine in the future.)

Closed and open questions

To ask about someone's future plans, use *Do / Does* for a closed answer (*Yes / No*).
Do you plan to study in France? – Yes, I do.
Does he want to be an engineer? – No, he doesn't.

Use *Wh-* question words (*What, Where*, etc.) to make open questions.
What do you hope to do next year? Where does she want to study?

1.3 Present simple and imperative: Giving information and instructions or advice

Use the imperative to give instructions or advice. The imperative form is the same as the infinitive form without *to*, e.g. *listen*.

Positive (+)	**Listen** carefully. Always **make** notes in lectures.
Negative (-)	**Don't write** on the examination paper. Please **don't make** a noise.

148 LANGUAGE REFERENCE

1.4 Sentences (1): Writing personal information

Verb *be*

Use the simple sentence pattern **subject** + ***be*** + **noun** or **adjective**.

I am a student.
s v n

His name is Adam.
   s v n

These textbooks are difficult.
      s   v   a

Other verbs

Use the simple sentence pattern **subject** + **verb** + **object**.

Subject	Verb	Object
I	enjoy	learning languages.
She	doesn't like	mathematics.
Our teacher	uses	new technology.

1.5 Linking language (1): *and, but, because*

Use *and* or *but* to join two sentences. To add something, use *and*. To show contrast, use *but*. Use a comma (,) before *but*.

*She now lives in Paris **and** she speaks French.*
*I enjoy learning languages, **but** I don't like mathematics.*

Use *because* to give a reason.

*I like learning English **because** it's an international language.*

Unit 2

2.1 Linking language (2): Sequencing and adding information

Linking language is words / phrases that help a listener or reader understand information.

Use *Firstly*, etc. to sequence information, i.e. put it in order. You can also use *Thirdly, Fourthly*, etc. to add more information.

***Firstly**, I plan to look at the home pages of education websites.*
***Secondly**, I'd like to talk about links to other pages.*
***Finally**, we'll look at the design of different web pages.*

Use *also* and *in addition* to add information.

***Also**, the website has links to other websites. / It **also** has links to other websites.*
***In addition**, the website has links to other useful websites.*

The words *firstly, secondly, finally,* and *also* are adverbs.

2.2 Noun phrases (1): Understanding a noun phrase

Academic texts present a lot of information in noun phrases. A noun phrase can be one word or a number of words. A noun phrase always has a head noun – this is the main noun in the phrase.

Common noun phrase patterns

One-word (noun or pronoun):
    websites, **information**, **it**, **they**

Determiner + head noun:
    a **user**, *the* **information**, *some* **websites**

Adjective + head noun:
    interactive **features**, *social* **networks**, *useful* **information**

Noun + head noun:
    home **page**, *news* **websites**, *search* **box**

Determiner + adjective + head noun:
    an entertaining **way**, *the main* **body**, *some design* **features**

The subject and the object of a sentence can be a noun phrase.

Subject	Verb	Object
Different **websites**	have	different **information**.
Other **websites**	offer	a **service**.
Some **websites**	include	moving **images**.
Web **designers**	use	different **colours**.

2.3 Noun phrases (2): Adjectives in noun phrases

Use adjectives to describe or classify a noun. Adjectives can be grouped into different types.

Type **A** describe the quality of the noun, e.g. colour, size, shape, age: *black, large, long, round, old, cheap, low, high …*

Type **B** often end in *-al* or *-ic*. They classify the noun, e.g. state its nationality or academic subject: *Chinese, Turkish, social, personal, national, global, financial, economic, cultural, online …*

Adjectives are very common in noun phrases. A noun phrase can have one or more adjectives. Put Type A adjectives first, then Type B.

a large global organization, a new cultural channel, a small local company
NOT a ~~global large~~ organization

2.4 Linking language (3): *in addition, also, so, or*

Use linking language to add more information or to explain something.

Adding information

Use *and* (see Unit 1.5), *also*, and *in addition* to add information to a statement.

Statement: *The BBC has global news channels.*
Additional information: *It offers local news.*

*The BBC has global news channels **and** it offers local news.*
*The BBC has global news channels. It **also** offers local news.*
*The BBC has global news channels. **In addition**, it offers local news.*

Explaining

Use *because*, *so*, and *or* to explain a statement.

Use *because* to give a reason.
> News websites are popular **because** people can read them anywhere.

Use *so* to give a result.
> The BBC is a very old news organization, **so** people think it's reliable.

Use *or* to give an alternative.
> People can read the news in newspapers, **or** on their smartphone.

Unit 3

3.1 Comparison (1): Comparative adjectives

Use comparative adjectives to compare two things, e.g. people, places, ideas. Add *than* after the comparative adjective.
> Istanbul is **larger than** Ankara. The Olympics is **more expensive than** the World Cup.

Adjective type	Comparative form
One-syllable adjectives with long vowel	➔ -er old - old**er**, few - few**er**
One-syllable adjectives with short vowel	➔ double the consonant + -er big - big**ger**, hot - hot**ter**
Adjectives ending in -e	➔ -r nice - nice**r**, large - large**r**
Two-syllable adjectives ending in -y	-y ➔ -ier happy - happ**ier**, busy - bus**ier**
Adjectives with two or more syllables	➔ more / less ... interesting - **more** interesting, expensive - **less** expensive
Irregular adjectives	good - **better**, bad - **worse**

3.2 Comparison (2): Superlative adjectives

Use superlative adjectives to compare three or more things. Use the same rules as for comparative adjectives with *the* + adjective + *-est*.
> Istanbul is **the largest** city in Turkey. London is probably **the most expensive** city in Europe. What's **the best** university in your country?

Adjective type	Superlative form
One-syllable adjectives with long vowel	➔ -est the old**est**, the few**est**
One-syllable adjectives with short vowel	➔ double the consonant + -est the big**gest**, the hot**test**
Adjectives ending in -e	➔ -st the nice**st**, the large**st**
Two-syllable adjectives ending in -y	-y ➔ -est the happ**iest**, the bus**iest**
Adjectives with two or more syllables	➔ most / least ... the **most** interesting, the **least** expensive
Irregular adjectives	the **best**, the **worst**, the **least**

3.3 Linking language (4): Comparing and contrasting ideas

Use linking language to compare and contrast ideas, i.e. to show the similarities and differences between the ideas.

Use *Similarly*, *In addition*, *also* to add a similar idea.
> The capital of Turkey is in the middle of the country. **Similarly**, the capital of Saudi Arabia is in the middle of the country.
> London is the UK centre of government. It is **also** the main financial centre.

Use *However*, *On the other hand*, *In contrast* to add a different, contrasting idea.
> Sydney and Melbourne are the biggest cities in Australia. **However**, the capital is Canberra.

Use *but* to join two sentences with different, contrasting ideas.
> Oxford Street is a great location for shopping, **but** it is expensive.

Punctuation

Use a comma (,) after Similarly, In addition, However, On the other hand, In contrast. Use a comma before *but* when it continues a sentence.

3.4 Word forms: *similar / different*

Use adjective, adverb, and noun forms of *similar* and *different* to compare and contrast. Use *between* after the noun form (*similarity / -ies between ...*, *difference / -s between ...*).

Adjective

similar / different:
> The size of the two capital cities is quite **similar**.
> The two countries are very **different**.

Adverb

similarly:
> The cost of houses is high. **Similarly**, office rents are expensive.

Noun

similarity (s.) / *similarities* (pl.):
> There are many **similarities** between London and New York.

difference (s.) / *differences* (pl.):
> There are many **differences** between Switzerland and Hungary.

3.5 Comparison (3): Expressing similarities and differences

Describing similarities

Use *as* + adjective + *as*, *both* + plural noun to describe similarities.
> Wales is **as beautiful as** Scotland.
> **Both countries** have a large highway network.

Describing differences

Use comparative adjectives, *more* + plural noun, *not as* + adjective + *as* to describe differences.
　Shanghai is **larger than** Beijing.
　There are **more airports** in London than in Paris.
　Frankfurt is **not as big as** Berlin.

3.6 Sentences (2): Writing about comparison

Introducing the comparison

Use *There are many / a number of similarities / differences between …*
　There are many differences between the capital cities Beijing and New Delhi.

Describing similarities

Use *Similarly, and, In addition, also, as* + adjective + *as*.
　Many of the buildings in Beijing are new. **Similarly**, the highways in Beijing are very modern. Beijing is **as modern as** Dubai.

Describing differences

Use *However, On the other hand*.
　The highways in Beijing are modern. **On the other hand**, the highways in New Delhi are mostly old.

Concluding

Use *Overall, In conclusion*.
　Overall, there are more differences than similarities between the two cities.

Unit 4

4.1 Data (1): Saying numbers exactly and approximately

Sometimes it is important to say numbers exactly.

Whole numbers

Say the whole number. Make clear the difference between '15' /fɪfˈtiːn/ and '50' /ˈfɪfti/, etc.
　0 – *zero*, 6 – *six*, 12 – *twelve*, 15 – *fifteen*, 50 – *fifty*,
　500 – *five hundred*, 1,000 – *a / one thousand*,
　5,500 – *five thousand, five hundred*

Long numbers

Say *and* before the final number.
　120 – *a / one hundred **and** twenty*
　1,235 – *a / one thousand, two hundred **and** thirty-five*
　10,540 – *ten thousand, five hundred **and** forty*
　100,000 – *a / one hundred thousand*
　1,000,000 – *a / one million*

Percentages

Say the number, then *per cent* (%).
　1% – *one per cent*, 12% – *twelve per cent*,
　22% – *twenty-two per cent*

Sometimes you can say numbers approximately, including in fraction form. Approximate numbers are easier for a listener to understand.

Numbers near round numbers

Round the number up or down to the nearest large number (e.g. 98 rounds up to 100). Use *approximately, about, around* + the round number. Use *nearly / less than* + number, or *over* + number.
　48.5% – *approximately fifty per cent*
　203 – *about two hundred*
　10.2% – *around ten per cent*
　993 – *nearly a thousand*
　79 – *less than eighty / nearly eighty / around eighty*
　91.5% – *over ninety per cent*

Fractions

Round the number up or down to the nearest fraction. Use approximate language.
　32% – *approximately a third*
　48% – *nearly half*
　74% – *around three-quarters*
　40% – *two fifths*
　54% – *over a half*
　9% – *less than a tenth*

4.2 Past simple: Talking about events in the past

Use the past simple to talk about finished events in the past.

Past simple regular verbs

I / you / he / she / it work**ed**	I worked at HSBC last year. India produced the most tea in 2013.

Past simple irregular verbs

Verb *be*: I / he / she / it **was** you / we / they **were** There **were**	It was more expensive last year. They were from Malaysia. There were two new students.
begin – **began**, buy – **bought**, do – **did**, go – **went**, make – **made**, sell – **sold**	Consumers bought over a million tonnes of chocolate. I went to university in Prague. Ford made its first car in the USA. IBM sold computers in over 100 countries last year.

See page 158 for a list of common irregular verbs.

Spelling

The verb is the same for all persons (except with the verb *be*). Add *-ed* after a regular verb → *He work**ed** in Oman in 2012*. Verbs ending *-e* → + *-d* (*lik**ed***), vowel – consonant → double the consonant + *-ed* (*plann**ed***), *-y* → replace *-y* with *-ied* (*stud**ied***). Many common verbs are irregular.

4.3 Data (2): Simplifying numerical information

Fractions

Use fractions *a quarter, a half, three-quarters, a fifth, a sixth, a tenth*, etc. to simplify numbers. Say fraction + *of* + plural noun.
　Three quarters of cars are imports.
　Four fifths of people live in cities.

You can leave out the *of* + main noun after the fraction.
　Half / A half are from Germany.
　A quarter are Chinese.

Use approximate language *nearly, over, about, around* + fraction.
> ***Nearly two-thirds*** *are from France.*
> ***Over a third*** *of tea is from China.*

Quantifiers

Use quantifiers *all, most, some, a few* + plural noun. You can leave out the main noun after the quantifier.
> *There are **a few** computer factories in Spain, but **most** factories are in Asia.*
> ***Some*** *tablets are from Europe, but **most** are from Asia.*

You can use *nearly* + *all* but NOT + *about / around / over*.
> ***Nearly all*** *tablets are from Asia.* NOT ~~Nearly over are …~~

Use *no* + noun or just *none* (*none* is a pronoun – it takes the place of a noun).
> ***No*** *customers are from Brazil.* NOT ~~None customers are from Brazil.~~
> ***None*** *are from Brazil.* NOT ~~No are from Brazil.~~

Unit 5

5.1 Defining (1): Definitions, explanations, and examples

The language of definitions is important in academic study to describe new terms and ideas. Definitions are often followed by more explanation and examples.

Definitions

Use the structure *x is / are y*, i.e. say what *x* (the new word or idea) means using other words (*y*). *y* = a defining phrase.
> *HTC **is** a Chinese brand of high-tech products.*
> *Appliances **are** machines for doing things in the home.*

Explanations

Use *In other words*, or a phrase such as *Let me explain* (*why / how … / by* + verb + *-ing …*) to introduce an explanation.
> *Dyson vacuum cleaners are bagless. **In other words**, they do not use bags to collect the dust.*
> *Biomimetics is the scientific study of design in nature. **Let me explain** (**why**). / **Let me explain how** this works. / **Let me explain by** showing you …*

Examples

Use *for example*, or a phrase such as *It / This is a good example of … / Let me give you an example* (*of …*) to introduce an example.
> *This computer has some great features, **for example**, wireless battery charging.*
> *Germany and South Korea **are good examples of** manufacturing countries.*
> ***Let me give you an example of*** *a biomimetic product.*

5.2 Defining (2): Identifying definitions, explanations, and examples

Common verbs and expressions introduce or add to a definition or show that a sentence contains an explanation or example.

Definitions

Look for forms of *be* (*is / are*), *mean, refer to, relate to*. The order is **word–verb–definition**.
> *Biology **is** the study of life.*
> *Biology **refers to** both animal and plant life.*
> *Biology **relates to** the life of animals and plants.*

Explanations

Look for the phrases *in particular* and *in other words*.
> *Many products are developing very fast. **In particular**, smartphones become old very quickly.*
> *All manufacturers focus on design. **In other words**, good design helps to sell a product.*

Examples

Look for the phrases *for example, such as, … is an example of …*
> *The Japanese bullet train **is a good example of** the application of design in nature to a man-made product.*

5.3 Defining (3): Writing definitions

Use a long noun phrase to write a definition. Use the pattern **new term** + **be** + **noun phrase**. Include a **prepositional phrase** in the noun phrase – this means you can add more information about the context.
> *A dishwasher is an appliance for washing dishes.*
> *Psychology is the scientific study of the mind and how it influences behaviour.*
> *HGVs are vehicles with long trailers.*

Common prepositions include *for, of,* and *with*. Use verb + *-ing* after *for*. Use another noun after *of / with*.

5.4 Linking language (5): Structuring definitions and explanations / examples

Use linking language to introduce explanations and examples after a definition. This helps a reader to understand the order of information.
> *Psychological factors in design relate to how the human mind influences people's behaviour. **In other words**, scientists can work out how people will behave in different situations and with different designs. **For example**, the design of a 4x4 car influences how the car driver behaves. **In particular**, the driver knows that their car is bigger than most other cars, so they drive differently.*

Unit 6

6.1 Changes and trends (1): Present progressive, present simple

Present progressive

Positive (+)

I**'m** he / she / it**'s** we / you / they**'re**	**learning**	*This semester I'm learning Spanish.* *You're working hard.*

152 LANGUAGE REFERENCE

Negative (-)

| I'm not
he / she / it isn't
we / you / they aren't | studying | We aren't using our textbook this term.
Prices aren't increasing. |

Question (?)

| Am I
Is he / she / it
Are we / you / they | working | Are you doing statistics this week?
Is the price of oil rising? |

Uses of the present progressive

Use the present progressive to talk about a situation that is changing. It describes something in progress now – in other words, it started in the past, but is not finished. This can be exactly now at the time of speaking, e.g. *I'm walking to the lecture room*, or it can be longer-term, e.g. *The population is going up*.

Time references

Use time expressions *at the moment, currently, now, these days, nowadays, this term, this week / month / year* with the present progressive to say when something is happening.

At the moment, prices are increasing.
You're working hard these days.

Present progressive v. present simple

Use the present simple to describe states or situations which are not changing.

She works at the local university.
Older people retire at 65.

Use present simple verbs *believe, know, understand, have, mean, say* to describe a state or condition.

I understand how to do algebra. NOT ~~I am understanding ...~~

6.2 Time, place, and quantity: Prepositional phrases

Use a prepositional phrase to say when, where, or how much / many. A prepositional phrase starts with a preposition, e.g. *in, at, from, to, by*, followed by a noun phrase or verb *-ing* form. Remember, *in* is for both time and place; *from ... to* is for both time and quantity.

Time

Use *in* to refer to months and years. Use *from ... to* for start and end dates. Use *by* for the end date.

House prices fell in July / in 2014.
Prices increased from 2005 to 2008.
The population of Istanbul will be 20 million by 2025.

Place

Use *in* for cities, countries, etc.

Our university has a campus in Hong Kong.
The fastest population growth is in Africa.

Quantity

Use *by* for quantities / amounts. Use *from ... to* for start and end quantities.

The population of Riyadh rose by 4 million over 50 years.
The population of London grew from 1 million in 1800 to nearly 7 million in 1900.

6.3 Changes and trends (2): Past and present tenses, *will*

Use the correct tense to express when changes happen.

Use the **past simple** for finished events in the past.
Unemployment went up last month.

Use the **present simple** to express states, situations, repeated actions and habits.
Millions of people move to cities every year.
A country with a strong economy usually has high employment and low unemployment.

Use the **present progressive** for changes and trends in progress now.
Tourism is growing by over 5% a year in many Asian countries.
The population of Russia is falling.

Use **will** + **infinitive without to** for predictions of changes and trends in the future.
The population of India will be larger than China by 2028.
Two thirds of the global population will live in cities by 2050.

6.4 Describing trends (1): Adverbs

Adverbs describe verbs. They say how something happens. Use **verb** + **adverb** to describe trends and changes.

↑ Use the verbs *go up, rise, increase, climb* to express rising trends.

↓ Use the verbs *go down, fall, decrease* to express falling trends.

Use adverbs *quickly / rapidly* to describe fast change. Use *slowly / steadily* to describe slow change. Use *slightly* to describe a small change.

The cost of houses in London went up rapidly in 2013.
The population of Shanghai is rising slowly at the moment.
The global population increased steadily from 1850.
Unemployment will fall quickly next year.
The number of universities decreased slightly from 1995 to 2015.

→ For no change, use *stay the same*.
The price of oil stayed the same this year.

Spelling of adverbs

Add *-ly* to the adjective (*quickly*). Adjectives ending *-y* → *-ily* (*steadily*).

6.5 Describing trends (2): Adjectives and adverbs

Adjectives describe nouns. Use an **adjective** + **noun** pattern to describe a trend or change.
*There was a **rapid fall** in unemployment.*

Use a **verb** + **adverb** pattern OR an **adjective** + **noun** pattern.
*The birth rate **will rise steadily**. → There will be a **steady rise** in the birth rate.*
*Prices **are falling rapidly**. → There is a **rapid fall** in prices.*
*The population **decreased slowly**. → There was a **slow decrease** in the population.*

verb	→ noun	adverb	→ adjective
rise	rise	rapidly	rapid
in<u>crease</u>	in<u>crease</u>	quickly	quick
fall	fall	slowly	slow
de<u>crease</u>	de<u>crease</u>	steadily	steady
grow	growth	slightly	slight
climb	climb		

Unit 7

7.1 Expressing opinions: Giving and supporting opinions, agreeing / disagreeing

Use different expressions to ask for, give, and support your opinion on a topic.

Asking for opinions

In a discussion, include other speakers and ask what they think.
What is your opinion?, What do you think?, Do you agree?

Giving your opinion

Introduce your own opinion clearly.
I think (that) …, I don't think (that) …, In my opinion …, In my view …

Supporting your opinion

Your opinion should be supported by other information, from your reading, your experience, or your knowledge of the world.
The textbook says (that) …, In my experience …, There are famous / good examples of …, X is a good example of …

Agreeing and disagreeing

I agree (with you). Yes, and …
I don't agree (with you). Yes, but …, Sorry, I don't agree with that.

7.2 Present simple passive (1): Describing facts and processes

Use the present simple in the passive form to describe facts and processes (they are generally true, rather than in progress). The focus is on the topic, e.g. *water*, *plants*. Use the present simple passive to describe what happens to it.
*Water **is used** in hydroelectric power. Plants **are grown** for biofuels.*

To form the present simple passive, use the present tense of the verb *be* (*is* / *are*) + the past participle of the main verb.

Positive	Water **is used** in hydroelectric power. Plants **are grown** for biofuels.
Negative	Water **isn't used** … Plants **aren't grown** …
Question	**Is** water **used** …? **Are** plants **grown** …?

The object of the active sentence becomes the subject of the passive sentence. The meaning of the two sentences is the same.

Active pattern (s–v–o):
Hydroelectric power uses water.
    s   v   o

Passive pattern (s–passive verb–prepositional phrase):
Water is used in hydroelectric power.
  s   v

Past participles

Add *-ed* to form the past participle of a regular verb (*heated*). Many past participles are irregular (*grow – grown*). See page 158 for a list of past participles of common irregular verbs.

7.3 Present simple passive (2): Describing a process

We often use the passive form to describe processes.

Passive pattern (s–passive verb–agent):
*Water **is heated** by the Sun.* (= the Sun heats the water)
*The turbines **are driven** by the wind.* (= the wind drives the turbines)

The phrase *by …* describes the **agent**, i.e. who / what does the action. Use the agent when it's important to say who / what does the action.

Passive pattern (s–passive verb–prepositional phrase):
Coffee is grown in several African countries.

Sometimes you don't need to say the agent (e.g. *by farmers*) if it's not necessary or not important. A prepositional phrase gives information to complete the sentence.

7.4 Linking language (6): Describing steps in a process

Signposting order

Linking language helps a listener or reader to understand the order of information.
First / Firstly / First of all → Second / Secondly → Then → Next → After that → Finally

Use linking language to signpost steps in a process. Linking expressions usually come first in the sentence.

1. Use a form of *First / Second / Third*, etc. in number order. You can say *Secondly, …*, etc. but NOT ~~Second of all, …~~
2. Use *then*, *next*, and *after that* in any order.
3. Use *Finally*, *Lastly* for the final step in the process.

154 LANGUAGE REFERENCE

4 Use *Overall, In general, To sum up, On the whole* to conclude and comment on the process.
*Solar energy can be used to heat solar water tanks in people's homes. **First of all**, cold water is pumped to solar panels on the roof. **Then** the water in the panels is heated by the Sun. **Next**, the heated water is transferred to a tank. It is stored in the tank. **Finally**, the water is sent to the taps in the house. **Overall**, solar energy is more efficient in hotter countries.*

When ... to link steps

Use a sentence pattern with *When* ... to link one step in a process to the next.
***When** the cold water reaches the solar panels, it is heated by the Sun.*
***When** the water is hot, it is transferred to a tank.*

Unit 8

8.1 Cause and effect (1): Verbs

Cause and effect relationships are common in academic study. It is important to be clear about which things are **causes** and which things are **effects**, e.g. *Building a new hotel* (= cause) *creates new jobs / traffic problems / more visitors* (= positive and negative effects).

Use the verbs *cause, create, lead to, produce* to express cause and effect relationships. In these s-v-o sentences, the subject is the cause, and the object is the effect.

```
     S              V         O
```
*The growth in air travel **causes** increased pollution.*
*New businesses **create** jobs.*
*More traffic **leads to** problems on the roads.*
*Coal **produces** CO_2. / Nuclear power **doesn't produce** CO_2.*

Use *-s* after the verbs with *he / she / it*.
*New businesses create jobs. A new hotel create**s** local jobs.*

In a cause → effect chain, an effect of one thing becomes the cause of something else.
New businesses create local jobs. More people with jobs leads to more traffic. More traffic causes problems on the roads.

Use *this* to refer back to a cause.
*More people with jobs leads to more traffic. **This** causes problems on the roads.*

This refers to 'more traffic' and the idea that 'More people with jobs leads to more traffic'.

8.2 Expressing possibility: Modals *could, might,* and *may*

Sometimes a cause → effect relationship is not 100% certain. In these cases, don't use the present simple. Use a modal verb *can, could, might,* or *may* + the infinitive form of a cause / effect verb.
lead to – *Building new hotels **can** / **could lead to** more tourists.*
cause – *Developing beach resorts **might cause** increased pollution.*
create – *More tourists **may create** local jobs.*

Use *might not* or *may not*. Don't use *could not*.
*Developing beach resorts **might not cause** increased pollution.*
NOT *...**couldn't cause** increased pollution.*

8.3 Cause and effect (2): Introducing cause with prepositions

As an alternative to a verb, use the prepositions *because of, as a result of, due to* to introduce a cause. Be careful to use the complete preposition (***Due to** tourism* ... NOT *Due tourism* ...).

Use the pattern **cause → effect** or **effect → cause**. Always put the preposition before the cause.

cause → effect
***Because of** the growth in tourism, cultures are becoming more mixed.*
***As a result of** the internet, booking a holiday is easier.*
***Due to** increased traffic, air quality is going down.*

Use a comma (,) after the cause phrase.

effect → cause
*Cultures are becoming more mixed **because of** the growth in tourism.*
*Booking a holiday is easier **as a result of** the internet.*
*Air quality is going down **due to** increased traffic.*

8.4 Cause and effect (3): Active and passive

When talking about cause and effect, you can use an active or a passive sentence pattern.

Active pattern:
*Tourism **creates** new jobs.*
*New jobs **produce** economic benefits.*

Passive pattern:
*New jobs **are created** by tourism.*
*Economic benefits **are produced** by new jobs.*

Note the position of cause and effect in active / passive sentences. The two sentences have the same meaning.

Use *lead to* in the active, but NOT in the passive.

8.5 Sentences (3): Writing about cause and effect

Use a variety of sentence patterns to write about cause and effect. Use a mixture of cause / effect verbs, active and passive sentences, and prepositions. Remember, use prepositions before the cause.

Active

Cause + verb + effect.
Tourism creates / leads to / produces economic benefits.

Passive

Effect + verb + *by* + cause.
Economic benefits are created / produced by tourism.

Preposition before the cause

Use a comma (,) after the cause phrase when it starts the sentence.
***Due to** tourism, there are economic benefits.*
***As a result of** tourism, there are economic benefits.*
*There are economic benefits **because of** tourism.*

Unit 9

9.1 Past events: Past simple and present perfect

Use the past simple and the present perfect to describe academic theories and discoveries.

Past simple

Use the past simple for finished events and discoveries in the past.

*Galileo **discovered** Jupiter's moons.*

Use a past time reference to show when the event happened.

*Galileo **discovered** Jupiter's moons in the early 17th century.*
*Charles W. Hull **invented** the first working 3D printer in 1984.*
*In the 19th century cities **had** much smaller populations.*

Present perfect

Use the present perfect to connect events in the past to the present. These events happened in the past, but they are still significant now.

*The discoveries of Galileo **have influenced** astronomers.*

Use a time reference to show the period up to the present.

*The discoveries of Galileo **have influenced** astronomers over the last 400 years.*
*The work of Shakespeare **has influenced** writers for 400 years.*
*Recently new technologies **have made** printing cheaper.*

9.2 Referring to evidence: Reporting verbs

Use a reporting verb + *that* to refer to evidence from sources (e.g. books, online articles).

Use an s–v–o pattern. Say *who / what* + **verb that** + what is reported.

***Dunbar* states that** *humans communicate with a maximum of 150 people.*

The verbs *say, state, show, report* are neutral. Use *believe, suggest* to be more cautious.

*Some scientists **believe that** Dunbar is correct.*
*Other research **suggests that** this number is too low.*

You can also use the verb *support*.

*The latest research **doesn't support** Dunbar's theory.*

9.3 Past simple passive: Describing discoveries and inventions

Use the past simple in the passive form to focus on a discovery or invention.

*Penicillin **was discovered** in 1928.*

To form the past simple passive, use *be* (*was / were*) + the past participle of the main verb. Add *-ed* to form the past participle of a regular verb (*discovered*). See page 158 for a list of past participles of common irregular verbs.

Use *by* + agent to emphasize who did the action.

*Penicillin was discovered **by Alexander Fleming**.*

Use the past simple passive form to describe steps in a process in the past.

*The Morse Code letters **were put** into the machine by a trained operator. Then they **were sent** over telegraph wires. Finally, the message **was received** at the other end.*

9.4 Perspective: Expressions and vocabulary

Perspective is very important in academic contexts. A topic or idea is often analysed from different perspectives, e.g. medical, economic, historical.

Often, the perspective is stated clearly.

***Economically speaking**, online shopping is profitable for businesses.*
***From a financial perspective**, online shopping can cause problems for the retailer.*
***In terms of education**, consumers need to learn about the new technology.*

Sometimes the perspective is stated using related vocabulary, e.g. the topic of *money* expresses a financial perspective.

*The latest proposal is interesting, but it will probably be **expensive**.* (financial perspective)
*Because people's **tastes** vary, companies adapt their food products for different parts of the **world**.* (cultural / global perspectives)

9.5 Sentences (4): Changing emphasis with active / passive / *by*

Choose the past simple active or passive to fit the focus of your writing.

Past simple active

Use the past simple active to focus on the person (e.g. inventor, writer).

*Spencer **discovered** that microwaves could cook food.*
*Shakespeare **wrote** Hamlet.*

Past simple passive

Use the past simple passive to focus on the thing (e.g. the invention, discovery, work, product). Use *by* + agent to refer to the person.

*Microwaves **were discovered** by Spencer.*
*Hamlet **was written** by Shakespeare.*

Tip: If you are writing about a person, e.g. Spencer and his life, use the past simple active and use *Spencer ... He ...* as the subject of most sentences. If your topic is a thing, e.g. the discovery of microwaves, use the past simple passive and use *Microwaves ... They ...* as the subject of most sentences.

9.6 Linking language (7): Using pronouns and determiners for cohesion

Pronouns and possessive determiners

Cohesion is how a text is connected in terms of meaning and language. Pronouns and determiners are important grammatical language for cohesion.

Use pronouns and determiners to avoid repetition of the main subject.

*Shakespeare was a writer. **He** was also an actor. **This** gave **him** the opportunity to understand how actors work with texts. **His** plays are still performed around the world.*

Use possessive determiners instead of possessive 's,
e.g. *Shakespeare's plays* → **his** *plays*.

Subject pronouns	Object pronouns	Possessive determiners
I	me	my
you (s.)	you	your
he	him	his
she	her	her
it	it	its
we	us	our
you (pl.)	you	your
they	them	their

Demonstrative determiners

Use demonstrative determiners *this / that / these / those* to refer back to a word or idea.

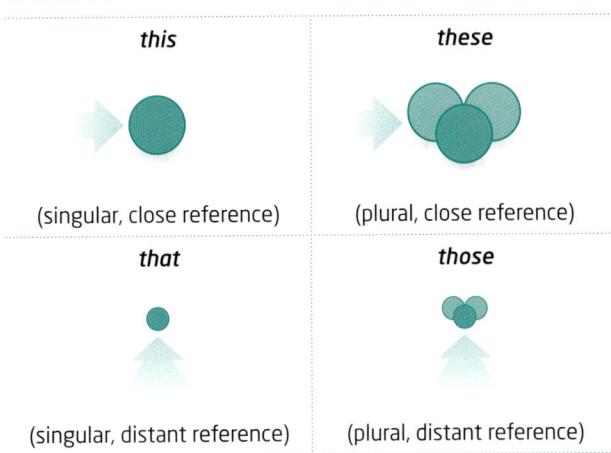

this
(singular, close reference)

these
(plural, close reference)

that
(singular, distant reference)

those
(plural, distant reference)

The most common demonstrative determiners in academic texts are *this* and *these*.
Shakespeare is famous for Hamlet *and* Romeo and Juliet. **These plays** *are performed all over the world.*

Unit 10

10.1 Questions (1): Open and closed questions

Open questions, e.g. *What's your name?* can have any answer. Closed questions have limited answers, usually *Yes* or *No*. Use a mixture of open and closed questions to get information.
   Why do businesses do research? **Does** *this research really help them?*

Open questions

Use open questions to ask for information on any topic.

Question words: *What, Where, Why, Who, When, How, How much / many, How often*, etc.
   What *are the benefits of historical research?*
   Why *do businesses do research?*
   How *do governments help businesses?*

Closed questions

Use closed questions to check something.

Question verb forms: *Is / Are … , Do / Does … , Have / Has … , Can … , Will …* , etc.
   Is *it easy to start a business in your country?*
   Does *he get a grant to study here?*
   Can *businesses get loans easily?*

You can add extra information when you answer a closed question:
   Is it easy for businesses to get loans in Italy? – Yes, but it can take a long time to get the money.

10.2 Collocation: Verb + noun

Collocations are two words which naturally go together, e.g. *give a presentation*. Verb + noun collocations are very common in academic texts. Often, a verb can go with a number of nouns.

Some common **verb** + noun collocations:
   do *research*, **discuss** *an idea*, **examine** *the evidence*, **give** *a presentation*, **list** *the main points*, **draw** *conclusions*, **record** *data*

Some **verb** + multiple noun collocations:
   analyse *data / feedback / results / a problem*
   ask for *information / feedback / an opinion / advice*
   carry out *research / a study / an experiment / a survey*
   explain *the meaning / the significance / the importance* (*of sth*)
   define *a word / a technical term / the objectives / the aim*

10.3 Questions (2): Form and tense

Use a variety of question forms and tenses for questions in a questionnaire.

Present simple

Closed	**Is** your house far from the university? **Do** you **stay** in expensive hotels?
Open	**Where** would you prefer to study? **How many** lectures **do** you **have** each week?

Present progressive

Closed	**Are** you **learning** a foreign language?
Open	**Why are** you **studying** Portuguese?

Past simple

Closed	**Were** your results good? **Did** you **have** an interview for the course?
Open	**When did** you **leave** school? **Which** school **did** you **go** to?

Present perfect

Closed	**Have** you **seen** this brand before? **Have** you **hired** a car in a foreign country?
Open	**How often have** you **used** the Student Union? **Which** other universities **have** you **visited**?

LANGUAGE REFERENCE 157

Modal verbs

Closed	**Will** you **buy** a new phone in the next year? **Would** you ever **change** banks?
Open	**Where will** you **study** next year? **Where can** you **buy** printers?

10.4 Sentences (5): The language of reports

Each stage of a report has a different purpose. Use key phrases to indicate the different stages.

The aim of this report is to find out what students think about the library facilities.

Stating aims and purpose

To say what you will cover and why.
The aim of this report is to …
This report aims to …
The purpose of the survey was to …

Explaining research methods and response rate

To say how you did the research and how many people responded.
The research was carried out by …
The research methods were …
The questionnaire focused on …
The response rate was …

Presenting results

To say what results you got.
With reference to / Regarding the question of …
According to 45% of the respondents, …
A majority of respondents reported that …
The responses show / suggest that …

Discussing results

To talk about the significance of your results.
These responses suggest that …
The results clearly show that …
(Overall,) the results are interesting / surprising because …

Common irregular verbs in OEAP A2

Present	Past simple	Past participle
be	was / were	been
become	became	become
begin	began	begun
build	built	built
burn	burned / burnt	burned / burnt
buy	bought	bought
choose	chose	chosen
come	came	come
cost	cost	cost
dig	dug	dug
do	did	done
draw	drew	drawn
drive	drove	driven
eat	ate	eaten
fall	fell	fallen
find	found	found
fly	flew	flown
get	got	got
give	gave	given
go	went	gone
grow	grew	grown
have	had	had
hear	heard	heard
keep	kept	kept
know	knew	known
lead to	led to	led to
learn	learned / learnt	learned / learnt
leave	left	left
make	made	made
mean	meant	meant
meet	met	met
pay	paid	paid
put	put	put
read	read	read
rise	rose	risen
run	ran	run
say	said	said
see	saw	seen
sell	sold	sold
send	sent	sent
show	showed	shown
speak	spoke	spoken
spend	spent	spent
swim	swam	swum
take	took	taken
teach	taught	taught
tell	told	told
think	thought	thought
understand	understood	understood
write	wrote	written

Writing Sample answers

Unit 1C Writing (2) TASK 3 (page 019)

My name's Drew Tomlinson. I'm 18 years old **and** I'm from Canada.[1] I have an international baccalaureate from my school in Vancouver. My favourite subjects are economics and politics. In my free time I like playing soccer in the summer and ice hockey in the winter. In the future, I **plan to** do a degree in management because I'm interested in business.[2]

▶ **Key features in Academic Writing**
[1] Join sentences with conjunctions.
[2] Use the correct verb form to refer to the present or future.

Unit 2C Writing (2) TASK 3 (page 033)

Microsoft is a **large, global** software company.[1] It is based in the **USA**, but it has offices all over the world.[2] You can buy its products from computer shops or order them online. **In addition,** when you buy computer equipment, it often comes with Microsoft products on it.[3]

▶ **Key features in Academic Writing**
[1] Use noun phrases with adjectives.
[2] Use capital letters when necessary.
[3] Join sentences with linking language.

Unit 3C Writing (2) TASK 3 (page 047)

There are a number of similarities and differences between the universities of Oxford and Cambridge.[1] **Both** universities are the most famous in England and about 100 kilometres from London. **Similarly,** they are the two oldest in the country.[2] On the other hand, the city of Oxford is bigger than Cambridge and has more students.[3] However, lots of international students go to both universities because the quality of the education is very high.[4]

▶ **Key features in Academic Writing**
[1] Introduce the comparison.
[2] Describe similarities using the language of comparison.
[3] Introduce differences.
[4] Conclude the paragraph.

Unit 4C Writing (2) TASK 3 (page 061)

The chart shows worldwide commercial vehicle production in 2012.[1] There are ten countries in total and over half of these countries produce more than one million vehicles per year.[2] The USA is the world's main producer, with **around** six million vehicles per year.[3] Next, China produces nearly four million and then Thailand, Canada, Japan, and Mexico produce over one million per year. The other four countries produce less than one million vehicles per year.[4]

▶ **Key features in Academic Writing**
[1] Introduce the title of the chart.
[2] Give general information about what the chart shows.
[3] Simplify the numbers.
[4] Give information about the main / other countries.

Unit 5C Writing (2) TASK 3 (page 075)

A webcam is a type of camera with a microphone for communicating through a computer or laptop.[1] In other words, it shows the speaker to another person at a different location. For example, people can see each other and show things while they speak.[2] **In particular,** the device is very useful for international business.[3]

▶ **Key features in Academic Writing**
[1] Define the term.
[2] Explain the definition with more detail and give an example.
[3] Use linking language.

Unit 6C Writing (2) TASK 3 (page 089)

The graph shows employed workers in the United Kingdom from 2008 to 2012.[1] Overall, there was a steady fall in the number of employed people.[2] In 2008 there were 25.4 million employed workers and this figure **fell rapidly** by 2009. However, there was **a slight rise** from 2010 to 2011 and then it stayed the same.[3] Experts think that employment will increase in the next few years.[4]

▶ Key features in Academic Writing
[1]Introduce the topic of the graph.
[2]Describe the overall trend.
[3]Describe other trends with verb + adverb and adjective + noun.
[4]Give a future prediction.

Unit 7C Writing (2) TASK 3 (page 103)

Solar energy is often used in hot climates for generating electricity. This diagram shows how the process works.[1] **First of all,** the Sun **heats** a solar PV panel. This generates electricity and a battery stores it. **Next,** the power **is converted** by an inverter and **finally** the electricity is used in the house.[2] Overall, it's a clean, efficient way to generate electricity.[3]

▶ Key features in Academic Writing
[1]Introduce the topic and the diagram.
[2]Describe the steps with linking language and sequencing words, and verbs in active and passive forms.
[3]Give an evaluation at the end.

Unit 8C Writing (2) TASK 2 (page 117)

Agri-tourism is a type of environmentally friendly tourism. It is when people stay on a farm or ranch for a holiday. For example, about 2.5 million agri-tourists visit farms and ranches in California every summer.[1] They learn about agriculture and this produces extra income for the farmers. In addition, agri-tourism creates employment for local people. The only negative impact is the increase in traffic in the countryside **because of** the tourists.[2/3] Overall, agri-tourism in California is a good example of how tourism can have a positive impact.[4]

▶ Key features in Academic Writing
[1]Introduce the term with a definition and example.
[2]Describe positive and negative impacts.
[3]Use cause and effect language.
[4]Conclude the paragraph.

Unit 9C Writing (2) TASK 4 (page 131)

Ajay Bhatt is an inventor and computer architect. He was born in India in 1957, but studied in the USA. In 1990, he joined the company Intel.[1] At Intel he **invented** different computer technologies and he **has become** famous for co-inventing USB technology.[2/3] Before the mid-nineties, computer devices were connected in different ways, but **his** USB invention solved the problem.[4] Nowadays, all computer devices use this technology.[5]

▶ Key features in Academic Writing
[1]Include information about the inventor.
[2]Refer to the invention.
[3]Use a range of tenses and verb forms.
[4]Use pronouns, determiners, and reference words for cohesion.
[5]Explain the impact of the invention.

Unit 10C Writing (2) TASK 3 (page 145)

The aim of the report is to look at how university students use technology. The purpose of the survey was to analyse the average time spent on the internet by students and the type of technologies used.[1] The research was carried out by an online survey and the response rate was approximately 33%.[2] With reference to the question of time spent on the internet, the survey **shows that** students use it for academic research and social media. According to most of the respondents, they use personal laptops, tablets, and mobile phones or handheld devices. Overall, the results **suggest that** most students use laptops and mobile phones to access the internet for their studies, but they also use it for leisure.[3]

▶ Key features in Academic Writing
[1]State the aim and purpose.
[2]Describe the method.
[3]Summarize and discuss the main results using reporting language.

Additional material from units

Unit 10A Listening & Speaking TASK 5 (page 137)

Student A

1 Read the information in the table about research methods. Some information is missing.
2 Ask Student B questions to find out the missing information about each research method. Note down the answers in the table.
3 Answer Student B's questions using the information in the table.

Useful questions

Can you explain what … is?
How does it work, exactly?

Why do people use this research method?
What are the advantages of this type of research?
Is there a disadvantage?

What does … mean, exactly?
Do you mean …?

Research method	Explanation	Advantage(s)	Disadvantage(s)
Personal interview	An interview conducted face-to-face in the street, in an office, or in a person's home	High quality results Can use materials (e.g. pictures, products) High response rate	Expensive Takes a lot of time Respondents are all in the same place
Telephone interview			
Email interview	A questionnaire sent by email – the respondent has to complete it and email it back to the interviewer	Easy for respondents Easy to reach a lot of people Not expensive	No control over the respondent Response rate can be low
Online questionnaire			
Focus group discussion		Provides a lot of information in a short time	Expensive The discussion can be difficult to manage Small number of respondents

SOURCE: Adapted from Bradley, N. 2010. p.138. *Marketing Research* 3rd ed. Oxford: Oxford University Press.

Unit 5A Listening & Speaking TASK 4 (page 067)

Student B

Smart materials

Smart materials are a type of material with special features. They can change colour, shape, and even temperature. Modern sunglasses are a good example of smart materials. Sunglasses with smart materials become darker when you are outside in the Sun and lighter when you walk inside a building.

SOURCE: Adapted from Russell, B. et al. 2011. p.128. *Design and Technology*. Cheltenham: Nelson Thornes.

Unit 6C Writing (1) TASK 3 (page 087)

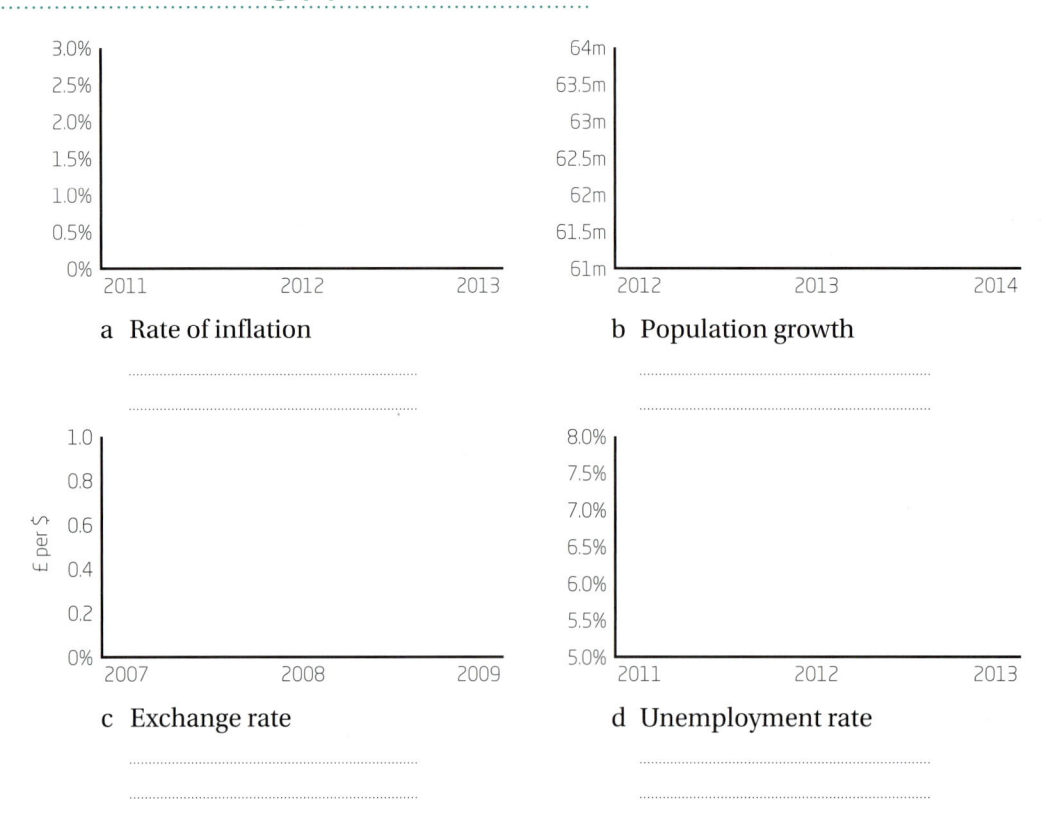

a Rate of inflation

b Population growth

c Exchange rate

d Unemployment rate

Unit 10A Listening & Speaking TASK 5 (page 137)

Student B

1 Read the information in the table about research methods. Some information is missing.
2 Answer Student A's questions using the information in the table.
3 Ask Student A questions to find out the missing information about each research method. Note down the answers in the table.

Useful questions

Can you explain what … is?
How does it work, exactly?

Why do people use this research method?
What are the advantages of this type of research?
Is there a disadvantage?

What does … mean, exactly?
Do you mean …?

Research method	Explanation	Advantage(s)	Disadvantage(s)
Personal interview			
Telephone interview	An interview on the telephone, where the interviewer calls the respondent	Fast - gives quick results. Interviewer can ask for more information	Interviewer cannot use any materials. People may not like being called
Email interview			
Online questionnaire	A questionnaire on a website which respondents go to via a link - they get this via email or text	Fast - gives quick results from a lot of respondents. Not expensive. Results are easy to analyse	No control over the respondent. Very low response rate
Focus group discussion	A small group of people who are asked to discuss and give their opinion on a specific subject		

SOURCE: Adapted from Bradley, N. 2010. p.138. *Marketing Research* 3rd ed. Oxford: Oxford University Press.

Answer key

Unit 1

Vocabulary

1 1 1 A V, B N
   2 A V, B N
   3 A V, B N
   4 A N, B V
   5 A V, B N
   6 A N, B V
 2 Student's own answers
2 1 1 <u>read</u>, textbooks
   2 <u>make</u>, notes
   3 <u>do</u>, exercises
   4 <u>watch</u>, videos
   5 <u>find</u>, solutions
   6 <u>listen to</u>, lectures
 2 1 repeat
   2 do
   3 develop
   4 give
   5 practise
   6 remember

Academic Language Check

1 1 1 'm
   2 doesn't want
   3 aren't
   4 plan
   5 's
   6 hope
   7 studies
   8 don't like
 2 1 N
   2 F
   3 N
   4 F
   5 N
   6 F
   7 N
   8 N
 3 3 Are history and geography difficult subjects?
   4 Do they plan to study science at university?
   5 Is he interested in information technology?
   6 Do we/they hope to work in the USA next year?
   7 Does she study economics at a business school?
   8 Do you/I like doing examinations?
2 1 1 you start
   2 you need
   3 try
   4 make
   5 listen
   6 talk
   7 's

 3 1 1 b
   2 d
   3 e
   4 c
   5 a
   6 f
 2 Student's own answers

Unit 2

Vocabulary

1 1 1 website
   2 home
   3 links
   4 PDFs
   5 search
   6 names
 2 1 2 organization
   3 entertainment
   4 presentation
   5 advertisement
   6 education
 2 Student's own answers.
 3 1 1 c
   2 g
   3 f
   4 e
   5 h
   6 a
   7 d
   8 b
 2 1 important
   2 useful
   3 easy
   4 modern
   5 expensive
   6 unreliable

Academic Language Check

1 1 1 Firstly
   2 Secondly
   3 Finally
   4 In addition
   5 Also
 2 1 1 <u>A search box</u> is <u>an important feature</u>.
   2 <u>A news website</u> has <u>information</u>.
   3 <u>A website</u> has <u>different links</u>.
   4 <u>A modern university</u> has <u>good resources</u>.
 2 a information
   b a search box, a news website
   c different links, good resources
   d a website
   e an important feature, a modern university

 3 1 1 Apple is a global IT company.
   2 Al Jazeera is an international TV news channel.
   3 Harvard is a famous American university.
   4 Google is a free search engine.
   5 *The Economist* is a popular weekly magazine.
4 1 1 but
   2 or
   3 so
   4 in addition
   5 also

Unit 3

Vocabulary

1 1 1 location
   2 cost
   3 rent
   4 customers
   5 expensive
   6 employees
   7 profit
 2 1 1 transport links
   2 office space
   3 sports facilities
   4 individual needs
   5 land costs
 3 1 1 f
   2 b
   3 g
   4 d
   5 e
   6 a
   7 c

Academic Language Check

1 1 2 high
   3 highest
   4 bigger
   5 busy
   6 most modern
   7 important
   8 more important
   9 least expensive
   10 good
   11 best
   12 worse

164 ANSWER KEY

2 1 The population of Los Angeles is ~~more~~ **larger** than the population of Atlanta.
2 São Paulo is **bigger** than Rio de Janeiro.
3 Dubai is **more modern** than Rome.
4 Shopping online is less **expensive** than shopping in the high street.
5 Accommodation in London is the **most** expensive in the UK.
6 Athens is one of **the oldest** cities in Europe.
7 I'm the ~~more~~ **youngest** in my family.
8 My city has the ~~most~~ **best** transport links in the world.

2 1 1 Similarly
2 But
3 addition
4 similarities
5 difference

2 1 e
2 c
3 b
4 d
5 a

Unit 4

Vocabulary

1 1 1 British
2 Germany
3 American
4 Canada
5 Chinese
6 Spain
7 Indonesian
8 Turkey
9 Australian
10 Saudi Arabia
2 Student's own answers

2 1 2 money
3 food
4 a country
5 a company

2 1 exports
2 spends
3 grows
4 visit
5 manage

3 1 1 look at
2 Moving
3 see
4 shows
5 is
6 Notice

Academic Language Check

1 1 1 33,000,000
2 ½
3 3,500,000
4 10,000,000
5 45%
6 95%
7 ¼

2 1 two thirds
2 A few
3 Most
4 A fifth
5 three quarters
6 Nearly a third
7 a half
8 two fifths

2 1 1 began
2 received
3 started
4 didn't have
5 joined
6 sold
7 bought
8 built
9 was
10 rented
11 paid

Unit 5

Vocabulary

1 1 1 Kevlar is a hard material.
2 ASIMO is a short, white robot.
3 Thermosetting plastic is a modern, heat-resistant material.
4 An integrated circuit is a small, square piece of technology.
5 Kingfishers have long, narrow beaks.
6 Time Warner is a large, global media company.

2 1 1 A N, B V
2 A V, B N
3 A N, B V
4 A N, B V
5 A N, B V

3 1 1 by
2 of
3 at
4 to
5 of
6 with
7 to
8 of
9 from
10 about

2 a verb + preposition: 1, 3, 4, 7, 9
a noun + preposition: 2, 5, 6, 8, 10

Academic Language Check

1 1 1 refers
2 example
3 particular
4 is
5 such as

2 1 d
2 b
3 e
4 h
5 a
6 g
7 c
8 f

3 1 The Greek word *ergon* relates to 'work' and 'organization'.
2 Kevlar has many useful features. In particular, it's a strong material.
3 CAD software is for creating new products. In other words, you can use it for design.
4 Ergonomic design refers to design for human use, for example, the modern keyboard.

Unit 6

Vocabulary

1 1 1 employs
2 employees
3 employers
4 Employed
5 Unemployed
6 employed
7 Unemployment
8 employment

2 1 ↑ climb, go up, grow, increase
↓ decrease, fall, go down
→ stay the same
2 Noun forms: a climb, a decrease, a fall, an increase

3 1 1 inflation
2 exchange rate
3 unemployment
4 population
5 tax
2 Student's own answers.

ANSWER KEY 165

Academic Language Check

1 1 1 is falling
      2 gets
      3 are staying
      4 means
      5 is going up
      6 don't understand
      7 is / rising
      8 do / pay
   2 1 invested
      2 had
      3 lost
      4 are putting
      5 are growing
      6 will continue
      7 has
      8 will become

2 1 1 In
      2 from
      3 to
      4 by
      5 In
      6 from
      7 to
      8 by
   2 1 T
      2 T
      3 T
      4 Q
      5 P
      6 Q
      7 Q
      8 T

3 1 1 a slight decrease
      2 a slow rise
      3 grew rapidly
      4 increases slightly
      5 a steady climb

Unit 7

Vocabulary

1 1 1 biofuel
      2 Wind
      3 hydroelectric
      4 oil
      5 Wood
      6 wave
      7 gas
      8 Nuclear
      9 Solar
     10 Coal

2 1 1 dangerous
      2 expensive
      3 reliable
      4 beautiful
      5 noisy
      6 useful

   2 2 dangerous, safe
      3 expensive, cheap
      4 reliable, unreliable
      5 beautiful, ugly
      6 noisy, quiet
      7 useful, useless

Academic Language Check

1 1 1 opinion
      2 examples
      3 agree
      4 with
      5 think
      6 what
      7 Yes
      8 says
      9 don't
   2 Student's own answers

2 1 1 Solar panels are heated
      2 Hydroelectricity is generated
      3 Turbines are designed
      4 Sea water is moved
      5 Plants are grown
   2 2 heats solar panels
      3 generates hydroelectricity
      4 design turbines
      5 moves sea water up and down
      6 grow plants for food but also for biofuel

3 1 1 First of all
      2 Then
      3 When
      4 Finally
      5 Overall

Unit 8

Vocabulary

1 1 1 impact
      2 travel
      3 Local
      4 leisure
      5 communities
      6 global
      7 beliefs
      8 footprint
      9 economic
     10 holiday
   2 2 NN
      3 AN
      4 NN
      5 AN
      6 AN
      7 AN
      8 NN
      9 AN
     10 NN

2 1 1 for
      2 on
      3 to
      4 on
      5 to
      6 of
      7 at
      8 in
      9 to
     10 from

Academic Language Check

1 1 Suggested answers:
      1 Online booking creates cheaper holidays.
      2 More aeroplanes produce noise pollution.
      3 More business creates more local jobs.
      4 More tourism causes more litter.
   2 1 Cheaper holidays are created by online booking.
      2 Noise pollution is produced by more aeroplanes.
      3 More local jobs are created by more business.
      4 More litter is caused by more tourism.
   3 1 Due to online booking, there are cheaper holidays.
      2 There is noise pollution as a result of more aeroplanes.
      3 There are more local jobs because of more business.
      4 Suggested answer: There is more litter because of more tourism.

2 1 1 New leisure facilities could **lead** to better health.
      2 The plan might **create** an increase in employment.
      3 More police on the street **may** (*or* **could**) lead to fewer crimes.
      4 Crowded beaches **might not** create a good atmosphere in the town.
      5 Improved public transport **might** (*or* **may**) not guarantee more tourists, but it's possible.

Unit 9

Vocabulary

1. 1. 1 economy
      2 educational
      3 historical
      4 medical
      5 politics
      6 sociological
      7 technology
      8 industry
      9 mathematics
      10 scientific
2. 1. 1 V, N
      2 N, V
      3 V, N
      4 V, N
      5 N, V
3. 1. 1 with, with a maximum of 150 people
      2 at, at the end of the 19th century
      3 by, by a group of scientists
      4 from, from Yale

Academic Language Check

1. 1. 1 has discovered
      2 made
      3 has recently published
      4 invented
      5 switched
      6 developed
      7 has grown
2. 1. 1 were discovered
      2 was invented
      3 were written
      4 was flown
      5 was reached
      6 was sent
      7 was made

3. 1. 2 your
      3 him
      4 she
      5 her
      6 it
      7 our
      8 them
   2. 1 it
      2 them
      3 He
      4 These
      5 Its

Unit 10

Vocabulary

1. 1. 1 interviews
      2 questionnaire
      3 online
      4 respondents
      5 results
      6 Research
      7 surveys
      8 Market
      9 objectives
2. 1. 1 set
      2 ask
      3 do
      4 set
      5 carry out
      6 set
      7 interview
      8 ask
   2. 1 have
      2 define
      3 draw / reach
      4 give
      5 analyse
      6 interview
      7 collect
      8 complete / fill in

Academic Language Check

1. 1. 1 Can
      2 How often
      3 Is
      4 What
      5 do
      6 Why
      7 does
2. 1. 1 **Are** you interested in our products?
      2 Does the university **help** you to find accommodation?
      3 How often do you **use** our hotels?
      4 Where **are** you currently studying?
      5 **Were** the exam questions difficult?
      6 When **did** Alexander Fleming discover penicillin?
      7 Did our representative **call** you back last week?
      8 Have you ever **used** our online library?
      9 How many times **has** she taken this exam?
      10 Will you **apply** to university next year?
   2. Student's own answers
3. 1. 1 e
      2 b
      3 c
      4 f
      5 a
      6 d

ANSWER KEY **167**

Transcripts

audio & video
audio only

Unit 1

1.1

design
engineering
English
geography
history
information technology
mathematics
media studies
physical education
science

1.2

I'm Shri Patel and I'm from India. We study hard at school in India because it's very difficult to enter a good university. You need high grades to enter the best universities. Maths and science are my favourite subjects at school, but at university I want to study management. Why? Well, I like management because the course is very practical. I like working in groups, but I don't like reading academic textbooks. So I think it's a good course for me.

1.3

I'm a student at university.
It's difficult.
Maths and science are my favourite subjects.

I like history.
They like watching videos.
She studies maths.

I'm not at university.
It isn't difficult.
They aren't my favourite subjects.

I don't like working in groups.
They don't like history.
She doesn't study English.

Are you a student?
Is she a lecturer?

Do you study science?
Do they like English?
Does he like reading?

1.4

I'm Leila Wong and I'm from Singapore. I was a chemical engineering student from the National University of Singapore, and now I plan to do a Master's degree in business. I like going to lectures, I like reading textbooks, and making notes. This works best for me. I want to study business because it's very useful for engineers – many engineers work for big companies and it's very important to understand how business works. In the future, I hope to become a project manager. I would like to work with people on international projects. So, that's me.

1.5

I plan to study business.
I hope to become a project manager.
She plans to work in logistics.
I don't want to study maths at university. I want to study management.

I'd like to study problems and find solutions.

Do you plan to study engineering?
Does she want to work in America?
What do you want to study?
Where does he hope to work?

1.6

Teacher Do you plan to study history at university?
Student No, I don't. I like history, but I'd like to work in business, so I want to do a business degree.
Teacher OK. Where do you hope to study?
Student Well, my brother plans to go to an American university next year. I'd like to go there too.

Unit 2

2.1 Extract 1

Hello. My name's Simon Philips. OK, today I'd like to talk about doing internet research for studying at university. We all use the internet because there's so much information out there. But how do you know which information is true? How do you know which websites can help you with research for your studies? So in this presentation, I'm going to talk about the features to look for in a website when you study.
My talk is in three parts. Firstly, the authority of a website. So, who writes it? Secondly, the design of a website. How does it look? How easy is it to use? And finally, information. What is good, useful content on a website?

2.2 Extract 2

OK, firstly, I'm going to talk about the authority of a website. When you look at a website for the first time, ask these questions: Is the website part of an organization or university? Who are the authors? What are their qualifications? In other words, check the authority of the website. Here's an example of an academic website with authority. The domain name ends in dot e-d-u which means it's an educational website. It also has a logo for a university. In addition, it has these headings for different subject areas.

Secondly, we'll look at the design of a website. Design is always important on a website. For example, this home page is very simple. It uses one image and one or two colours, so it looks academic and it has a search box at the top, so you can look up keywords and find information quickly. Also, the links are easy to read.

Finally, I'll talk about the information on a subject page. I clicked on *Research* and now I can see more information and there's an article as a PDF, and I can click on the PDF to open it. But before I read the whole article, I look at the title and the information about the author. I can look up the author's name on other websites if necessary.

OK. So, to sum up, before you use websites for research, check the authority of the website. Also, consider the design. Does it look academic and is it user-friendly, easy to use? And finally, check the information carefully. Are there any questions?

🔊 2.3

Firstly, …
Secondly, …
Finally, …
Firstly, I'm going to talk about the authority of a website.
Secondly, we'll look at the design.
Finally, I'll talk about the information on a subject page.

It also has …
In addition, …
Also, …
The domain name ends in dot e-d-u.
It also has a university logo.
In addition, it has subject headings.
Also, the links are easy to read.

🔊 2.4

I'm going to talk about the library's online resource. Firstly, we'll look at how you register on our website. Secondly, I'll talk about using the home page. And finally, I'll talk about the information on the site. In addition, I'll show you how to find specific information for your courses. We'll also have time for questions at the end.

Unit 3

▶ 3.1   Extract 1

OK, good morning. Welcome. So, 'Planning the Olympic Games'. Today we're going to focus on what the people who plan the Olympics think about when they choose an Olympic venue. I'm going to look at three factors. Firstly, the location of the Games. Secondly, transport links. And finally, the cost.

▶ 3.2   Extract 2

So, first let's start with the location of the Olympics. The Olympics is a major event, so location is important because you need space for the sports facilities such as the stadium, the swimming pools, and so on. So, the location of an Olympic Games has to be a big city. For example, London held the Olympics in 2012 and it's the biggest city in the UK. However, Olympic cities don't always have to be the biggest. In China, in 2008, Beijing was the city for the Olympics and it's smaller than Shanghai. And in Brazil in 2016, Rio de Janeiro is the Olympic city, but the city of São Paulo is bigger than Rio.

This brings me to my second point. The size of the city is important, but actually transport links are more important than size. Thousands of people travel to the Olympic Games, so the location needs good air, rail, and road links. So, for example, in 1996, the Games were in Atlanta in the USA. Again, Atlanta is not the biggest city in the USA, but it has a busy international airport. In fact, it's probably the busiest airport in the world.

Finally, let's look at cost. The Olympic Games are very expensive, so a city needs a lot of money from its government and sponsors. For example, the cost of the 2014 Winter Olympics in the Russian city of Sochi was very high, at around $50 billion. It was the most expensive Olympic Games in history …

🔊 3.3

London is older than Atlanta.
The cost of transport is higher than the cost of many facilities.
The location is more important than the size of the city.
Paris is less expensive than London.
This location is better because it has good transport links.
Road and rail transport are worse in this city.

🔊 3.4

Berlin is the biggest city in Germany.
Shinjuku station in Tokyo is the busiest train station in the world.
I think location is the most important factor.
People say that Bucharest is the least expensive city in Europe.
Is Rome, Sydney, or Delhi the best city for the next Olympic Games?

Unit 4

🔊 4.1

Brazil is in Latin America.
Canada is in North America.
Germany is in Europe.
Ghana is in Africa.
Indonesia is in Asia.
Oman is in the Middle East.

4.2

So firstly, let's look at this chart. It shows exports of cocoa around the world. So these figures are the world's main cocoa producers and these are the percentages of their exports. For example, Indonesia exports 13%, Ghana exports 15%, Brazil 8%, and so on. And notice this. The Ivory Coast exports nearly a half of the world's cocoa. So, as you can see, most of the exporters of cocoa are African or Latin American countries, with two countries in Asia.

Moving on, here you can see the major consumers by country and the amount of cocoa here, in thousands of tonnes. So, the USA imports around 900,000 tonnes per year. Germany imports a third of that and here are other European importers like France, the UK, Italy, and Spain. Russia imports approximately 150,000 tonnes. But this is interesting because Brazil is the only major Latin American consumer. So those countries on the first chart were the main producers, but most of them aren't the main consumers.

OK. Now let's see how much a cocoa producer actually earns in this process. This is my final chart. It's a chart of where your money goes when you buy a bar of chocolate in the UK. The chocolate costs one pound in the shop and about half of this is for the chocolate company. More than a fifth is for the shop, with 15 pence in tax for the UK government. And look at this number – the cocoa farmer earns only seven pence out of every pound.

4.3

0, 11, 15, 71, 101, 1,010, 101,000, 1,000,000
3%, 13%, 33%
99.2, approximately one hundred, about one hundred, around one hundred
a half, a quarter, three quarters, a third, two thirds, a fifth
35%, more than a third, 24%, nearly a quarter, 22%, less than a quarter

4.4

19% – approximately a fifth
48% – nearly a half
51% – around a half
66% – about two-thirds
75% – three quarters
99% – nearly one hundred per cent

4.5

1 Ecuador exports 3% of the world's cocoa.
2 Nearly two thirds of the price is for the supplier.
3 Brazil consumes about 100,000 tonnes of chocolate per year.
4 Farmers receive around 5% of the total price.
5 We export half of our production every year.
6 A quarter of the costs is transportation.

Unit 5

5.1 Extracts 1–3

1 Biomimetics is the scientific study of design in nature and its application in the design of man-made objects. In other words, an engineer or an architect can get ideas for new buildings by studying design in the natural world. Let me explain by giving you a famous example.
2 This is the Japanese bullet train, or Shinkansen. It's a good example of 20th-century engineering. It can travel very fast – at around 300 kilometres per hour. It carries over 150 million people per year and it has a 100% safety record. The Shinkansen is also a good example of biomimetic design. Let me explain why.
3 The design of the train is based on this. A kingfisher. It's a very fast bird with a long, narrow beak. The train's chief engineer Eiji Nakatsu was a keen birdwatcher and he watched how a kingfisher flies quickly from open air into water because of the shape of its beak. As a result, Nakatsu designed the front of the train like the beak of a kingfisher, so it can travel at very high speeds.

5.2

This is the Japanese bullet train, or Shinkansen. It's a good example of 20th-century engineering. It can travel very fast – at around 300 kilometres per hour. It carries over 150 million people per year and it has a 100% safety record. The Shinkansen is also a good example of biomimetic design. Let me explain why.

The design of the train is based on this. A kingfisher. It's a very fast bird with a long, narrow beak. The train's chief engineer Eiji Nakatsu was a keen birdwatcher and he watched how a kingfisher flies quickly from open air into water because of the shape of its beak. As a result, Nakatsu designed the front of the train like the beak of a kingfisher, so it can travel at very high speeds.

5.3

Biomimetics is the scientific study of design in nature.
Kingfishers are very fast birds with a long, narrow beak.
In other words, …
Let me explain why.
Let me explain by giving you a famous example.
It's a good example of 20th-century engineering.
For example, …
Let me give you an example.
This is a good example of …

5.4

Fibre optics is the science of using glass or plastic fibre to transmit light. In other words, light can travel through cables made of fibre optics. Let me give you an example of fibre optics used in the telecommunications industry.

5.5 Extracts A and B

A

Thermosetting plastic is a special heat-resistant plastic for manufacturing electrical household appliances. In other words, it can become very hot, but it doesn't change shape. For example, a modern electric kettle is a household appliance made of thermosetting plastic.

B

An integrated circuit is a tiny piece of silicon with electronic circuits. Let me explain by showing you the inside of a computer. A computer has thousands of electronic components. This is a good example of an integrated circuit.

5.6

biology
bibliography
chronology
geography
psychology
physiology
sociology

Unit 6

6.1

employ
employee, employer
employed, unemployed, self-employed
employment, unemployment
full-time employment, part-time employment

6.2 Extract 1

All governments want high employment in their country. The working population is important because working people earn money and they spend it; in other words, it means you have a strong economy. On the other hand, you can never have 100% employment. Countries always have a dependent population. These people include students, older and retired people, parents with young children, or unemployed people who can't find a job or who don't want to work. Economists often measure the strength of an economy by comparing the percentage of the working population with the dependent population. For example, in a country like Brazil, with a total population of over 200 million, the working population is currently increasing and at the same time the dependent population is decreasing. That's because the number of younger people in work is rising and, especially, more and more women these days are going to work instead of staying at home. On the other hand, in a country such as Spain, the dependent population is increasing because the number of older and retired people is going up. In addition, the number of younger people in Spain is going down. That's because they're leaving Spain for new jobs in other countries. So at the moment the working population is falling.

6.3 Extract 2

… For example, in a country like Brazil, with a total population of over 200 million, the working population is currently increasing and at the same time the dependent population is decreasing. That's because the number of younger people in work is rising and, especially, more and more women these days are going to work instead of staying at home. On the other hand, in a country such as Spain, the dependent population is increasing because the number of older and retired people is going up. In addition, the number of younger people in Spain is going down. That's because they're leaving Spain for new jobs in other countries. So at the moment the working population is falling.

6.4

The working population is increasing.
Prices are falling.
The dependent population isn't rising.
Government taxes aren't going down.

The working population is currently increasing.
Prices are falling at the moment.

6.5

A Unemployment in my country is rising at the moment.
B Why is it rising?
A Because the population is increasing and there aren't any new jobs for young people.

Unit 7

7.1

Tutor So, in our seminar last week we talked about non-renewable energy resources such as oil and gas and renewables such as solar power and wind power. And if you remember, I also asked you to read the section in the textbook on nuclear power and to research some information about nuclear power online, because in our seminar today I'd like to discuss this question: 'Is nuclear power the best choice?' So, … Adam, what's your opinion?

Adam OK, well, the information in the textbook says that nuclear power is an effective alternative to fossil fuels and I agree. You need one gram of uranium fuel to produce the same amount of energy as eight kilos of fossil fuels. I also think it's better because it doesn't produce CO_2, so it's cleaner than fossil fuels. In addition, well, in my country, the UK, there are never any problems with power stations, so it's safe. I think we should build more nuclear power stations because, in the future, wind power and solar power won't produce enough energy.

Tutor OK, thanks Adam. Some good points there. Travis, what do you think? Do you agree with Adam?

Travis Well, I agree about fossil fuels and using cleaner energy, but in my opinion, nuclear power is very dangerous. Especially when you think about …

Adam Yes, but not if you store the waste safely …

Tutor One moment Adam. Let Travis finish.

Travis Sorry, I don't agree that it is safe. There are famous examples of nuclear accidents, such as Chernobyl in 1986 and Fukushima in 2011. Those were big environmental disasters. That's why in Germany the government plans to close all of the nuclear power stations over the next ten years. And Adam, you come from the UK with all that wind and sea. I think you should use more wind and wave power.

Adam Yes, I think we should too. But only 15% of the UK's energy comes from renewables, so in my opinion the UK can't live without nuclear power.

7.2

What's your opinion?
What do you think?
Do you agree?

I think …
I don't think …
In my opinion …

The textbook says …
In my experience …
There are famous examples of …
There are good examples of …

I agree.
I agree with you.
Yes, but …
I don't agree.
Sorry, I don't agree.

Unit 8

8.1

A OK, so we have to discuss the different impacts of tourism. First of all, who's going to take notes?
B I will.
A Great, thanks. OK, well let's start with the positive economic impact of tourism. Tourists spend money. So tourism creates more local business.
B Right. So business owners employ more people and this produces more jobs.
A OK. What about negative points? I can't think of any.
C Well, one negative point is seasonal employment because tourism could produce higher employment in the summer, but it may not create new jobs in the winter.
B Yes, I see. So there are fewer jobs out of season. OK. Got that.
A So what about social impact?
C I think facilities are important here. New facilities for tourists lead to better leisure facilities for local people as well.
B OK, local people might want better leisure facilities. But the facilities for tourists may be too expensive for local people.
C Er, yes, I suppose so …
A Actually, I think you're both right. But, anyway, that gives us a positive and a negative point for 'social impact'. Which just leaves the environmental impact, which is an easy one. I mean, for example, air travel causes pollution all over the world.
C Well, that's a negative point. What about a positive impact?
B Well, local people could plant trees and build parks. This might create a better environment for tourists and locals.
A Yes, exactly. In fact, in the town my family comes from, that's what local people have done …

8.2

Air travel causes pollution.
Tourism creates more local business.
More advertising leads to more visitors.
More business produces more jobs.

More advertising leads to more visitors. This creates more local business.

8.3 Extracts 1–3

1 One negative point is seasonal employment. Tourism could lead to higher employment in the summer, but it may not create new jobs in the winter.
2 Local people might want better leisure facilities. But the facilities for tourists may be too expensive for local people.

3 Local people could plant trees and build parks. And that might create a better environment for tourists and locals.

🔊 **8.4**

New facilities lead to more tourists.
New facilities could lead to more tourists.

More business creates jobs in the summer.
More business might create jobs in the summer.

Busy roads cause traffic problems.
Busy roads may cause traffic problems.

New facilities may not lead to more tourists.

Unit 9

▶ **9.1 Extract 1**

In anthropology, 150 is a famous number. In fact, it has a name – 'the Dunbar number' – because of the man who discovered it. Robin Dunbar is Professor of Anthropology at the University of Oxford. And over the last 20 years, he has developed the theory that humans prefer to be in groups with approximately 150 members because, he argues, 150 is the maximum number of people we can have close social relationships with at one time.

▶ **9.2 Extract 2**

Some of Dunbar's arguments are based on historical evidence. He has studied how people lived in the past and found that, in ancient times, groups of people often lived in communities of about 150 individuals. In military history, the number of soldiers in a typical military unit was around 150 and today this is still true in many modern armies.

More evidence for the Dunbar number has come from the world of business. In 1958, a man called Bill Gore started the clothing company Gore-Tex; he ran the company from his house and only employed a few people. As the company became more successful, he opened a factory and employed more and more people. Then one day, Bill Gore realized that he didn't know the names or the faces of all his employees. As a result, he decided that 150 was the maximum number of employees that should work in one factory. Since then, whenever the number of employees in a Gore-Tex factory has reached 150, the company has opened a new factory to create a new working community.

More recently, Dunbar and other anthropologists have researched human relationships on social media sites. In a study published in the journal *Proceedings of the National Academy of Sciences*, Dunbar worked with an international team and studied the social communication of 24 students. The results showed that when a student made a new close friendship, they spent less time communicating with an older friend. In other words, they didn't increase the communication, but they limited the number of friends to around 150. So even though you might have 1,000 friends or followers on social media sites like Facebook or Twitter, you probably only communicate with a maximum of 150 of these people.

🔊 **9.3**

In ancient times, groups of people often lived in communities of about 150 individuals.
In 1958, a man called Bill Gore started the clothing company Gore-Tex.
Over the last 20 years, Dunbar has discovered groups of humans with approximately 150 members.
More recently, anthropologists have researched human relationships on social networking sites.

🔊 **9.4**

A So Dunbar believes that 150 is the number of people we can have meaningful relationships with at one time. What do you think?
B Well, the evidence from Gore-Tex shows that you can't work with more than 150 employees in one place. Also, Dunbar's research states that people communicate with an average of 150 friends on social media. I know many people who communicate with more than 150 Facebook friends, including me! But overall, I think his theory works and his evidence supports the theory.
A Actually, I don't agree with all the evidence … because one study by the anthropologist Russell Bernard and a scientist called Peter Killworth suggests that the average number for a social network is 291. And another study in the *Journal of the American Statistical Association* reports that it's 611. So not everyone agrees with Dunbar.

🔊 **9.5**

Dunbar states that humans communicate with a maximum of 150 people.
Dunbar's study shows that people talk to an average of 150 friends on Facebook.
Their research suggests that Dunbar's theory is wrong.
Other research doesn't support this theory.

Unit 10

▶ **10.1 Extract 1**

Lecturer So when a person or a company is starting a new business, perhaps the most important thing is to do proper research. And doing research – any kind of research – basically means asking the right questions. You need to know which questions to ask, in order to get the information you need. So when you're starting a business, you need to ask questions like: How big is the market? Who are my customers? How much will they pay for my product or service? Who is the competition? How big is their share of the market? And so on ... And of course, one very important question is – how much money will I need?

The next very important question is: What are the possible sources of finance I can use? If you have done your research properly, and if you can show that you have done this in your business plan, then it's more probable that you will get access to the finance you need to start your business. Now, according to Bloomberg, the business and financial data news company, about 80% – eight zero – 80% of all new businesses fail in the first 18 months because they run out of money. And in many cases, this is because they didn't do enough research. What this means is that a lot of banks won't give loans to new businesses. And even if they do give a new business a loan, they'll charge a very high interest rate. That can be very expensive for a new business. So doing proper research into finance is really important. Now, before we move on, are there any questions about sources of finance?

Student Yes, I read that some new businesses can get a grant to get started. Can you explain how that works?

Lecturer Basically, it's when a government or another organization gives money to new businesses.

Student So ... is a government grant like an interest-free loan?

Lecturer Yes and no. The business doesn't pay any interest and it also doesn't have to pay back any money. Even if the company fails.

Student Why does the government give away the money?

Lecturer Well, because, in theory, grants encourage new businesses, which will create jobs and help the wider economy ...

10.2 Extract 2

A OK, so I did some research on businesses that use a new source of finance called 'crowdfunding' to get started. This information is all online. So this is Emilie Holmes and she started a business called the Good & Proper Tea Company. It sells high-quality, fresh tea in central London. As you can see, Emilie operates from a van. To start up her company, she needed around £10,000. She looked at different ways to finance her company, including a bank loan, but in the end she chose a crowdfunding website called 'Kickstarter'.

B I have a question. What is crowdfunding?
A Well, this is when you have a business idea and you create a project on a special website. People read about your business idea and they give you small amounts of money. They become investors in your business. And hopefully they will share this with other people, and so more people hear about your business and you get more investors. You offer your investors rewards. So Emilie offered her investors rewards like bags of tea.
B Why didn't she take out a bank loan?
A Because the interest on the loan that the bank offered her was 19%. But with crowdfunding, you don't pay any interest on the loan.

10.3 Extract 3

A So, what do we have to do?
B OK, we have to choose the best source of finance for a company which sells educational equipment to schools. The company is two years old and it wants to expand into selling to universities as well. So, what do you think?
A Well, first of all, I think they should get a bank loan because the business is two years old and the bank probably knows about them.
B Well, yes, but bank loans usually have a high interest rate. So I think we should look into other ways as well.
A Other ways? Do you mean like a family loan? Or borrowing money from friends?
B Well, for example, maybe they could apply for a government grant.
A Do you think the government will give them money? After all, they aren't a new business.
B Yes, but they're an educational business ...
A Well, not really. They sell equipment to schools, but that's not the same thing ...

10.4

What are the advantages of doing proper research?
Why do governments not give loans to some businesses?
How do you start a business with crowdfunding?
Can you explain what you mean by a grant?

Does the government give grants for free?
Is it difficult to get a loan?
Are they expensive?

Can you explain what you mean by a grant? Do you mean, it's like a loan?

Oxford source material used in this course

The Reading and Listening & Speaking skills modules of *Oxford EAP* include extracts from the following source material published by Oxford University Press. For more information about any of these titles, please visit: **www.oup.com**

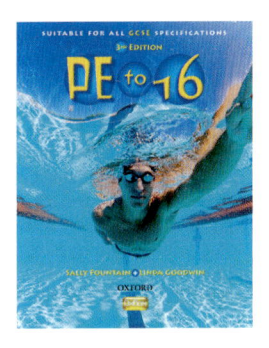

pages 013 and 015
PE to 16

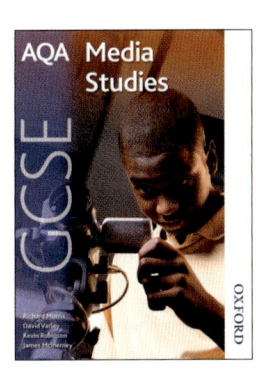

pages 026 and 028
AQA GCSE Media Studies

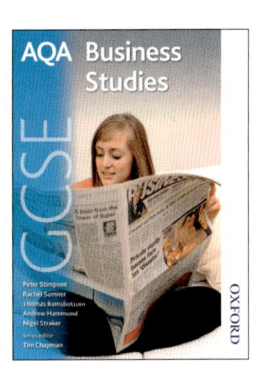

pages 041 and 042
AQA GCSE Business Studies

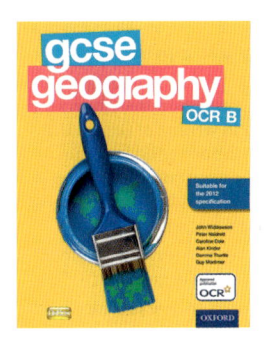

pages 055 and 056
GCSE Geography OCR B

pages 067, 068, 070, and 162
AQA Design and Technology: Product Design

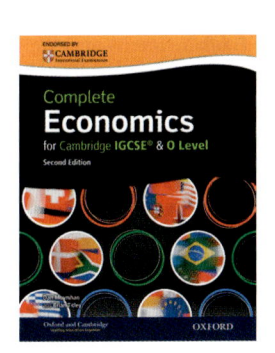

pages 079, 082, and 083
Complete Economics for Cambridge IGCSE and O Level

pages 093, 096, and 098
GCSE Science Higher

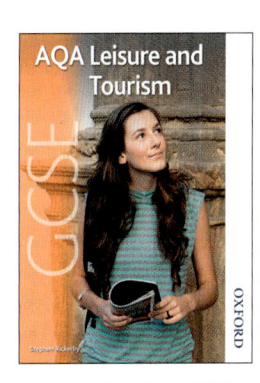

pages 107, 110, and 112
AQA Leisure and Tourism GCSE

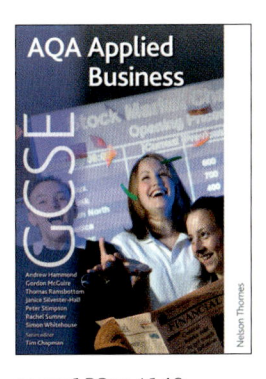

pages 138 and 140
AQA Applied Business GCSE

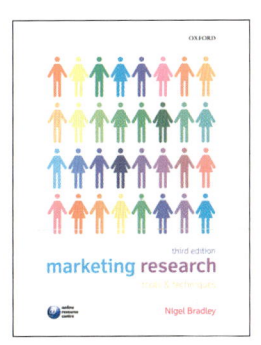

pages 161 and 163
Marketing Research

OXFORD
UNIVERSITY PRESS

Great Clarendon Street, Oxford, OX2 6DP, United Kingdom

Oxford University Press is a department of the University of Oxford. It furthers the University's objective of excellence in research, scholarship, and education by publishing worldwide. Oxford is a registered trade mark of Oxford University Press in the UK and in certain other countries

© Oxford University Press 2015

The moral rights of the author have been asserted

First published in 2015

2019 2018 2017 2016 2015

10 9 8 7 6 5 4 3 2 1

No unauthorized photocopying

All rights reserved. No part of this publication may be reproduced, stored in a retrieval system, or transmitted, in any form or by any means, without the prior permission in writing of Oxford University Press, or as expressly permitted by law, by licence or under terms agreed with the appropriate reprographics rights organization. Enquiries concerning reproduction outside the scope of the above should be sent to the ELT Rights Department, Oxford University Press, at the address above

You must not circulate this work in any other form and you must impose this same condition on any acquirer

Links to third party websites are provided by Oxford in good faith and for information only. Oxford disclaims any responsibility for the materials contained in any third party website referenced in this work

ISBN: 978 0 19 400205 9

Printed in China

This book is printed on paper from certified and well-managed sources

ACKNOWLEDGEMENTS

The authors and publisher are grateful to those who have given permission to reproduce the following extracts and adaptations of copyright material: p.026 Extracts from *AQA GCSE Media Studies Student Book* by Richard Morris, David Varley, Kevin Robinson and James McInerney (Nelson Thornes, 2009), reproduced by permission of the publishers, Oxford University Press. p.028 Common eye movement pattern from "The Best of Eyetrack III: What We Saw When We Looked Through Their Eyes" by Steve Outing and Laura Ruel, www.poynter.org, 2004. Reproduced by permission of the Poynter Institute. p.055 Extracts from *GCSE Geography OCR B Student Book* by John Widdowson, Caroline Cole, Alan Kinder, Peter Naldrett and Gemma Thurtle (Oxford University Press, 2011), reproduced by permission of Oxford University Press. p.079 Extracts from *Complete Economics for Cambridge IGCSE and O-level* by Dan Moynihan and Brian Titley (2e, Oxford University Press, 2012), reproduced by permission of Oxford University Press. p.093 Extracts from *Twenty-First Century Science: GCSE Science Higher Student Book* by Ann Fullick and Andrew Hunt (2e, Oxford University Press, 2011), reproduced by permission of Oxford University Press. p.107 Extracts from *AQA GCSE Leisure and Tourism Student Book* by Stephen Rickerby (Oxford University Press, 2009), reproduced by permission of Oxford University Press. p.161 Tables adapted from page 138 of *Marketing Research: tools and techniques* by Nigel Bradley (Oxford University Press, 2010), reproduced by permission of Oxford University Press. p.138 Extracts from *AQA GCSE Applied Business* by Andrew Hammond, Gordon McGuire, Thomas Ramsbottom, Janice Silvester-Hall, Peter Stimpson, Rachel Sumner and Simon Whitehouse (Nelson Thornes, 2009), reproduced by permission of the publishers, Oxford University Press. p.084 Graphs "Population Growth and Projections" and "Rural and Urban Population", http://www.un.org/. Reproduced by permission of United Nations.

Sources: *AQA GCSE Design and Technology Product Design Student Book* by Jeff Draisey, Brian Russell, Krysia Balance, Andrea Bennett and Nicola Deacon (Nelson Thornes, 2009) *Global online shopper report* by WorldPay (2012), www.worldpay.com 2012 Production Statistics by OICA, www.oica.net Social Networking Fact Sheet by Pew Research Center, www.pewinternet.org www.bloomberg.com

The publisher would like to thank the following for permission to reproduce photographs: 123RF pp.45 (Massachusetts Hall/Jannis Werner), 45 (Yale University/Peter Spirer), 46 (University of Singapore/Jordan Tan), 47 (Riyadh, Saudi Arabia/Fedor Selivanov), 57 (bale of raw cotton/Robert Byron), 60 (Skoda Volkswagen open doors day/Nataliya Hora), 61 (vans for sale/stocksolutions), 66 (light up kettle/Konstantin Labunskiy), 71 (smoke detector/Jesus Castro Fernandez), 71 (toothbrush with toothpaste/maxpayne222), 72 (red mini/zirtae), 103 (sunflowers/Surasak Tapanavongvet); Alamy Images pp.16 (young woman portrait/UpperCut Images), 17 (young man by sea/itanistock), 26 (BBC News website/Bhandol), 26 (1960s advertisement for Lurpack/Antiques & Collectables), 27 (iPad computer/Pixellover RM 1), 30 (BBC offices/Justin Kase zsixz), 31 (CNN building/age fotostock), 40 (Jones Bootmaker/Sam Barnes), 46 (Hong Kong University/icpix_hk), 47 (Ankara/Hilke Maunder), 56 (harvesting beans/Simon Rawles), 57 (picking cotton/Joerg Boethling), 64 (high speed train/JTB Media Creation, Inc.), 66 (integrated circuit chip/David J. Green), 71 (Apple iPad 2 tablet computer/David J. Green), 71 (commuter on a fold up bicycle/Philip Bramhill), 71 (cinema/Peter Forsberg), 72 (Italian Carabinieri police officer/Military Images), 72 (bricklaying wall/Radharc Images), 74 (engineers designing industrial clutches/Cultura Creative), 75 (business people video conferencing/Hero Images Inc.), 82 (street in Tokyo/FocusJapan), 97 (tidal turbine in Northern Ireland/Paul Lindsay), 99 (Crosby Beach and Liverpool Docks/Paul Gisby Photography), 102 (solar water heater/Christian Delbert), 110 (ancient sun dial/Jack Sullivan), 113 (aeroplane/Charles Polidano/Touch The Skies), 114 (iPhone screen showing Expedia travel website/iPhone), 115 (recycling/Maskot), 116 (Khao Sok National Park, Thailand/Igor Prahin), 117 (horse riding/parkerphotography), 122 (Roman soldiers at Jerash, Jordan/Michele Burgess), 124 (3D printer/Piero Cruciatti), 125 (3D printed bionic ear/Piero Cruciatti), 125 (3D scanner/Richard Levine), 127 (care homes website/Helen Sessions), 128 (antique telegraph machine/Anyka), 129 (Benjamin Franklin/Niday Picture Library), 131 (microwave/Flirt), 131 (British police body armour/Martin Brayley), 162 (sunglasses for sale/Dave Pattison); Bridgeman Images p.120 (a detail from the so-called 'Standard of Ur', side B/Werner Forman Archive); Corbis p.131 (Ajay Bhatt, European Inventor Award/Evert Elzinga/epa); Getty Images pp.8 (biology students in classroom with teacher/yellowdog), 13 (coach and young players watching soccer game/Jetta Productions), 22 (binary code/AnthiaCumming), 32 (News Corporation offices/Bloomberg), 36 (Reading Room at The British Museum/James Osmond), 37 (Olympic stadium, London/Mark Chivers), 39 (Cibeles Palace/Driendl Group), 39 (West Bay, Qatar/Michael Gerard Santos Ceralde), 39 (Suleymaniye Mosque, Istanbul/Richard Cummins), 40 (Tesco Cheetham Hill/View Pictures), 50 (tulip fields in the Netherlands/Darrell Gulin), 55 (coffee cups on kitchen counter/Jupiterimages), 57 (Divine milk chocolate bar/Clynt Garnham Food & Drink), 65 (kingfisher/Andrew Howe), 70 (chairs in a Lobby/Rich Legg), 70 (creative businesswoman typing on laptop at office/Klaus Vedfelt), 71 (flight controls/Jason Edwards), 78 (business meeting/suedhang), 94 (worker at the Fukushima nuclear plant/Shizuo Kambayashi), 106 (Copacabana/Marcelo Nacinovic), 110 (beach in the Maldives/Mohamed Shareef), 129 (original Benjamin Franklin stove/Werner Wolff), 130 (Gutenberg's press, c 1430/Science & Society Picture Library), 134 (pathologists analysing samples from under microscope/Medic Image), 135 (tea van/AFP), 135 (pouring tea/AFP), 140 (young people looking at tablet in the street/Xavier Arnau); Oxford University Press pp.12 (task 2), 23 (university students on campus/Moodboard), 26 (Economics), 43 (London Tower Bridge/Medioimages), 43 (Eiffel Tower/Shutterstock), 85 (college lesson/Monkey Business Images), 92 (wind turbines/chinaface), 175; Rex Features pp.32 (The Simpsons/FoxSearch/Everett), 32 (House TV still/c.20thC.Fox/Everett); Science Photo Library p.101 (zebra grass/Gustoimages); Shutterstock pp.44 (Durham Castle/Robin Nieuwenkamp), 44 (Bristol Cathedral and University/pjhpix), 67 (robot/catwalker), 68 (shoe shop/pio3), 71 (bus station/villorejo), 71 (playground/Iakov Filimonov), 72 (space satellite/Andrey Armyagov).

Illustrations by: Peter Bull pp.92, 93, 96, 100, 101, 102, 103; Richard Ponsford/Libro pp.28, 44, 51, 53, 54, 55, 58, 60, 61, 80, 82, 84, 86, 87, 88, 89, 145 157 ; Mariko Yamazaki/Dutch Uncle p.79.

Commissioned photography by: Mark Bassett pp.9, 10, 24, 26, 37, 52, 65, 80, 94, 121, 136; Oxford University Press p.12 (task 1).

Cover photograph by: Gareth Boden.

Design by: Richard Ponsford/Libro.

The authors and publisher would like to thank the following individuals for their valuable advice and assistance in developing the material for this course: Asmaa Awad (University of Sharjah, United Arab Emirates), David Bozetarnik (Sharjah Women's Higher Colleges of Technology, UAE), Jim Echelberry (University of Fukui, Japan), Fatos Ugur Eskicirak (Bahcesehir University, Istanbul, Turkey), Ana Silvia Ferreira (São Paulo University, Brazil), Jeff Gibbons (King Fahd University of Petroleum & Minerals, Dhahran, Saudi Arabia), Claire Graham (Sino British College, Shanghai, China), Yakut Ilyas (Meliksah University, Kayseri, Turkey), Professor Narahiko Inoue (Kyushu University, Japan), Tanisaya Jiriyasin (University of the Thai Chamber of Commerce, Bangkok, Thailand), Alev Küçük (Eastern Mediterranean University, North Cyprus), Jill Newby (Foundation Institute, University of Nizwa, Oman), Gary Pathare (Higher Colleges of Technology, Dubai, UAE), Adrienne Radcliffe (RMIT University, Ho Chi Minh City, Vietnam), Gordon Reisdorf (Konan University, Kobe, Japan), Lynne Robinson (Petroleum Institute, Abu Dhabi, UAE), Walaiporn Tantikanangkul (Chiang Mai University, Thailand), Kate Tindle (Zayed University, Dubai, UAE), Bob Wenn (Abu Dhabi Men's College, UAE).

Special thanks to: Kate Chomacki